SACRED PARTNERSHIP

Jesus and Mary Magdalene

FOREWARD BY MARVIN MEYER

"He knew her completely and loved her devotedly."
GOSPEL OF MARY 10:10

JOHN BEVERLEY BUTCHER

the apocryphile press
BERKELEY, CA
www.apocryphile.org

Dedicated to Marie
My Beloved Daughter

a p o c r y p h i l e   p r e s s
BERKELEY, CA

Apocryphile Press
1700 Shattuck Ave. #81
Berkeley, CA 94709
www.apocryphile.org

Cover Icon: Chalices of Mystery by iconographer Lewis Williams, copyright 2009. The Icon is available in a variety of formats from www.trinitystores.com

TABLE OF CONTENTS

FOREWORD

WHAT MIGHT THE STORY OF JESUS OF NAZARETH AND
Mary Magdalene look like, John Beverley Butcher asks, if Jesus and
Mary are given the places in the gospel story that they occupy in
such recently discovered texts as the Gospel of Thomas, the Gospel
of Mary, and the Gospel of Philip? Butcher's answer to this question
is provided in the present book, *Sacred Partnership*, a narrative volume that most resembles a modern-day gospel. Written in the present tense, the volume narrates a powerful story of ancient wisdom,
holy mystery, and sacred partnership, with disarmingly contemporary overtones. In the story Jesus announces, "The kingdom of the
Father and Mother is within you," and somewhat later Mary echoes
this announcement by observing, "The Seed of True Humanity is
within you." Liturgies for Sacred Rituals based upon the wisdom of
Jesus and Mary are given at the conclusion of the volume.

John Butcher is well prepared to formulate this dramatic retelling
of the life and teachings of Jesus of Nazareth and Mary Magdalene.
He is an ordained priest in the Episcopal Diocese of California and
the author of *The Tao of Jesus* (Harper, 1994), *Telling the Untold Stories*
(Trinity Press International, 2001), and *An Uncommon Lectionary*

(Polebridge, 2002). For some time he has been a member of the Jesus Seminar, and he brings to expression many of the insights voiced by scholars within that group. In the books he has written and the workshops he has led, Butcher explores multifaith religious possibilities linked to the arts and liturgy. It is precisely this set of commitments that empowers and inspires the vision of good news in *Sacred Partnership*.

Marvin Meyer
Griset Professor of Religious Studies, Chapman University
Editor, The Nag Hammadi Scriptures, *HarperOne, 2007*

INTRODUCTION

I HAVE BEEN FASCINATED WITH JESUS ALL MY LIFE AND with Mary Magdalene for almost as long. There is something about them that draws me like a magnet. I need to study all the information about them that I can get my hands on.

Our database on Jesus of Nazareth and Mary Magdalene has been substantially and dramatically expanded by the discovery of the Gospel of Thomas, the Gospel of Peter, the Gospel of Mary, the Gospel of Philip and many other significant sacred texts.

Most notable was the discovery of the Nag Hammadi Scriptures in 1945, the same year that the atomic bomb was first used on other human beings: one discovery leads to destruction and death, the other provides us with wisdom for rebuilding life.

Since that time there has been intense research by many competent scholars leading to a creative explosion of new books on Jesus and on Mary Magdalene. The implications are enormous and challenge us to rethink our understanding of these two people, their relationship, and their wisdom teachings.

The conventional New Testament has scant information on Mary Magdalene which diminishes her and keeps her mainly in the background. With the new data available to us, we can see clearly that she is the closest woman companion to Jesus. She works closely with him in their shared ministry of teaching and serving as catalysts for healing both before and after his crucifixion.

What might the Gospel story look like and how might it read if Mary Magdalene were to be returned to her rightful place? My task is twofold: to put her back into the story where she belongs and to restore the neglected wisdom teachings from her and from Jesus.

According to the research of the Jesus Seminar scholars and many others, the first written records are the "sayings Gospels": Gospel of Thomas and the Q Gospel. Their first editions were produced about the year 50 C.E., just two decades after the crucifixion of Jesus. Mark comes later about 70 C.E., Matthew about 80 C.E., Luke and John about 90 C.E.[1]

Thomas and Q provide us with wisdom teachings usually standing on their own without providing any specific context. In studying the sayings Gospels and arranging the teachings, I began to understand from the inside how the other Gospel writers of Mark, Matthew, Luke, and John were creating scenes to embody the teachings in a coherent fashion. I am following their example by creating contexts to hold the newly discovered vibrant teachings alongside the familiar ones.

I am excited about our expanded database[2] and have been searching all the information I can find that is available in English translation. I want to know more about the Gospel writers' own spiritual experiences behind their wisdom teachings.

Those who hear Jesus and Mary are often astonished at their teachings since they speak on their own authority and not as the scribes.[3] I am convinced that their authority originates with their experience of Sacred Mystery within, between, around, and beyond themselves. In other words, first comes the experience, then comes the teaching.

What were their experiences? And who were the people who were most influential in their lives? These are among the questions that energize me in researching the documents and doing my writing.

In the pages that follow, I offer you my best effort in restoring Mary Magdalene to her rightful place alongside Jesus in the Gospel tradition. I am seeking to rediscover and reclaim them both as historical and archetypal characters.

I am also committed to verifying and supporting their companionship which is best summarized, "He knew her completely and loved her devotedly."[4]

In addition, I am wondering what would happen if both Jesus and Mary were to be integrated more fully into rituals of baptism and eucharist? In the concluding section of this book I provide new rituals and invite you to consider using them in your own communities of faith as I have since 1994.

Please note that this book is heavily foot-noted. If you are reading and find yourself asking, "Where did John Butcher get that idea?" simply consult the footnotes for the chapter and verse of a sacred text or writings from reliable scholarly sources.

You will find that normally the words and actions of Jesus are rooted in actual citations from sacred scripture. Words and actions ascribed to Mary Magdalene are from original sources plus what I trust are credible expansions.

I now recognize that Mary Magdalene, along with women whom I have perceived as carrying her energies, has been the object of my own intense projections for many years. Gradually my view of Mary Magdalene has shifted. I am seeing her more clearly as a person in her own right. With this shift I am able to see other women more clearly as well.

This book is not a novel. What you have in your hands is my understanding of Jesus and Mary in their Sacred Partnership. How might their life and teachings enable us to enter more fully into our own partnerships and express our true humanity?

John Beverley Butcher, San Francisco, California,
Mary Magdalene Day, July 22, 2010

NOTES

1. For dating of Gospels, see the chart on page 6 of *The Complete Gospels*, Robert J. Miller, Robert W. Funk, Polebridge Press, Santa Rosa CA, 1992, and the extensive research and literature of the Jesus Seminar.

2. Database for Jesus and Mary Magdalene is on page 344.

3. Luke 4:32, Scholars Version

4. Gospel of Mary 10:10, Scholars Version

5. Translations by the Jesus Seminar scholars in *The Complete Gospels*, Robert J. Miller, Robert W. Funk, Polebridge Press, Santa Rosa CA, 1992.

CHAPTER 1:
WHEN DO JESUS AND MARY MEET?

WHEN DO JESUS AND MARY FIRST MEET EACH OTHER? Jesus is from Nazareth, a Jewish peasant village set in the hills of Galilee. He is growing up with his mother, Mary, who loves him dearly, guides him and holds each part of his development closely to her heart.[1] She has her own deep and abiding practical faith. Jesus observes how his mother does things: how she uses leaven to make bread rise, how old fabric is used to repair worn garments, how moths and rust work to frustrate even the most careful homemaker. When he goes to the market with his mother, he notices the cost of everything and how merchants vary their measure of a bushel.[2] Jesus is also known as the carpenter's son.[3] Apparently Jesus learns the carpenter's trade.[4] The word for carpenter in Greek is *tekton* which means not merely one who is skilled in making cabinets or furniture, but a designer, construction engineer, or architect.[5] He also observes how day laborers stand waiting for work.

If Mary Magdalene is from Magdala-Tarichaea[6] an important fishing and dried fish export center on the west shore of the sea of Galilee, then the home towns of Mary and Jesus are about fifteen miles apart. The most direct road from Nazareth to the inland Sea of

Galilee ends up at Magdala. Might Jesus and Mary have met as children playing on the beach? Or as teens with youthful explorations? Or perhaps as young adults? In all likelihood, members of Mary's family are in the fishing business. Perhaps Jesus meets her when he buys salted fish from her stand to take home to his family?

As Jewish people, both Jesus' and Mary's families normally travel to the Temple in Jerusalem for the major festivals of the year, especially Passover in the springtime. Perhaps Jesus from Nazareth and Mary from Magdala meet in Jerusalem during one of the festivals?

If, however, the term "the Magdalene" refers not to her place of origin, but rather is a description of who she is as a person, then perhaps she is the Mary whose home town is Bethany.[7] This would place her in a town just a couple of miles east of Jerusalem. She and Jesus might have first met when he was in the City for one of the festivals.

In this case, Mary would be a Judean and Jesus a Galilean, which creates an interesting scenario of the city girl meeting the country boy.

Another possibility is that both of them might have been attracted to the ministry of John the Baptizer down at the Jordan River. Might they have met through John or their baptisms?

The important point is that Jesus and Mary do meet, even if the exact time and place is uncertain.

They share a common context. Both Jesus and Mary are Jews living in a land occupied and dominated by the Roman Empire. Like all empires before and after, Rome follows a simple strategy: conquer, install puppet governments who will cooperate, extract natural resources, and exploit cheap labor. The system runs on force and fear for controlling the subject people.

Jesus and Mary are very aware of the ever present power of the Empire with its centurions, tax collectors, and toll takers on public roads. They witness the cruelty, the beatings and the very public crucifixions of their people. They feel the terror and fear all around them.

As they grow up and become adults living in an occupied country, Jesus, Mary and their families face choices. They can cooperate with the ruling powers as do the Herodians, the Jewish bureaucrats working for Rome, and the religious authorities who are allowed to practice their religion as long as they do not disrupt Roman control. The bottom line is to keep the masses obedient to Roman rule, which is euphemistically and ironically known as the Pax Romana, The Peace of Rome.

Or Jesus and Mary can decide to join those who are resisting the Empire. The main groups are the Zealots who are planning the violent overthrow of their Roman oppressors and the Sicarii, who are skillful in using the sicarius, a blade easily concealed under one's clothing until it is needed for swift assassination of people who are cooperating with Rome.

Will Jesus and Mary align themselves with those who are cooperating with the power structures? Will they join movements who are opposing Roman authority? Will they follow the majority who take the line of least resistance and simply stay out of the power struggle, get along as best they can, and hope and pray that things will get better? Or will they seek out and discover other alternatives?

Will Jesus and Mary do some traveling together? Interestingly, a trip to Damascus in the north is not much further than a trip to Jerusalem in the south.[8] Damascus is the main junction of the Silk Road connecting China with the Middle East. Jewish, Syrian, and Chinese merchants meet primarily for commercial purposes but their conversations would inevitably include a sharing of beliefs, teachings and customs.

Damascus in the first century is a fascinating city that is attractive to any adventurous young person in search of new ideas and experiences. Perhaps Jesus and Mary travel to Damascus individually or together? To stretch our imaginations a bit further, might they have joined a caravan traveling on the Silk Road into China?[9] Whether they actually go to China or not, they could meet travelers and be exposed to ideas of Lao Tzu, Confucius, and other Chinese thinkers.

Who are their role models? Whom will they choose to emulate? What teachings will they follow? As they become adults, what choices do they each make? And where will their choices converge? Which spiritual practices will they embrace? How will they be energized to live creatively in the context of Empire?

I invite you to join me in seeking answers to these and other questions as we accompany Jesus and Mary on their journeys through Galilee, Judea, and beyond. We will walk along side them as they encounter Life in all its richness and complexity with an eye toward the Way in which they face not only the outer pressures and opportunities, but also the inner mysterious life of their souls.

NOTES

1. Luke 2:19

2. *Mary, the Imagination of Her Heart*, Penelope Duckworth, Cowley Publications, 2004, p. 47.

3. Matthew 13:55

4. Mark 6:03

5. Definition of tekton from Margaret Starbird, *Magdalene's Lost Legacy*, p. 53

6. *The Anchor Dictionary*, volume IV pps. 463-464, Doubleday, New York 1992

7. See the careful research of Margaret Starbird in her *Mary Magdalene, Bride in Exile*, Bear & Company, Rochester, Vermont, 2005, especially chapter 3.

8. Nazareth to Damascus is about 75 miles. Nazareth to Jerusalem about 60 miles.

9. *Jesus in China*, Wee Chong Tan, Canadian College for Chinese Studies, 2004, p. 31

CHAPTER 2:
JESUS HEARS THE
MESSAGE OF JOHN

WHEN JESUS TURNS THIRTY HE FINDS THAT THE persistent questions of life are welling up inside him with greater intensity: "Who am I really?" "What shall I do with the rest of my life?" As he is pondering these and other pressing questions he hears that John is preaching and baptizing people down at the Jordan River. People from the Judean countryside and all the residents of Jerusalem are streaming out to hear him.[1] Jesus feels enormous curiosity regarding what is going on and decides to make the trip down south to the place where people are gathering along the west bank of the river, just a short distance before it empties into the Dead Sea.

Jesus invites his friend Mary Magdalene to accompany him on the journey which is over sixty miles from home. Even though it takes several days on foot to get there, they have the persistent feeling that the trip will be worth it.

Arriving on the scene, they are a bit startled at John's appearance: he is wearing a mantle of camel hair and a leather belt around his waist. Jesus thinks to himself, "John looks more like Elijah the prophet and nothing like the teachers or the priests."[2]

John is an itinerant preacher who is calling for baptism and a change of heart that lead to forgiveness of sins.[3] People are riveted to

John and the message he is delivering with tremendous force and conviction.

Many are moving toward John and confessing their sins. When they are ready, they remove their outer clothing and take John's hand as he walks with them into the river. When they are about waist deep, John immerses them in the water for their cleansing. Coming out of the water, they seem to be changed: faces shining and voices shouting for joy.

When people ask, "What should we do now?" John replies, "Whoever has two shirts should share with someone who has none; whoever has food should do the same."[4]

Even tax collectors and toll takers who work at checkpoints along the roads come for baptism and ask, "Teacher, what should we do?" and John replies, "Charge nothing above the official rates."[5]

Even Roman soldiers show up and ask, "What about us?" And John looks them in the eye and says, "No more shakedowns! No more frame-ups either! And be satisfied with your pay."[6]

Some of the Pharisees and Sadducees have come out to investigate what is going on. John spots them in the crowd, points an angry finger at them and says, "You brood of vipers! Who warned you to flee from the impending doom? Well, then, if you are serious, start producing fruit suitable for a change of heart, and don't even think of saying to yourselves, 'We have Abraham for our father.' Let me tell you, God can raise up children for Abraham right out of these rocks. Even now the axe is aimed at the root of the trees. So every tree not producing choice fruit gets cut down and tossed into the fire."[7]

Most of the Pharisees and Sadducees feel insulted and angry, shake their fists at John, and return to Jerusalem. But some are taking the message to heart and move toward him, confessing their sins and asking to be baptized. John appears to be more surprised than anyone else, but recognizing their sincerity, takes them gently into the water and immerses them for their cleansing.

Jesus has just seen ordinary peasants, people who work for the Romans, and even soldiers and religious officials changing their ways and being baptized. Something very deep is resonating within him: the message of change of heart and forgiveness of sins.

Jesus realizes that there are changes he needs to make within himself.

Perhaps Jesus is reviewing his own life up to this point, recognizing things he wishes he had not done, aware of failing to do the things he could have done. Is he also getting in touch with the attitudes behind his actions or lack of action? Is he feeling the need for a course correction in the direction of his life? Even more deeply, is he getting in touch with a feeling of emptiness that needs filling? The more Jesus examines his own life, the more he is feeling the impulse to walk toward John and ask to be baptized.

Notes

1. Mark 1:5

2. The prophet Elijah's appearance is described in II Kings 1:8

3. Mark 1:4

4. Luke 3:11

5. Luke 3:12-13

6. Luke 3:14

7. Matthew 3:7-10

CHAPTER 3:
JESUS IS BAPTIZED[1]

MANY OTHERS HAVE COME OUT OF THE CROWD TO BE baptized. The moment comes when Jesus knows that now is the right time for him. He goes right up to John and says,

"I am ready for baptism."

Removing his clothing, stripping himself of all outer appearances, Jesus enters the water just as he is. While being immersed into the flowing water, Jesus simultaneously goes into the depths of his own soul, down through the layers of his psyche. The deeper he goes, the greater the darkness and the pressure. It is time for him to be open to whatever he discovers within himself.

The baptism itself is accomplished in a moment of time, but the inner exploration is timeless; Jesus is entering into the unknown eternal depths embracing the entire history of the human race back to the beginnings, even to the Big Bang, the origins of all things where Being emerges out of Nothingness.

What appears as a quick dip is actually a trip into the Place of Knowing and Not Knowing all at once. And it is there that he hears the Voice, "You are my dear son: I delight in you."[2] Jesus feels and knows that he is connected: now there is Nothing between him and the Source of his life. Immersion in Mystery goes beyond the ability of anyone to describe: but here he knows the I AM, the Eternal Verb, the inexpressible now being expressed in and through him!

As Jesus emerges from the water, he breaks through into the Heavens and knows what it means to be born anew. The whole fountain of the Holy Spirit has come down on him.[3] Jesus experiences a tearing and opening of soul, followed by a deep sense of peace like a dove.[4] He feels the Spirit gently resting on him.[5]

The old text from the psalm resonates in him, "Today I have begotten you."[6] Jesus comes out of the water laughing.[7] Perhaps he is laughing for joy. Or he may be laughing at the stupidity and absurdity of the present world order. Laughter gives him joyous release.

Along with Jesus, the One who is metaphorically described as "sitting on the throne in heaven" is also laughing.[8] Perhaps they are enjoying the cosmic joke together. Jesus knows exhilaration and freedom.[9]

Jesus, who was begotten before everything, has been begotten anew. Jesus, who was once anointed, has been anointed anew. He who is now redeemed is able in turn to assist in the redemption of others.[10]

Jesus has died and risen again right here in the waters of the Jordan River at the hands of John. Some of his old ideas have been shattered and are being replaced by a new awareness of Being One with All. Those who say they will die first and then rise are in error. If they do not first receive the resurrection while they live, when they die they will receive nothing.[11]

Coming out of this intense, yet calm and peaceful experience, Jesus has a mind full of questions centered in one: what will he do next?

NOTES

1. Evidence regarding the Baptism of Jesus has been expanded through the Nag Hammadi Scriptures which I will be citing in the retelling of the story.

2. Mark 1:11, William Tyndale translation, 1526 C.E.

3. Gospel of the Hebrews 3:1

4. Mark 1:10

5. Gospel of Hebrews 3:2

6. Psalm 2:7

7. Gospel of Philip 98

8. Psalm 2:4

9. Gospel of Hebrews 3:1

10. Gospel of Philip 81

11. Gospel of Philip 90

CHAPTER 4:

JESUS GOES ON
A VISION QUEST[1]

HEART OVERFLOWING, MIND FLOODING WITH questions, Jesus knows he must go somewhere to sort things out. After saying a quick "Goodbye" to Mary, he heads out into the wilderness of the desert and the wilderness of his own soul.[2] Jesus feels both driven[3] and led[4] by the Spirit simultaneously. Pushed and pulled at the same time, he enters the wilderness alone for what will become his Vision Quest.

This is a time for fasting: no need for food now. And it is a time for prayer: deep inner dialogue. After walking some distance, Jesus finds a comfortable rock and sits down to rest. In a moment he sees a serpent rising up like a cobra before the charmer. Jesus has the immediate intuitive feeling that here is the same Serpent who rose up to greet Adam and Eve in the Garden of Eden.[5]

Next Jesus sees on his left all kinds of wild animals racing toward him. Some are desert creatures he has seen before, but there are others, strange and unfamiliar. Simultaneously Jesus discovers a host of angels on his right: it feels like they are standing with him no matter what happens. Jesus wonders to himself, "Am I dreaming?" so he pinches himself; but this is no dream, he is wide awake! He has been going without food, and says to himself, "Am I hallucinating?" These forces rising up from within him are demanding his full attention. Whatever is happening, it is very real.

The Serpent in the Center calls Jesus by name and starts asking questions: "If you are the son of God, prove it: why don't you just turn these rocks into bread?"[6]

Being very hungry, Jesus knows it would be great to have some food right now.

But attention to food is only a distraction, so he turns down the offer, and finds himself giving voice to a new awareness, "Human beings are not to live on bread alone, but on every word that comes out of God's mouth.[7] Speak, I am listening!"[8]

The dialogue continues with the Serpent who is his Instructor, embodying Wisdom, the Feminine Spiritual Presence.[9] The Serpent says to Jesus, "Lay aside immaturity, and live, and walk in the way of insight."[10]

As though lifted by the hair of his head,[11] Jesus feels himself being transported out of the wilderness, into the holy city of Jerusalem and onto the pinnacle, the highest part of the temple, where crowds below gaze at him. He hears a Voice saying to him, "You can show your power by jumping off this pinnacle—and the angels will catch you with their hands: you won't even stub your toe."[12]

A verse from the Scriptures flashes to mind and Jesus replies, "You are not to put the Lord your God to the test."[13]

One more imaginary yet very real scene occurs: Jesus finds himself on a very high mountain from which he can see all the kingdoms of the earth with all their power and prestige: he hears a voice saying, "I'll give you all these, if you will kneel down and pay homage to me."[14]

What a tempting scene: how much good he could do if he was in a position of power! He could control an Empire even greater than that of the Roman Caesars! Jesus thinks it over and then responds, "Get out of here! Remember, it is written, 'You are to pay homage only to the Lord....'"[15]

Pondering the Vision, Jesus realizes that the wild animals on one side are his own natural energies and powers, wild, free and ready for him to use. The angels on the other side are there to bring messages and provide guidance. Jesus knows he will need both his energies and his guidance as he faces the questions of Life.

The powerful vision fades, but its impact and the persistent questions remain: How will Jesus use his new power? Will he yield to the temptation to use his power to dominate other people? Jesus looks at the domination options and says "No" to them.

Now it is quite clear to Jesus: he will live his life not by might, not by power, but by the Spirit.[16] Like Abraham and Sarah,[17] Jesus knows that it is time for him to leave all that is familiar and go into a new life, a new way of living in places and situations yet to be revealed. This he knows from deep within himself: he is willing to move in faith and face whatever will be required of him.

NOTES

1. This chapter is rooted in the Synoptic Gospels and related texts.

2. Mark 1:12

3   Mark 1:12

4. Luke 4:1

5. Genesis 3

6. Matthew 4:3

7. Matthew 4:4

8. I Samuel 3:10

9. The Nature of the Rulers formerly known as the Hypostasis of the Archons 89:31-90:12, *Nag Hammadi Scriptures*

10. Proverbs 9:6

11. Gospel of the Hebrews 4

12. Matthew 4:6, Psalm 91:11-12

13. Matthew 4:7, Deuteronomy 6:16

14. Matthew 4:9

15. Matthew 4:10

16. Zechariah 4:6

17. Genesis 12:1

CHAPTER 5:
MARY IS BAPTIZED₁

AS JESUS COMES OUT OF THE WILDERNESS AND RETURNS to the place along the river Jordan where John had baptized him, there is a strange stillness. At first he sees no one—all seem to have vanished, swept away. Even John is nowhere to be seen.

Just then Mary Magdalene appears. Jesus is both startled and pleased to see her and asks, "Have you been waiting out here for me?"

"Yes and no," she replies. When we said our 'Goodbyes,' I wanted you to have the time you needed to be alone out there in the wilderness. I stayed here listening to John and the more I heard his message, the more he seemed to be speaking directly to me. Like you, I knew that there are changes I need to make. So I walked toward John and asked him to baptize me as well.

"After my baptism as I was coming out of the water, I knew that what had bound me had been slain, and what surrounded me had been destroyed, and my desire had been fulfilled, and my ignorance had been replaced with knowing who I am. The chains of forgetfulness had fallen away. I am free and can rest in silence.²

"The experience touched me deeply and I realized that I also needed some time alone in the wilderness. I found an isolated spot that seemed to be calling to me and there I spent my own forty days.

"Now I need just one more thing, Jesus, will you join me in prayer?"

Jesus lays his hands upon Mary and prays that she will receive the full anointing of the Spirit. His energized spirit comes upon her and meets the same Spirit welling up from within her in a burst of transforming power. Each of her seven chakra energies are being transformed from the root to her crown, on into the two beyond.[3] She is being empowered to live and act more creatively than ever before.[4] Her initiation is complete. Both she and Jesus know that they have become living chalices of Mystery. They know that the pulsating energy of the Universe is within, between, around, and beyond them.

Jesus and Mary have been fasting for a long time. Now they need to resume eating and gain the physical strength they will need for the long journey back home to Galilee. Along the way, they share deeply their experiences in baptism and in the wilderness. They are experiencing the pulsating Energy of the Spirit of Mystery and know intuitively that they are becoming sacred partners empowered for living creatively. Where will the Spirit be leading them next?

NOTES

1. From Luke 8:1-3 we learn that Mary Magdalene has been traveling with Jesus from the beginning of his ministry. The story of her baptism is missing. Perhaps it is recorded in the first missing chapters of the Gospel of Mary. Until that information is in our hands, I offer this chapter as my best attempt at reconstructing what may have occurred.

2. Gospel of Mary 9:27-29

3. Luke 8:2

4. For a fuller description see the Cameo Essay on Demons and Chakras p. 28.

CAMEO ESSAY 1:
WHAT ARE DEMONS AND CHAKRAS?

SOME CONCEPTION OF EVIL SPIRITS OR DEMONS WAS held universally by the religions of the ancient world. Many of these religions had developed a rather extensive demonology. Egyptian religion included the use of magical incantations to ward off disease and misfortune caused by malevolent spirits. Greek popular belief postulated a class of spirit beings, possibly spirits of the dead, between men and gods. These beings could afflict people with madness and sickness. Zoroastrianism conceived of a dualism in the spirit world, with a dark kingdom of demons under the direction of Ahriman warring against the spirits of light led by Ahura Mazda.[1]

The Hebrew concept of the Lord's sovereignty minimizes the development of demonology in the Torah scriptures, but Jesus, Mary, and many other Jewish people around them are being influenced by the thinking which says that anyone with any kind of problem, especially the more serious ones, must be under the spell or control of malevolent spirits

The word "demon" comes from *daimon*, a Greek word for power. Demons, or evil spirits, are conditions of mind, or states of consciousness, that have developed because creative energies have been misdirected or used in an unwise or ignorant way.[2]

It can be tempting to ascribe negative energies to outside forces. Blaming demons is also a convenient way to avoid responsibility. In other words, "The devil made me do it!"

Facing the powers within oneself is difficult, but much more realistic. One may experience an overwhelming sense of gripping power when feeling driven, compulsive, or running out of control, like Paul who says, "I do not understand my own actions. For I do not do what I want, but I do the very thing I hate."[3]

Essentially, demons are powers, energies within every person that can be used beneficially or detrimentally within oneself and/or toward others. The number seven is very significant and may refer to the chakras, the seven symbolic energy centers of the body:

"Chakra" is a Sanskrit term meaning circle or wheel. There is a wide literature on chakra models, philosophy, and lore that underpin many philosophical systems and spiritual energy practices, religious observance, and personal discipline. Theories on chakras fit within systems that link the human body and mind into a single unit, sometimes called the 'bodymind' (Sanskrit: *namarupa*). The philosophical theories and models of chakras as centers of energy were first codified in ancient India.[4]

Knowledge of chakras would have been pervasive in the middle east world of Jesus and Mary Magdalene. Awareness of chakras has spread more recently to the west especially through the trailblazing work of C.W. Leadbeater in his book, *The Chakras*, first published in 1927, and numerous other philosophical and spiritual pathfinders such as Caroline Myss in her book, *Anatomy of the Spirit: The Seven Stages of Power and Healing*.[5]

The root chakra is located at the base of the spine and contains the basic energy of life. The second chakra, located in the pelvic area, is the creative energy of partnership. The third chakra, located in the solar plexus, is a constellation of energy and its use and misuse of one's power. Then comes the heart chakra and relationship issues. Next comes the throat chakra known as the Third Ear at the base of the neck which symbolizes the ability to hear and speak from a Source greater than oneself. Likewise, the Third Eye in the center of the forehead contains the ability to see beyond normal eyesight, to have a vision; like the potential of all the other chakras, this one may create visions that may be used beneficially as with Dr. Martin Luther King and his famous "I have a Dream" speech or misused by someone like Adolf Hitler who envisioned the Third Reich with a pure Aryan race dominating or destroying all others.

On the top of the head is the crown chakra representing a higher consciousness and awareness. In some symbolic systems, there are two more energy centers: the Eighth located above the head and the Ninth which is way out there in the farthest reaches of the Cosmos! The purpose in working with the chakras is to begin with the root chakra and raise energy through each of the energy centers of the body and out the top of the head into space and the higher consciousness of the Eighth and the Ninth.[6]

The energy of the primary root Chakra gains additional strength and momentum as it rises through the body, rather like a seven stage rocket, until it releases freely into the Cosmos and enters the Deepest reaches of outer Space. When we make the reverse trip and return to our earthly bodies, the energies of seven chakras plus two can enliven and empower us for living creatively in the world.

Once activated, we need to ask ourselves questions: will our chakra energies be used for our own enjoyment alone or will we choose to put them to work for worthwhile purposes in the world?

Will we use our energies for selfish purposes of control and dominance over others, or in the service of liberation, freedom, love, respect and a spirit of cooperation in the rebuilding of the Earth and the healing of humanity?

The chakra challenge is simple: think globally and cosmically. Then use chakra energies to act locally and personally.

NOTES

1. *Anchor Bible Dictionary*, Doubleday, 1992, volume 2, p. 140

2. *Metaphysical Bible Dictionary*, Unity Books, 2003, p. 170.

3. Romans 7:15, *New Revised Standard Version*

4. Wikiepaedia

5. Caroline Myss, *Anatomy of the Spirit: The Seven Stages of Power and Healing*, Three Rivers Press, New York, 1996.

6. On the Eighth and the Ninth, *The Nag Hammadi Scriptures,* Harper One, 2007.

CHAPTER 6:
COMPANIONS
WITH SHARED MINISTRY

BOTH JESUS AND MARY HAVE INTENSE INNER LIVES. BOTH know what it is like to venture into the depths of their soul and face whatever is to be discovered. Their respect and love for each other deepens and it is clear to others that their relationship is becoming a very strong and creative bond.

Jesus loves Mary more than any other woman.[1] They have become companions[2] and they kiss each other often.[3] When they kiss, their souls meet, they conceive and give birth[4] to new awareness, fresh possibilities, and so much joy. Jesus says, "When you drink from my mouth you will become like me; I myself shall become you, and the hidden things will be revealed to you.[5]

Mary is a woman who fully understands.[6] Both she and Jesus have strong intuition. One truly understands the other quickly without having to spend too much time explaining things. One sentence is worth many paragraphs. Sometimes their conversation leapfrogs forward at a rapid pace. Sometimes they simply relish being in the moment. Perhaps they are teaching each other how to "Be here now."

They enter freely into each other's inner world with compassion and understanding. They discover how to hold up a mirror to each

other to see the beauty and loveliness while taking an honest look at *crtation?*
those parts that may be difficult to face.

Jesus knows Mary completely and loves her devotedly.[7] The
reverse is also true: Mary knows Jesus completely and loves him
devotedly.

Springing out of his vibrant companionship with Mary and his
deep encounters with the Mystery of Life, Jesus feels profound
insights welling up from within. His cup is full and running over.[8]
He says, "When you make the two into one, and when you make the
inner like the outer and the outer like the inner, and the upper like
the lower, and when you make male and female into a single one, so
that male will not be male nor the female be female... then you will
enter into the Kindom[9] of Father and Mother, the Way of Mystery."[10]

Jesus goes even further and says, "When you make eyes in place
of an eye, a hand in place of a hand, a foot in place of a foot, an
image in place of an image, then you will know the Kindom of the
Father and Mother, the *Way of Mystery.*"[10] Like stepping into fresh
clothing, they have put on their true humanity to wear in public for
all to see.[12]

What they have experienced within is now being expressed and
lived in their relationships, their work, and the way they pace themselves.

NOTES

1. Gospel of Mary 6:1
2. Gospel of Philip 32
3. Gospel of Philip 55
4. Gospel of Philip 31
5. Gospel of Thomas 108
6. Dialogue of the Savior 20:2
7. Gospel of Mary 10:10
8. Psalm 23:5
9. See Cameo Essay #2

10. Gospel of Thomas 22:4-5

11. Gospel of Thomas 22:6-7

12. Gospel of Philip 24

CAMEO ESSAY 2:
"KINGDOM OF GOD" OR "KINDOM OF FATHER AND MOTHER?"

JESUS AND MARY MAGDALENE LIVE UNDER THE oppressive influence of the Roman Empire, yet they discover a way of living freely. Their wisdom teachings are centered in proclaiming how to experience and live this new freedom.

In the written documents that come down to us, we find that the very heart and core of their teaching about how to live freely is in the Greek phrase *Basileia tou theou.*

Greek is the language of the Gospels but Aramaic would have been the primary language spoken by Jesus and Mary so perhaps there was an Aramaic phrase behind *Basileia tou theou*. Yet it is next to impossible to know exactly what their original phrase might have been. Greek would have been their second language so perhaps they also used *Basileia tou theou*. How, then, might this phrase be best translated into English?

Scholars who produced the King James Version translated the phrase *Basileia tou theou* as Kingdom of God. Variations include Kingdom of Heaven and Kingdom of the Father. In the late sixteenth and early seventeenth centuries, a time of monarchies,

Kingdom was clearly understood by readers and hearers. This wording would have been fully endorsed by King James, the sponsor of the translation project, who was determine to solidify his right to the British crown.

In our twenty-first century context, inherited monarchies are more likely to be symbolic than political. In the United States and many other countries we are attempting to create and maintain democracies. Consequently, the use of Kingdom does not resonate well as a valid expression of what Jesus is trying to convey to us. So, again, how might *Basileia tou theou* be best translated in our context?

Jesus Seminar translators tell us that they "went in search of a term or phrase that would satisfy three basic requirements: (1) the phrase had to function as both verb and noun, to denote both activity and region; (2) the phrase had to specify that God's activity was absolute; there could be no suggestion of democracy or shared governance; (3) the phrase should have feeling tones of the ominous, of ultimate threat, of tyranny—associations going with the end of the age and the last judgment, since it often appears in such contexts."

Some members of the Jesus Seminar proposed empire as an appropriate ancient and modern counterpart, since it called to mind both the Roman Empire and the evil empires of the nineteenth and twentieth centuries. But empire could not serve as a verb; for this purpose something like "rule" or "reign" was required. And Jesus' own use of the phrase, particularly in connection with his parables, called for a phrase that was perhaps less ominous, yet no less absolute. The happy solution the panel reached was to combine imperial with rule to gain the nuance of both terms.

When a spatial term is required by the context, it was decided to utilize domain: in his domain God's dominion is supreme. When Matthew substitutes "Heaven" for "God," Jesus Seminar scholars translate, "Heaven's imperial rule" or "Heaven's domain" as required by the context."[1]

Unfortunately, the terms "Imperial rule," and "domain" still come across as variations on the word "Empire" with the connotations of a Dominator mode of thinking. Historian Riane Eisler in her insightful work, *The Chalice and the Blade* demonstrates clearly that Jesus replaces the Dominator model with Partnership which proved to be threatening to both the governing authorities of the Empire and the patriarchy of religion.

The issue of how to translate *Basileia tou theou* is further complicated by the fact that in their wisdom teachings Jesus and Mary never define what they mean. Instead they say that it is like a mustard seed, it is like a pearl, it is like a woman kneading leaven into bread, it is like this, it is like that. If you don't understand, they provide yet another symbolic metaphor. Eventually, perhaps we "get it." Once we understand experientially, then we have the same problem Jesus and Mary have: how shall we put into words the Mystery who is beyond all definition?

One further consideration is that in their Hebrew tradition the Holy Name was never spoken. It was understood that if you spoke the Name you would die: it is rather like splitting the atom where you cannot survive the Energy release. Hebrew custom was to refrain from saying the word aloud and in its place to say Adonai meaning Lord.

This we know clearly: Jesus and Mary Magdalene are inviting people to let go of their fear of the Roman Empire and commit themselves to another reign or rule, a Way of Living that emerges out of Mystery. The disciples of Jesus and Mary Magdalene became known as followers of the Way.

There is an additional language problem that remains to be addressed: the use of the word "God" which so often conveys maleness, patriarchy, and oppression of many kinds. In reaction, some people switch to worshiping only a "Goddess."

When we study the record of the experience of Jesus in his Baptism we hear him saying, "Abba," Father. He also says, "My True Mother gave me Life."[2] We are now learning from some texts in the Nag Hammadi Scriptures that in the early communities of faith people referred to God as both Father and Mother and beyond. Is there an English word that we can use that includes both the feminine and the masculine at once?

Search the English language and it is difficult, if not impossible, to find such a word.

For example, when the Jesus Seminar scholars are translating the Greek word *logos* in the opening lines of the Gospel of John they use four English words, "In the beginning there was *the divine Word and Wisdom*." "Word" is masculine and "Wisdom" is feminine.

The good news is that in the Chinese language there is a single word that includes both the word and the wisdom, the masculine and the feminine, the yang and the yin, and more, much more. That single word is Tao. The Chinese language has come to our semantic rescue! Perhaps the time has come to add to our vocabulary the word Tao (pronounced "Dao") which is both a noun and a verb simultaneously.

How then shall we understand the full meaning of Tao? The Chinese classic Tao Te Ching opens by saying, "The Tao that can be told is not the eternal Tao. The name that can be named is not the eternal name."[3] Later in the text it says, "Those who know do not say; those who say do not know."[4] The issue remains: we are attempting to name what is beyond naming. It remains an indefinable Mystery.

Words are symbols that function like a finger pointing toward Reality, but the finger must not be confused with the Reality itself. In the final analysis, all words are inadequate.

There is One Amazing Mystery within, between, around, and beyond us. The more we enter into and experience this Mystery the more the Empires of today will lose their grip on us. As we increase our awareness of Mystery we will discover more freedom, joy, and empowerment for living creatively.

When Jesus is saying, "Abba,"[5] Father, and also, "Mother"[6] he is using relational words reflecting a deep sense of connection with the Source of Life, with the Ground of Being, with Ultimate Reality.

The troublesome word, "Kingdom" remains. Perhaps the time has come, as some[7] are suggesting, to drop the letter "g" and refer to the Kindom of Father and Mother.

Since there is no adequate English translation of the word, *baslieia*, some scholars are suggesting that the word be left in the Greek.[8]

The inadequacy of words persists. And a further consideration calls out to us. The Gospel of Philip clearly states that Jesus, the Teacher, does everything in a Mystery.[9]

Reminding ourselves that all attempts to Name the Unnamable will fail, I have finally decided that in this book *Basileia tou theou* will appear in English as "Kindom of Father and Mother," followed by the italicized phrase *the Way of Mystery*.

NOTES

1. *The Complete Gospels*, p. 12

2. Gospel of Thomas 101

3. Tao Te Ching 1

4. Tao Te Ching 56

5. Gospel of Mark 14:36

6. Gospel of Thomas 101:3

7. Caroline Casey, mystical activist, on KPFA Radio, the Pacifica network.

8. Shelly Matthews and Melanie Johnson DeBaufre during the Jesus Seminar on the Road in Sahuarita, Arizona, February 26, 2010.

9. Gospel of Philip 68, *Nag Hammadi Scriptures* 67:27

CHAPTER 7:
A CIRCLE OF SEEKERS BEGINS FORMING

AS JESUS AND MARY ARE WALKING ALONG TOGETHER, they notice one of the disciples of John the Baptizer coming toward them with a distressed look on her face. Mary greets her and asks, "Is something wrong?" And John's disciple replies, "John has been arrested!"[1]

On the one hand the news is a shock, but on the other hand it is no surprise. After all, how long would the authorities allow this kind of preaching to go on? it is much too empowering for the listeners and much too threatening for those in authority. Mary asks the disciple, "So how is John? What are they doing to him in prison?"

The disciple tells them as much as she knows. Then Jesus asks, "Then who will carry on his work, his vital ministry?" Jesus turns toward Mary and as their eyes meet, they both know the answer to this question: John's ministry has been given to them. They will pick up where John left off. Ready or not, they will do this together.

They have the feeling that some parts of John's message will remain the same, other parts will go deeper into the soul, perhaps even further than they themselves realize.

Entering Galilee together, Jesus and Mary are sharing their experience and proclaiming the Good News to whoever will listen. "The time is up: old power structures are crumbling and the Kindom of the Father and Mother, the *Way of Mystery*, is breaking in. A new order is beginning! Expect major changes within you and around you! Change your ways! Be aware! Become part of this new movement of the Spirit![2]

"Seek and keep on seeking. Do not stop seeking until you find. And when you find you will be troubled. And then you will marvel and be astonished: you will be amazed! Then you will reign over All: you will have a new perspective over everything! And then you will rest![3] You will feel the rhythm of Life, the movement and the rest![4]

Walking along the shore of the Sea of Galilee, Jesus spots two men he knows: Simon and Andrew, brothers in the fishing business together. Mary also recognizes them as fishermen who have often taken their catch to Magdala for sale. Many times she has bought their catch and salted it away.

But today is different and the greeting to Simon and Andrew rings out clear as a bell, "Forget the fish! Come, join us in fishing for people!"[5]

Who in his right mind would quit a good fishing business and go off somewhere with a stranger and no clear plan of what is involved? It seems impulsive, even foolish, but who cares? This is what Simon and Andrew spontaneously feel compelled to do.

After going a little further down the road, Mary and Jesus catch sight of two more fishermen, James and John, who are mending the nets in their boat. Hearing the same ringing call, they leave their father Zebedee in the boat with the hired hands and join the growing circle of seekers.[6]

As Jesus, Mary, and the fishermen are walking along together, Jesus gives them a new understanding of fishing by telling a story. "The one who discovers how to be a truly human being is like a wise fisherman who cast his net into the sea and draws it up from the sea full of little fish. Among them the wise fisherman discovers a fine large fish. He throws all the little fish back into the sea, and easily chooses the larger fish. Anyone here with two good ears had better listen."[7]

Someone calls out, "Yes, we already know that story: it's one of Aesop's fables! Why don't you tell us one of your own stories?"

And Mary replies, "Aesop had a point: we all go fishing. But did Aesop tell you that we need to drop our nets down into the sea of our own souls and pull up whatever we find there? Did he tell you that we need to sort out what we find and select what is most important? So, you see, we are fishing inside ourselves as well as fishing for people."

At Mary's urging, they go into Magdala. "I have some friends I would like you to meet, Joanna and Susanna. I've known them both for a long time. I know what they are going through. And right now is prime time for them to have something new happen in their lives. Perhaps together we can walk with them and help them find new direction and release new energy."

So Mary and Jesus visit with Joanna and Susanna; this is the dark night of their souls and a time of healing for each of them.[8] Living out her new awareness becomes especially difficult for Joanna because of her home situation: her husband, Chuza, is making a good living which is fine, but he is working as a steward for Herod. The Herodians are cooperating with the Roman occupation authorities. Joanna has been increasingly uncomfortable living with Chuza. With her new awareness of the Way moving within her, Joanna knows the day is coming when she will have to leave her husband and take her dowry with her.

Susanna is from a wealthy family with Herodian connections. She knows that if she joins up with Jesus and Mary and starts traveling with them her action will be seen as scandalous by her family and friends. This may be costly for her but she knows she must take the risk.[9] Susanna and Joanna talk it over together and decide to make the break and go on the road with Jesus and Mary.

The next day Jesus and Mary spot Philip who is down from Bethsaida. They invite him to open himself to the Way that is within, between, around, and beyond him. He knows in his heart that this is right and with great enthusiasm calls out to his brother Nathanael to join them.

When Nathanael learns that Jesus is from Nazareth, an insignificant little village of less than five hundred people,[10] he asks, "Can anything good come from that place?" Philip knows there is no sense arguing with his brother so he says, "Come and see."[11]

Jesus likes Philip right away and says, "You are a genuine person—there is not a trace of deceit in you."[12]

A circle of disciples is forming around Jesus and Mary. A core group is already taking shape and they often come in pairs: Peter and Andrew, James and John, Joanna and Susanna, Philip and Nathanael. Sitting in a circle one evening in Mary's home in Magdala, Jesus says, "You are my friends: our friendship is coming out of our knowing our true Mother and Father."[13]

Mary and Jesus are in touch with the Spirit and know that they will be following their sense of inner direction each step of the Way. It is too soon to go back to Nazareth. People in his hometown will remember him as a boy growing up. They knew what he was like before his immersion in Mystery. Would they be open to hear what he has to say now? Perhaps some other time? Right now the next stop is Capernaum.

NOTES

1. Mark 1:14

2. Mark 1:14

3. Gospel of Thomas 2

4. Gospel of Thomas 50

5. Mark 1:16-17

6. Mark 1:19-20

7. Gospel of Thomas 8

8. Luke 8:1-3

9. *Anchor Bible Dictionary*, Volume 6, p. 246, Doubleday, New York 1992

10. *Anchor Bible Dictionary*, Volume 4, p. 1050, Doubleday, New York 1992

11. John 1:46

12. John 1:47

13. John 15:15, Gospel of Thomas 101:3

CHAPTER 8:
A VERY FULL DAY
IN CAPERNAUM₁

JESUS AND MARY ARE WALKING ALONG THE LAKE together with their new followers, Simon Peter, Andrew, James and John, Susanna and Joanna, Philip and Nathanael. They arrive in Capernaum on the sabbath day and go directly to the synagogue. Jesus walks right in and starts teaching people on his own authority, unlike the scholars.

Jesus says, "If your leaders say to you, 'Look, the Father's rule is in the sky,' then the birds of the sky will precede you. If they say to you, 'It is in the sea,' then the fish will precede you. Rather, the Kindom of the Father and Mother, the *Way of Mystery*, is inside you and outside you. When you know yourselves, then you will be known, and you will understand that you are the children of the living Father. But if you do not know yourselves, then you live in poverty, and you are that poverty."[2]

Jesus says, "Know what is in front of your face, and what is hidden from you will be disclosed to you. For there is nothing hidden that won't be revealed and nothing buried that won't be raised."[3]

Anointed with the power of the energetic Spirit moving within him, Jesus speaks directly from his own experience and does not need to quote a text to prove or justify his point. There is no secondhand religion for Jesus. His daring and his clarity come across with the full force of personal conviction. People are feeling sincerity in the way he teaches. He weaves questions into his teaching and gets into dialogue with people. For those who have some education, Jesus reminds them of the style of Socrates. His message has many layers of meaning. Literate or illiterate, everyone is astonished by his teaching and the way he says it.

Jesus keeps on his theme and says, "If you bring forth what is within you, what you have will save you. If you do not have that within you, what you do not have will kill you."[4]

Just then someone in the congregation stands up and shouts out, "Jesus! What do you want with us, you Nazarene? Have you come to get rid of us? I know who you are: God's holy man!"[5]

With this loud interruption, there is a rustle among the people. Many in the congregation think of this man as being possessed by an unclean spirit. Perhaps Peter is thinking to himself, "I wonder how Jesus will deal with this guy?" Perhaps James or John, who are known for being "sons of thunder," are wondering if they should throw this fellow out before he causes any further disruption. Mary stays calm and lets her own energy flow into the situation. She knows in her heart that Jesus will know just what to do.

Jesus yells back at the unclean spirit, "Shut up, and get out of him!"[6] The confrontation has begun and the man is thrown into convulsions until he lets out a loud shriek and the spirit comes out of him.[7]

People are wondering what is happening here. Perhaps the man has just gone through an epileptic fit. Perhaps he is wrestling with his own inner demons. Someone murmurs under his breath, "Reminds me of when Jacob was wrestling with an angel all night!"[8] "Yes," says someone close by, "only this is happening in broad daylight!"

Whatever this episode is all about, it is now over. Jesus and the man are talking quietly with each other and Jesus wraps up his message with a few more memorable thoughts, "You are the salt of the earth."[9] "You are the light of the world."[10]

On the way out of the synagogue, people are saying to one another things like this, "What in the world did he mean by us being salt of the earth and light of the world?" Others are saying, "I may not fully understand, but this I know, when I am near him, I am near the fire!"[11]

Jesus, Mary, and the other disciples are the last to leave. They decide to go over to Peter and Andrew's house and have something to eat. As soon as they arrive, they learn that Peter's mother-in-law is in bed with a fever.[12] Jesus goes up to her, takes hold of her hand, raises her up, and the fever disappears. The connection of healing energy running between them cools the fever and she is feeling much better. Feeling responsibility for her guests, she gets up out of bed and begins preparing and serving a meal. Perhaps Mary is wondering, "She has not been well and even though she is better now, why does she feel so obligated to do the serving?"

Word spreads rapidly about the scene in the synagogue and by evening the whole town is crowding around the door. People with various kinds of diseases and personal problems come to Jesus and Mary. Especially notable are those struggling with their inner demons, conflicting forces causing distress. Because of her own healing and compassion, Mary is well prepared for healing ministry. She takes time patiently with each person, assisting them in encountering, transforming, and redirecting their chakra energies.[13]

After a very full day, Jesus and Mary and the others spend the night in the home of Peter and Andrew. Rising early the next morning, they slip away to a quiet and isolated place for prayer, centering and rejuvenating their energies.[14] But Peter and those with him hunt them down and when they find them, Peter says, "They're all looking for you."

But Jesus replies, "Let's go somewhere else, to the neighboring villages, so I can speak there too, since that's what I came for."[15]

NOTES

1. Mark 1:21-39. In Mark's Gospel, the synagogue in Capernaum in the first synagogue where Jesus teaches. Luke rearranges the sequence and says that Jesus begins in his home town of Nazareth, which is unlikely. Luke also provides Jesus with a text

for his inaugural teaching: Isaiah 61:1-2, but the earlier Gospel of Mark says that Jesus is teaching "from his own authority." So what might his message have been in his "first sermon"?

2. Gospel of Thomas 3, Scholars Version

3. Gospel of Thomas 4, Scholars Version

4. Gospel of Thomas 70, Scholars Version

5. Mark 1:23-24

6. Mark 1:25

7. Mark 1:26

8. Genesis 32:22-32

9. Matthew 5:13

10. Matthew 5:14

11. Gospel of Thomas 82

12. Mark 1:29-30, Matthew 8:14-15, Luke 4:38-39

13. Regarding Chakra Energies, see Cameo Essay One, page 28.

14. Mark 1:35

15. Mark 1:36-37

CHAPTER 9:
ON THE ROAD AGAIN

IF THE COUNTRY SINGER WILLIE NELSON HAD BEEN ONE of the disciples traveling with Jesus and Mary Magdalene, his song, "On the Road Again" would have resonated with everyone:

On the road again, just can't wait to get on the road again,
The life I love is making music with my friends.
I can't wait to get on the road again.

As Jesus and his band go down the roads of Galilee, sometime their songs bring harmony, sometimes discord. Everywhere they go people seek them out. Authorities become uneasy and fearful that Jesus may cause unrest and upset the system.

The music of Jesus, Mary and the disciples follows the rhythm of "movement and rest,"[1] prayer and action, solitude and mixing with people. Jesus is both present and detached. His motto is "Be Passersby."[2] Each time his friends hear Jesus say this they wonder what exactly does he mean?

All kinds of people approach him, even lepers, outcasts with whom no one wants to associate, let alone touch in any way.

A leper comes up to him and says, "Teacher, Jesus, in wandering around with lepers and eating with them in the inn, I became a leper myself. If you want to, I'll be made clean."

Mary is thinking to herself, "This man has shown compassion to others with this skin condition and has even shared food with them. He took the risk of compassion, became infected himself and now people are avoiding him. How unfair that is!"

Jesus says to him, "Okay—you're clean!" And at once the affliction vanishes from the leper. Mary knows in her heart what has just happened: the man has seen his wholeness in Jesus which is reflected back to him. Healing is also in the eye of the beholder.

Jesus then says to him, "Go and have the priests examine your skin. Then offer for your cleansing what Moses commanded—and no more sinning." Jesus snaps at him and dismisses him curtly.[3]

Mary is bewildered by Jesus' attitude, and taking him aside asks, "Why did you snap at this man? Why were you so curt with him? Sometimes I just do not understand you!"

Jesus does not answer, so she asks again, "Were you afraid of something? Afraid you might get leprosy also, the way he did when he associated with the other lepers?"

Jesus replies slowly, "Yes, I must admit I was afraid. I do not want to be infected!"

Mary: "So you are going to avoid people with leprosy just like everyone else?"

Jesus: "I'm just being careful."

Mary: "You, careful? Yes, usually you are full of care, but your caring seems to go away when you are afraid."

Jesus: "Yes, I'll admit that is true."

Mary: "So what are you going to do about it?"

Jesus: "I'd like to feel differently..."

Mary: "And what is all this about telling him, 'No more sinning?' What has sin got to do with it?"

Jesus: "I always thought that when people were sick it was because they had sinned."

Mary: "Now you sound like the friends of Job!"

Jesus: "I really do not want to be that way..."

Mary: "Then how about a little more compassion? Mark my word, the day will come when you will say, 'There is no such thing as sin.'"[4]

They walk along in silence awhile. Their disciples are bringing up the rear and pondering the conversation they have just overheard.

Meanwhile, the leper who has experienced healing starts telling everyone and spreading the story. People continue to come from just about everywhere so that Jesus can no longer enter a town openly, but has to stay out in the countryside.[5]

As they settle down for the night under the stars, Jesus says, "You know, Mary, foxes have dens, and birds of the sky have nests, but those living from their true humanity have nowhere to rest their heads."[6]

[handwritten margin note: Interesting translation. "Son of Man"]

Mary replies, "I hear our heavenly Mother and Father saying to us 'Come to me, all you who travel and are weary, and are carrying heavy burdens, and I will give you rest.'"[7]

Still pondering what Mary has said, Jesus feels he needs time to think things over and get cleansed of his negativity. So he says, "Tomorrow, let's get in a boat and go over to Gadara and soak in the hot springs."[8]

NOTES

1. Gospel of Thomas 50

2. Gospel of Thomas 42

3. This story of the leper is taken from the Egerton Gospel 2:1-3. It is also found in Mark 1:40-45, Matthew 8:2-4, and Luke 5:12-14. The Jesus Seminar scholars offer this commentary: "Jesus did not cure this leper of Hansen's disease—the ailment known to modern medicine as leprosy. In biblical times the term leprosy embraced a wide range of disorders, including rashes, acne, eczema, psoriasis, and other forms of dermatitis. Biblical leprosy consisted of scaly or flaking skin, accompanied by white spots and white hairs; the skin may also have developed red spots or streaks and may have been broken. Leprosy was sometimes regarded as divine punishment for sin, but it was not considered an incurable disease. The Fellows of the Jesus Seminar agreed by a narrow margin that Jesus cured the "leper" of some form of dermatitis. They were much more certain that Jesus declared the leper clean. Under conventional circumstances, only a priest could declare a leper clean and thus eligible to reenter society. Jesus seems to have usurped this priestly function. Whether

Jesus actually cured the ailment is less certain." *Acts of Jesus,* Robert Funk & The Jesus Seminar, HarperSan Francisco, 1998, page 62

4. Gospel of Mary 3:3

5. Mark 1:45

6. Matthew 8:20 and Luke 9:58

7. Matthew 11:28

8. Near Gadara are the hot springs of el Hamme. *Interpreter's Dictionary of the Bible*, Volume E-J, Abingdon Press, 1962, p. 335

CHAPTER 10:
ROMAN OCCUPATION DRIVES A MAN CRAZY[1]

WHEN THEY COME TO GADARA AT THE OTHER SIDE OF the Sea of Galilee, they get out of the boat. A man under the influence of an unclean spirit comes out from the tombs where he has been living. He is wild and crazy. Nobody is able to control him. Even though he has often been bound with fetters and chains, he breaks the fetters and pulls the chains apart. Day and night he howls among the tombs and keeps bruising himself on the stones.

When he sees Jesus from a distance, he runs up and kneels before him. Jesus says, "Come out of that fellow you filthy spirit!"

The man shouts at the top of his voice, "What do you want with me, Jesus, you son of the most high God? For God's sake, don't torment me!"

Jesus starts questioning him, "What is your name?"

The man replies, "My name is Legion, for there are many of us."

"Yes," replies Mary, "The Roman Legion[2] has done this to you, making you so crazy! Inside you there is a sensitive, compassionate Spirit who needs to heal your inner torment, release your demons, and set you free!"[3]

Some of the people with a vivid imagination see a herd of two

[handwritten margin notes: "interesting connection", "In Mark, it is Jesus."]

thousand pigs stampeding and running off a cliff into the sea: "There they go, the demon spirits of the Roman legion are drowning like the pigs they are!"

With or without the imagination, people have heard the commotion and then feel the calm. They come with curiosity, asking, "What happened?" And there they see the man who had been tormented, sitting peacefully, clothed, and in his right mind.[4]

As the curious become satisfied and move away, Mary asks the man who has become well, "We are on our way to the hot springs: care to join us?" He accepts her invitation and off they go together, just the three of them.

On the way Mary and Jesus ponder in silence the events of the day and people who are excluded by others because of their outer appearance, like skin conditions, and those who are excluded because of their inner torments that seem so out of control. Jesus, Mary, and their new friend, a former lunatic, arrive at the hot springs and enjoy a refreshing soak in the healing waters.[5]

Coming out of the waters, Jesus emerges with a new insight, "When an unclean spirit leaves a person, it wanders through waterless places in search of a resting place. When it doesn't find one, it says, 'I will go back to the home I left.' It then returns, and finds it swept and refurbished. Next it goes out and brings back seven other spirits more vile than itself, who enter and settle in there. So that person ends up worse off than when he or she started."[6]

And Mary replies, "Our demons are transformed when we are immersed in the waters of the Spirit. I know because it happened to me when I was baptized and filled with the Spirit!"

NOTES
1. The story is found in Mark 5:1-20. cf. Matthew 8:28-33, Luke 8:26-39
2. A legion consisted of four to six thousand soldiers in the Roman army used to conquer and control the people of occupied countries.
3. Mark 5:11-14
4. Mark 5:14b-15

5. Near Gadara are the hot springs of el Hamme. *Interpreter's Dictionary of the Bible*, Volume E-J, Abingdon Press, 1962, p. 335

6. Luke 11:24-26

CHAPTER 11:

THE STORY OF THE TWO SONS

AFTER THEIR REFRESHING SOAK IN THE HOT SPRINGS, Jesus, Mary, and the former lunatic have returned to Capernaum. Word gets around that they are at home. Disciples come into the house and begin asking questions. Mary invites them to sit in a circle on the floor and Jesus begins asking them questions in return. Underlying all their shared teaching is one persistent and pervasive message: "Seek, and do not stop seeking until you find. When you find you will be disturbed. When you are disturbed, you will marvel, and will rule over all, and then you will rest."[1] The disciples ask Jesus what he means by each phrase and as they begin exploring the meaning more deeply, additional people enter the house and a second circle forms around the first.

Jesus tells stories illustrating his central message of seeking and finding. He begins by asking, "Is there any woman with ten silver coins, who if she loses one, wouldn't light a lamp and sweep the house and search carefully until she finds it? When she finds it, she invites her friends and neighbors over and says, 'Celebrate with me, because I have found the silver coin I had lost.'"[2]

People keep coming into the house and soon there are several concentric circles of people seated for teaching and learning together. Before long the house is full and there is no more room. People crowd around the door, listening and trying to catch the words as best they can.

PRODIGAL
SON

Jesus then tells the story of parents who had two sons.[3] The younger of them said to his father,"Father, give me the share of property that's coming to me." So he divided his resources between them.

Not many days later, the younger son got all his things together and left home for a faraway country where he squandered his property by extravagant living. Just when he had spent it all, a serious famine swept through that country, and he began to do without.

So he went and hired himself out to one of the citizens of that country, who sent him out to his farm to feed the pigs. He longed to satisfy his hunger with the carob pods, which the pigs usually ate; but no one offered him anything.

Coming to his senses he said, "Lots of my father's hired hands have more than enough to eat, while here I am dying of starvation! I'll get up and go to my father and I'll say to him, 'Father I have sinned against heaven and affronted you; I don't deserve to be called a son of yours any longer; treat me like one of your hired hands.'" And he got up and returned to his father.

But while he was still a long way off, his father caught sight of him and was moved to compassion. He went running out to him, threw his arms around his neck, and kissed him. And the son said to him, "Father, I have sinned against heaven and affronted you; I don't deserve to be called a son of yours any longer."

But the father said to his slaves,"Quick! Bring out the finest robe and put it on him; put a ring on his finger and sandals on his feet. Fetch the fat calf and slaughter it; let's have a feast and celebrate, because this son of mine was dead and has come back to life; he was lost and now is found." And they started celebrating.

Now his elder son was out in the field; and as he got closer to the house, he heard music and dancing. He called one of the servant-boys over and asked what was going on.

He said to him,"Your brother has come home and your father has slaughtered the fat calf, because he has him back safe and sound."

But he was angry and refused to go in. So his father came out and began to plead with him. But he answered his father, "See here, all these years I have slaved for you. I never once disobeyed any of your orders; yet you never once provided me with a kid goat so I could celebrate with my friends. But when this son of yours shows up, the one who has squandered your estate with prostitutes—for him you slaughtered the fat calf."

But the father said to him, "My child, you are always at my side. Everything that's mine is yours. But we just had to celebrate and rejoice, because this brother of yours was dead, and has come back to life; he was lost, and now is found."

After Jesus finishes telling this story, there is a pregnant pause. Then Mary says, "Jesus, your story seems to illustrate what you were saying about seeking and not to stop seeking until you find, and when you find being troubled and then amazed and then resting!" Then Mary turns toward the people and says, "Many of you here are parents. How do you feel about the younger son's asking for his inheritance early?"

↓ ALL SPECULA-TION

"Outrageous!" says one man. "He should have done the work at home like his older brother and wait until the old man dies for his inheritance!"

A younger man speaks up and says, "If he waits that long, he would be an old man himself and never have any chance to go traveling and exploring on his own! Why wait around? I say he had a lot of courage!" The younger men all agree and the older men try to shout them down.

Just then a woman speaks up and says, "It is always the same, generation after generation. Everyone does the same thing. Nothing changes. I like the younger son's initiative: he wants to make something of himself. Of course, I would miss him terribly while he was gone."

Mary then asks another question, "How do the rest of you think the parents might have felt when their younger son was away?"

A mother says, "If I didn't hear from him, I would worry and start imagining all kinds of terrible things. So I would want him to send word back as often as he could so I would know he was all right."

A father says, "Well, I would have confidence in my son: I think he could handle whatever comes up and if he makes some mistakes he might learn from them. If I had taught him well enough and he had paid attention, he would be okay."

Another father says, "You mean give him enough rope and he'll hang himself? What kind of father are you, anyway?"

The first one replies, "I would trust my son. That's enough."

As the argument starts to get very heated, Mary intervenes and says, "Let's look at the story from the point of view of the younger son: what might it be like for him when he finds himself out on his own?"

Responses come quickly, especially from the younger men. "If it were me, I would feel free! No responsibilities! Do whatever I like. No one telling me what to do! Just have a good time!"

Mary then focuses attention on another character in the story, saying, "There are two brothers in the story. What might the older brother have been feeling while his younger brother was away on his adventures?

One person says, "He was slaving away, working hard, doing everything he had to do, not having any fun. I imagine he would have been very angry and resentful! Here he is working hard and his brother is out there with all these wild women, all these prostitutes!"

"Hold on a minute," says another young man. "Jesus didn't say that the younger brother actually was hanging out with prostitutes. It was the older brother who was imagining it."

"Right," says another. "It was the older brother who wished he could get some of that!"

Everyone laughs and Mary then asks, "And what is it like for the younger son?"

"Well he does go through his money. Traveling and meeting new people, and getting new ideas, when he suddenly discovers he is out of funds and has to take whatever job he can get!" says someone else.

"Yes, and that's when he starts thinking even more deeply about things. He has been learning so much and figuring out what is really important to him. Family really does matter and he decides to go home."

And another,"The plain truth is the man is broke and has to go home!"

And Mary says, "Whatever the case, and it is probably different for every person who is willing to take the risk and go on the journey, he or she does come to his senses, feels a shift inside, and decides to return home. And how are his parents feeling now?"

"Thanks for talking about both parents, Mary," says a woman in the group. "Jesus only mentioned the father, but as far as I'm concerned the mother would have been just as excited about her younger son coming home and would have welcomed him back just like the father. And besides, who do you think would have ended up actually cooking the calf for the party?"

Just then Jesus pops into the conversation, "Sorry about not mentioning his mother. Perhaps I took her for granted!"

"And what is the real point of the story?" says Mary. "You have to make the journey, leave the familiar, explore, wake up, and return and see who you are and your true home for the first time!" People are becoming excited and are asking more questions.

NOTES

1. Gospel of Thomas 2, from the Greek version

2. Luke 15:8-9

3. Luke 15:11-31

NFV has no mention of mother either.

CHAPTER 12:

JESUS AND MARY IN AN OPEN HOUSE₁

RIGHT IN THE MIDST OF THEIR TEACHING THERE IS A BIG commotion. People are breaking a hole in the roof, setting the roof tiles aside. Sunlight streams in as though the heavens were being opened!

All who have been seated begin standing up and moving back to form an open space in the center.

Two men jump down through the hole into the room and two other people are gently lowering a stretcher into the room. The man on the stretcher seems to have something wrong with him: looks like he may be paralyzed.

As the man is laid gently on the floor, one of the men says, "Sorry for the interruption, but we just had to get our friend to you, Jesus, and there was no way we could get into the house: too many people crowding around outside. We will fix the roof later, promise! But our paralyzed friend just has to see you!" The man is resting on the floor right between Jesus and Mary.

People are surprised at the interruption and the commotion. Some are objecting and yelling, "What do you think you are doing?" Many are speechless at these strange circumstances. The more spiritually aware sense the rising energy and know in their hearts that something unusual is about to occur. Amazement, curiosity, and anticipation flood the room.

Jesus and Mary are calm and soon all the people in the room become quiet.

With Jesus on one side and Mary on the other, they center their chakra energies and focus their attention on the man who is paralyzed. Looking intently at him, Jesus says, "Son, your sins are forgiven." Mary massages his feet. Jesus holds his head gently. A resonant connection is made from Mary through the man to Jesus. As they pray with him aloud and in silence, healing energy runs through the man's entire body with rhythmic, pulsating power.

Simultaneously, skeptical scholars in the room are saying to themselves, "Why does this fellow say such things? He's blaspheming! Who can forgive sins except the one God?" There is the risk that their negativity might draw energy away from the man and prevent his healing.

Jesus senses in his spirit that the scholars are raising questions like this among themselves, so he turns toward them and says, "Why do you entertain questions about these things? Which is easier to say to the paralytic, 'Your sins are forgiven,' or to say, 'Get up, pick up your stretcher and walk'?"

Having deflected the opposing energies from the scholars, Jesus and Mary continue running healing energies through the man's body from his feet through the crown of his head. The force field formed between them is doing its work. Jesus and Mary are awakening the true humanity lying asleep within the man who has been paralyzed and unable to function fully for such a long time.

As new vitality flows through his soul and body, old wounds are healed, blockages are opened, and vitality is restored. Jesus speaks and Mary echoes the heart of the message one more time, "I say to you, stand up, take up your stretcher, and go home!"

Revitalized by this encounter and in touch with his own true humanity, the man stands up on his feet. His new energy opens a path like Moses parting the waters of the Red Sea. He walks straight through the crowd and right on out the door into his new spirit filled life.

Everyone looks on in amazement and all become ecstatic, praising the Wondrous Mystery and exclaiming, "We've never seen anything like this!"

This healing has served as climax to the teaching. One by one the people leave in silent wonder. Before long, Jesus and Mary are left alone with each other, still basking in the joy of being catalysts of healing power.

"Thank you, Mary, for sitting opposite me in the circle today."

Mary replies, "That put me near the door where I could welcome people and invite them into the circle."

"That was good hospitality, but there was more, much more. Your being across from me where I can see you helps so much. I look at you and draw strength. The expressions on your face and your little gestures give me clues. Your questions and your comments are so helpful. I work so much better when I am in resonance with you."

"Jesus, today I began feeling that you and I are teaching and empowering people together!"

"Yes, that's it, exactly. Our task is to empower others. And what a joy that is! Thank you for being my companion and my partner in this work."

"We are in this together, Jesus, whatever comes. But I am concerned that the authorities won't like what we are doing," Jesus replies, smiling, "Then that will have to be their problem. It has been a long day, Mary. Let's center ourselves, pray a little more, then get some rest..."

NOTES

1. The story of the Paralytic is found first in Mark 2:1-12 with parallels in Matthew 9:1-8 and Luke 5:17-26

CHAPTER 13:
A BENT WOMAN STANDS UP₁

IT IS THE SABBATH. JESUS HAS BEEN TEACHING ABOUT the prophet Ezekiel hearing the Voice within him saying, "Stand up on your feet!"² Jesus expands the message and says, "Listen to the Voice within you. See the vision set before you. Live out your true humanity. Act without fear."

Coming out of the synagogue, Mary notices a woman who had not been in the service. She is walking around very bent over. It is clear that in her life she sees more sandals than faces. Only by turning her face to one side or the other can she get a glimpse of anyone.

Mary says, "Look at her, Jesus." And Jesus replies, "Yes, I know, she's been that way for a very long time. I remember her from right after my Bar Mitzvah. It was just about then when something happened to her, I don't remember exactly what it was."

"You mean to tell me she has been this way for eighteen years and no one has done anything about it?" says Mary.

"I have always felt sorry for her and like everyone else I have just accepted it."

"You have been accepting it? How do you think it has been for her? The worst situation is when a woman is resigned about her con-

63

dition and thinks there is nothing she can do about it. How long is she going to continue being bent over like that?"

Jesus replies, "We might be able to do something, but she has to do something herself as well." Then he calls out, "Woman, come over here!" She is startled because rarely does anyone speak with her. But she responds to the call and moves toward Mary and Jesus. When they have come close to each other, Jesus places his right hand on her lower back and his left hand on the top of her head: a rush of energy begins moving with gentle force up through her body to the crown of her head. With all her energy centers activated, she stands up straight! In amazement she finds she is able to move with ease. With head raised high and arms lifting up, she praises God with all her heart and Energy!

People see her doing a little dance and are very surprised. Everyone thinks that what has just happened is a wonderful thing except the leader of the synagogue. When he hears the commotion he comes outside to see what is happening. Sizing up the situation, he says, "Don't you know that there are six days which we devote to work? You people can come here on any of those days and be healed, but not on the sabbath day."³

Jesus responds angrily and says, "You phonies! Every last one of you unties your ox or your donkey from the feeding trough on the sabbath day and leads it off to water, don't you? This woman, a daughter of Abraham who has been kept in bondage for eighteen long years—should she not be released from these bonds just because it is the sabbath day?"⁴

People hearing Jesus telling off the synagogue leader start shouting, "That's right!" And they join Jesus and Mary in dancing with the woman. People start singing familiar songs with new energy.

Later, after everyone has left and the woman has gone home, Jesus and Mary sit down together on the ground and she says, "You know, Jesus, I've seen so many women like her, lots of them, yielding to whatever the men want. Going along obediently, carrying whatever burdens are put on their backs. They are just like her, only it doesn't show so obviously. Their spirits are broken."

"And it is not just women, Mary. Farmers are being forced into debt from heavy taxes and then their land is confiscated. Next thing you know they go back to work the same land as tenant farmers, producing for the new owners with barely enough left over for themselves and their children. They might as well be slaves. Everyone tells them what to do: landlords, officers, Roman soldiers, and those pious leaders in the synagogue, let alone the priests up in the Temple in Jerusalem. The people working for Herod know that they are part of this oppressive system, but they are afraid of losing their jobs. Everyone is so afraid! There are more of us than the people who are controlling us, but no one does anything effective to set the people free! It makes me angry, very angry!"

"And don't forget the children, Jesus. They take the brunt of it! They get the beatings when their parents are frustrated and upset. Their bright eyes start looking sad: they run and hide behind their mothers' skirts a lot. They are learning to be afraid at a very young age!"

"I know, Mary, and the only people doing anything about it are the Zealots organizing for revolution and the Sicarii carrying out targeted assassinations. But whenever they take out a few people, Rome just cracks down more and more. Violence is not the answer. There has to be another way: we've got to help set people free from the inside out! Looks like we've got our work cut out for us, Mary."

"Yes, Jesus, and somehow I have the feeling that the key to unlocking the fears and releasing their freedom lies with a fresh look at their innocent children."

NOTES

1. The story of the bent woman is told only in Luke 13:10-17.

2. The phrase, "Stand up on your feet," Ezekiel 2:1.

3. Luke 13:14

4. Luke 13:15-16

CHAPTER 14:
CONVERSATIONS WITH CHILDREN

JESUS IS ENGAGED IN LIFELONG LEARNING ACCELERATED by his baptism and wilderness experience, enabling him to see more clearly, listen more carefully, and give focused attention. His learning is enhanced by his centering prayer and his conversations and encounters with everyone he meets including children.

Walking through the marketplace with Mary, Jesus notices especially the infants and children. Jesus says, "The person old in days won't hesitate to ask a little child seven days old about the place of life, and that person will live."[1]

Jesus sees some babies nursing and says to his disciples, "These nursing babies are like those who enter the Kindom, the *Way of Mystery*." They reply, "Then shall we enter the *Way of Mystery* as babies?"

"Look how the Mother and Child are one, giving and receiving from each other. When you make the two into one, and when you make the inner like the outer and the outer like the inner, you will enter the Way of Mystery."[2]

Mary adds, "Most children are so trusting, so spontaneous, and so in touch with their instincts. I love their native curiosity. Are these some of the qualities we adults have lost and need to recover?"

Oneness

Noticing how attentive Jesus and Mary are to children, parents start bringing their children to them so they can lay hands on them. But the disciples scold the parents and try to get them to go away. Jesus becomes indignant and says to his disciples, "Let the children come up to me, don't try to stop them. After all, the Way belongs to people like that. I swear to you, whoever doesn't accept the Way as a child would, certainly won't ever set foot on that path!" And he would put his arms around them and bless them, and lay his hands on them.[3] "And any of you who misleads one of these trusting souls would be better off if you had a millstone hung around your neck and were thrown into the sea!"[4]

A child with a flute says to her playmates, "Let's play wedding", but no one seems interested. Another child says, "Let's play funeral!" and no one responds. Finally another says, "Well, what do you want to play?"[5]

Jesus smiles and says, "So many people these days are just like these children! No matter what you suggest, no one wants to play. No one wants to get involved!"

Just then Jairus, one of the leaders of the synagogue, starts coming toward Jesus, who says, "I wonder what he wants? Ready to offer more criticism?" And Mary replies, "No, I think it is something else: look at the anxious expression on his face!"

Jairus comes closer and drops to his knees. He starts pleading and begging, "My little daughter is on the verge of death, so come put your hands on her so she may be cured and live! She is only twelve years old and I love her so much, please come and help!"[6]

They start out with Jairus to his home and along the way a crowd forms. In the midst of the crowd is a woman who has had continuous vaginal bleeding for twelve years; she has been to many doctors and spent all her money but nothing has helped and her condition has gotten worse.

Having heard about Jesus, she says to herself, "If I can just touch his cloak, I'll be cured!" She works her way through the crowd, comes up behind Jesus, and touches the hem of his cloak. Her vaginal flow stops instantly and she senses in her body that she is cured of her illness.

Jesus, realizing that power has drained out of him, says, "Who touched my clothes?"

His disciples say to him,"You see the crowd jostling you around and you're asking, 'Who touched me?'"

Jesus starts looking around to see who had done it. Although the woman is scared and starts trembling, realizing what she has done, she comes and falls down before him and tells him the whole truth. Jesus looks compassionately at her and says, "Daughter, your trust has cured you. Go in peace, and farewell to your illness."[7]

While Jesus is speaking with the woman, the synagogue officials approach and say to Jairus, "Your daughter has died; why keep bothering the Teacher?"

Overhearing this conversation, Jesus says to Jairus, "Don't be afraid, just have trust!"

He wouldn't let anyone follow along with him except Mary, Peter, James, and John. When they come to Jairus' house, Jesus notices a lot of clamor; people are crying and wailing. Jesus enters the house and says to them, "Why are you carrying on like this? The child hasn't died; she's sleeping."

They start laughing at him. So he runs everyone out of the house and takes the child's father and her mother and his companions and goes in where the child is. He takes the child by the hand and says to her, "*Talitha koum*" (which means, "Little girl, get up!"). And the little girl gets right up and starts walking around.

Everyone is ecstatic. Jesus gives them strict orders that no one should learn about this, and he tells them to give her something to eat.[8]

As they are leaving, Mary says to Jesus, "You've had so much trouble from the leaders of the synagogues, but you haven't let that keep you from caring for this child. I'm proud of you!"

And Jesus replies, "Why blame the children for their parents behavior?"

There is a pregnant pause in their conversation and then Mary says lovingly to Jesus, "Do you think we may have a child of our own someday?" And Jesus replies,"Who knows?"

NOTES

1. Gospel of Thomas 4

2. Gospel of Thomas 22

3. Mark 10:13-16

4. Mark 9:42, cf. Luke 17:1-2, Matthew 18:6

5. Luke 7:31-32

6. Mark 5:21-24, cf. Matthew 9:18-19, Luke 8:40-42a

7. Mark 5:24-34, cf. Matthew 9:20-22, Luke 8:42b-48

8. Mark 5:35-42, cf. Matthew 9:23-26, Luke 8:49-56

CHAPTER 15:
A BIRTHDAY PARTY
FOR KING HEROD ANTIPAS[1]

"JESUS, DO YOU EVER WONDER WHAT YOUR LIFE MIGHT have been like if you hadn't gone down to the Jordan to hear John?" asks Mary.

"Now, Mary, that is a very scary thought! Without hearing John's message that led me to my baptism and my vision quest in the wilderness my life would be entirely different. Would I ever have discovered how to be centered in the One in whom we live and move and have our being? Would I still be doing some carpentry and daydreaming about what I should be doing with my life?"

Mary smiles and says, "Now you are a new kind of carpenter helping people rebuild their lives."

"Yes, Mary, now we are both architects and carpenters helping people redesign and rebuild their lives! Without John, would we ever have started this teaching and healing ministry, empowering people? Can you imagine having no disciples doing the work with us? I don't even want to think of how it might have been!"

Jesus pauses and then adds, "From Adam to John the Baptist, among those born of women, no one is greater than John the Baptist.[2] The interesting thing is that anyone who becomes as a lit-

tle child and recognizes the the Kindom of Father and Mother, the **ɔFV(?)**
Way of Mystery, will become greater than John."³

Just then two men arrive at the door with bad news: John is still
in prison in Sepphoris, a city Jesus knows well because it sits on a
hill just a few miles north of Nazareth where he grew up. When
Herod the Great died, which was about the same year Jesus was
born, his son Herod Antipas took over as tetrarch of Galilee and
Perea and made Sepphoris his northern capital. As a boy Jesus was
very much aware of the rapid expansion of this city. He knew that
Herod Antipas had built himself a palace in Sepphoris, with a theatre that seated 3,000, and an upper and lower city with an upper
and lower market. The upper city was predominantly Jewish. Many
craftsmen in Nazareth and other villages found work in Sepphoris.⁴
Now John is in custody there and these two men have come to Jesus
with a message from John.

One of them says, "John has had many reports about you since
you were anointed and empowered with the Holy Spirit. John has a
question, 'Are you the one who is to come or are we to wait for
another?'"⁵

Jesus responds and says, "Go report to John what you have heard
and seen: the blind see again and the lame walk; lepers are cleansed,
and the deaf hear; the dead are raised and the poor have the good
news preached to them. Blessings to those who don't take offense at
me."⁶

Not long afterwards, Joanna comes in and says to Mary, "My husband, Chuza, is in charge of a big birthday party for Herod Antipas.
He needs more people to help with the preparations and the serving. He wants me to come and find some other women who will
help out. He sounds desperate. And since I have been away traveling everywhere with you and Jesus, I feel I should be there and help
at least this once. Susanna says she will work. How about you, Mary?
Will you come with us?"

Mary replies, "Not my favorite thing to do, but I will help you this
one time if it will make a difference for you."

So Mary, Susanna, and Joanna go over to help Chuza in the
kitchen and in the serving. Before long everything is ready for
Herod's big birthday party. Guests come from far and wide. Officials

from Herod's court, leading men of Galilee, and dignitaries from Rome arrive. The food is lavish and superb.

As the evening progresses, there is some exotic dancing. The dancer who totally captivates Herod is Salome. Herod is so pleased with her that he makes a wild promise, "Ask me for whatever you wish and I'll grant it to you!" Then he swears an oath to her: "I'll grant you whatever you ask for, up to half my kingdom!"[7]

Salome goes and asks her mother, Herod's wife, what she should ask for. Her mother had been married to Herod's brother Philip. John had publicly criticized Herod for taking his brother's wife, which is against Jewish law. As a result of this criticism, her resentment against John had been running high and now is the opportunity for revenge. Salome's mother says, "Ask for the head of John the Baptist."

Returning to King Herod, Salome approaches him and makes her request, "I want you to give me the head of John the Baptist on a platter right now!"

The king feels regretful, but, on account of his oath and the dinner guests, he doesn't want to refuse her.[8]

Joanna, Susanna, and Mary are shocked at what they are witnessing and hurry off together and ask themselves, "Is there anything we can do to stop this madness?" They even ask Chuza, "Can you talk some sense into Herod?"

But the situation is too far gone. Herod calls for the executioner and commands him to bring John's head. Everything moves very quickly. John is beheaded in prison and the executioner brings in John's head on a platter supplied by Chuza and presents it to Herod who presents it to Salome who gives it to her mother.

John's disciples claim his body and put it in a tomb.[8] The three women return, weeping, to Jesus and relate all that has happened.

Everyone regroups around Jesus who says, "Come alone to an isolated place and rest a little."[10]

John's disciples either scatter, go into hiding, or join up with Jesus and Mary. Those who gather in the isolated place are given a brief orientation. When they ask Jesus, "What is the place to which we shall go?" Jesus replies, "Stand in the place that you can reach." Then Jesus puts it even more simply, "Be passersby."[11]

NOTES

1. This chapter is rooted in the story of the beheading of John the Baptist

2. Gospel of Thomas 46

3. Gospel of Thomas 46

4. Background information on Sepphoris is from *The Anchor Bible Dictionary*, Doubleday, 1992, Volume 5, pps. 1090-1091.

5. Matthew 11:2-3

6. Matthew 11:4-6

7. Mark 6:21-23

8. Mark 6:24-26

9. Mark 6:27-29

10. Mark 6:30

11. Gospel of Thomas 42

CHAPTER 16:
DINNER WITH LEVI, THE TOLL COLLECTOR₁

ANYONE TRAVELING ANYWHERE IN GALILEE ON ALMOST any road can expect to be stopped at a checkpoint by a toll collector. Everywhere you turn, the Empire exerts its control on the movement of people and seizes additional opportunities to collect tolls. The more fearful people allow themselves to be intimidated; they remain in their villages minding their own business. Those who have already been pushed to their limits form roving gangs of bandits who take whatever they need or want.

Instead of avoiding the system or fighting it, Jesus and Mary take another approach. When they come upon yet another toll collector, they engage in conversation with him as they do one day with a toll collector named Levi.

Mary asks, "You are from the tribe of Levites, the ones who are responsible for priestly work in the Temple?" Levi does not answer, but Mary senses that she has hit a nerve: perhaps this man Levi has been excluded from the ranks of priests. In order to survive and make some sort of living to support his family he has taken this job as a toll collector. This means that he is excluded from the ruling classes and is also despised by everyone else who hates the constant surveillance by the Empire and the additional taxes.

Jesus surprises everyone, including his own disciples, by looking Levi right in the eye and saying, "Follow me!" Levi is so startled to be invited, that he accepts and walks off the job. The next moment Levi extends an invitation of his own, "Come over to my house for dinner!" Jesus and Mary accept the offer of hospitality and off they go to Levi's house.

Having found such immediate acceptance from Jesus and Mary, Levi in his exhilaration decides to make it a big party by inviting all the other toll collectors and outcasts he knows. Having already walked off the job, he has nothing else to lose so he might as well party! Besides, maybe some other toll collectors and their outcast friends will decide to join up with Jesus!

Jesus and Mary smile at each other knowing that instead of fearing the system or fighting it, they have simply started undermining it.

Some of the disciples catch on quickly and see what Jesus is doing. Others, especially those who remember bad experiences with officials like Levi are muttering to each other, "So now we are supposed to accept this toll collecting scum?"

Word runs rapidly by way of the grapevine to the Pharisees and their scholars that a former priest who had become a toll collector has just joined up with Jesus. They come to the disciples of Jesus and ask, "Why does your teacher eat with toll collectors and sinners?"[2]

When these comments circle back around to Jesus, he has a crisp reply, "Those who are well don't need a doctor."[3] So who are the well? And who are the sick? Jesus leaves everyone trying to figure it out.

Meanwhile, it is time to get on with this impromptu party with many party crashers, all of whom are made to feel welcome. The toll collectors, who are skilled at making a little extra on the side, have the wherewithal to make their contribution to the festivities. As a result of divorce or other dire circumstances, some women have become sex workers as their last resort for making a living. They are especially welcome at the party.

Delicious food and good wine are passed around. When everyone is feeling fine and happy someone calls out, "Well, Teacher, what do you have to tell us?"

Mary whispers into Jesus ear, "How about telling them your dinner party story? They would love it!"

As the crowd quiets down and lends their ears, Jesus says, "A person was receiving visiting guests. When he had prepared the dinner, he sent his slave to invite the guests. The slave went to the first and said to that one, "My master invites you." That one said, "Some merchants owe me money; they are coming to me tonight. I have to go and give them my orders. Please excuse me from dinner."

The slave went to another and said to that one, "My master has invited you."

That one said to the slave, "I have bought a house, and I have been called away for a day. I shall have no spare time."

The slave went to another and said to that one, "My master invites you." That one said to the slave, "My friend is to be married, and I am to arrange the banquet. I shall not be able to come. Please excuse me from dinner."

The slave went to another and said to that one, "My master invites you." That one said to the slave, "I have bought a farm and I am going to collect the rent. I shall not be able to come. Please excuse me."

The slave returned and said to his master, "Those whom you invited to dinner have asked to be excused." The master said to his slave, "Go out on the streets and bring back whomever you happen to meet to have dinner."[4]

After Jesus finishes his story, the people start applauding. They are feeling so warmly accepted.

Mary whispers again in Jesus' ear and says, "Now that you have their attention, maybe they are ready to go a little further: why not give it a try?"

Jesus fixes his gaze on the crowd and speaks clearly and distinctly in a tone that everyone senses is coming in deep sincerity,

"Let me tell you the truth: I take my stand in the midst of the world and have found everyone intoxicated. I do not find any of them thirsty.

"My soul aches. I feel pained and saddened for the children of humanity, because they are blind in their hearts. They are mentally blind and do not see, for they come into the world empty, and they also seek to depart from the world empty. But meanwhile they are drunk. When they shake off their wine and sober up, then they will have a change of heart and change their ways."[5]

There is a hush and then a flood of questions about what Jesus really means. Many are feeling that partying is fine, but there is more to life than that. If so, what might it be? Many guests leave, but those who remain for further teaching begin to understand very deeply when Jesus concludes by saying, "Whoever drinks from my mouth will become like me; I myself shall become that person, and the hidden things will be revealed to him."[6]

Those who are entering into a deeper Reality share the Shalom, the Peace, with one another before leaving for their homes.

NOTES

1. This story is rooted in four parallel accounts: Mark 2:14-17, Matthew 9:9-13, Luke 5:27-32, and Gospel Oxyrhynchus 1224. In Mark and Luke the toll collector who becomes a disciple of Jesus is named Levi. The Gospel of Matthew changes the name to Matthew. Oxyrhynchus simply says that Jesus "reclined at table in the company of sinners." Presumably Jesus had more than one meal with tax collectors and sinners.

2. Matthew 9:11

3. Gospel Oxyrhynchus 5

4. The basic story most likely told by Jesus is Gospel of Thomas 64:1-11 without the interpretive 64:12 which says, "Buyers and merchants will not enter the places of my Father." Luke 14:16-24 expands the story with additional details. Matthew 22:1-10 goes even further and imposes an interpretation attempting to provide an explanation as to why the City of Jerusalem was a destroyed in 70 C.E.! How much better it is to have the Thomas version without the overlays!

5. Gospel of Thomas 28

6. Gospel of Thomas 108

CHAPTER 17:
BARTIMAEUS REGAINS HIS SIGHT[1]

ON EITHER SIDE OF THE JORDAN RIVER, JUST BEFORE IT flows into the Sea of Galilee, are two fishing villages that provide centers of operations for Jesus and Mary Magdalene and from which they venture out for their itinerant teaching. Bethsaida is located on the eastern side of the river. Capernaum is just a bit west of the Jordan. The two villages are only a few miles apart. Bethsaida is the hometown for Andrew and his brother, Peter[2] who married a woman from Capernaum and moved in with his in-laws. Bethsaida is also the hometown for Philip and Nathanael.[3]

Jesus, Mary, and their disciples are walking from Capernaum to Bethsaida and are met by a crowd of people who are bringing with them a man who is blind and lives by begging. People in the crowd ask Jesus to touch and heal him.[4]

Hearing that it is Jesus of Nazareth coming into town, the blind beggar calls out, "You son of David, Jesus, have mercy on me!"[5]

Many in the crowd start yelling at him to shut up, but he shouts all the louder, "You son of David, have mercy on me!"[6]

Jesus pauses and says, "Tell him to come over here!" They call to the blind man, "Be brave, get up, he's calling you!"[7]

So he throws off his cloak, and jumps to his feet, and goes over to Jesus.[8]

Jesus turns toward the blind man and asks him, "What do you want me to do for you?" The blind man says to him, "Rabbi, I want to see again."[9]

Jesus says to him, "Follow me," and the blind man places his right hand on Jesus' left shoulder and follows him in a trust walk outside the village where they can speak privately.[10]

On the way Mary asks him, "What is your name?" And the man replies, "Bartimaeus." And Mary says, "So they are calling you, "Son of the Unclean One?"[11]

"Yes, I have been living with insults against me and my father for a long time; I just can't face those people or look them in the eye anymore."

The three talk further about what has happened in this man's life and the feelings that have been stored within him for so long. Understanding and insight begin to dawn.

Then, at the climax of their conversation, Jesus takes the man's head into his hands, holds it gently and firmly, clears his throat, spits into one eye and then the other, and then says, "Do you see anything?"[12]

Shocked and startled, the man experiences his sight beginning to come back. The first thing he says is, "I see human figures, as though they were trees walking around."[13]

Jesus then spits on the ground, makes a paste with his spit and treats the man's eyes with it.[14] A few moments later Jesus says, "Now go and rinse off."[15] So the man goes, rinses off his eyes, and returns to Jesus and Mary with his sight restored.[16]

Looking him straight in the eye, Mary says, "They called you *renames him.* Bartimaeus, Son of the Unclean One. Now your name is Adam, Son of the Earth."[17]

His new name gives him a new identity and freedom.

Then Jesus sends him home, saying, "Don't bother to go back to the village."[18]

As Jesus and Mary walk back into Bethsaida together without the man who had been blind, people begin asking, "What happened? Where is the Blind Son of the Unclean One?"

Without offering an explanation, Mary invites the people to sit down. When all are seated, the teaching begins with Jesus saying, "Your eye is the body's lamp. When your eye is clear, your whole body is flooded with light. When your eye is clouded, your body is shrouded in darkness. Take care, then, that the light within you is not darkness."[19]

Jesus says, "If a blind person leads a blind person, both of them will fall into a hole."[20]

Mary adds, "Some who claim to see are actually blind; some who are blind have insight."

Jesus says, "Love others like your own soul, protect them like the pupil of your eye."[21]

Jesus says, "You see the sliver in your friend's eye, but you don't see the log in your own eye. When you remove the log out of your own eye, then you will see well enough to remove the sliver from your friend's eye."[22]

Mary then asks a few questions, "Think of someone you dislike intensely." A man in the crowd blurts out, "You mean like that dirty Bartimaeus?"

Mary interjects quickly, "Don't say any names—just think to yourself who this person is." The people laugh. "Now ask yourself, 'What is it about this person I dislike so much?' Don't say anything aloud." The people are thinking quietly. Mary pauses and then asks, "Might there be any ways in which you are doing the very things you dislike so much in the other person? Don't be too quick to deny it."

Some faces in the crowd reveal that they are beginning to understand; others seem angry and start to walk away.

Mary calls out, "Before you leave, I have two or three questions for you, ones that I think you will like.

"Imagine someone else that you greatly admire." A woman in the crowd says, "You mean like you or Jesus?"

And Mary replies, "Whoever it is, think of that person and the qualities of that person that are so attractive to you." She pauses for a moment and then says, "Now ask yourself: might these qualities be also in me? Don't be too quick to deny the possibility. Perhaps you have those same good qualities that need to be expressed more."

A woman in the crowd who has the courage to speak says, "So sometimes the splinter we see in another person is actually our own log? And sometimes the sparkle we see in another's eye is a reflection of our own?"

Jesus says, "I will give you what no eye has seen, what no ear has heard, what no hand has touched, and what has never occurred to the human mind."[23]

Sensing that this is enough teaching for one day, Mary and Jesus slip out of the crowd and go on their way to the home of Philip and Nathanael for supper and to spend the night.

NOTES

1. The Fellows of the Jesus Seminar by a narrow majority concluded that Jesus cured at least one blind person. By a similar majority they were inclined to the view that he employed either mud or spittle, or both, to effect the cure, in addition to the more customary touch. Jesus did not use spittle or mud as a kind of primitive medicine, but as a part of the ritual employed by the charismatic healer in the ancient world. The seminar took the view that the blindness Jesus was able to cure was subject to psychosomatic therapy. In arriving at these conclusions, the Fellows were drawing on the evidence provided by three stories: the blind man at Bethsaida, blind Bartimaeus (Mark 10:46-52) and the man born blind (John 9:1-7). This retelling combines elements from several accounts: Mark 10:46-52 with parallels in Matthew 20:29-34 and Luke 18:35-43 plus a similar story involving two blind men in Matthew 9:27-31 and the account in John 9:1-41. Additional dialogue is also provided.

2. John 1:44

3. John 1:45

4. Mark 8:22

5. Mark 10:47

6. Mark 10:48

7. Mark 10:49

8. Mark 10:50

9. Mark 10:51

10. Mark 8:23

11. The name Bartimaeus means "son of the unclean." *Interpreter's Dictionary of the Bible,* George A. Buttrick, editor, Abingdon Press, Nashville, 1962, Volume A-D, p. 361

12. Mark 8:23

13. Mark 8:24

14. John 9:6

15. John 9:7a

16. John 9:7b

17. Adam means, "Earth Man" or "Truly Human Being"

18. Mark 8:26

19. Q Gospel, Luke 11:34-35

20. Gospel of Thomas 34

21. Gospel of Thomas 25

22. Gospel of Thomas 26

23. Gospel of Thomas 17

CHAPTER 18:
A DEAF MUTE REGAINS HIS HEARING AND HIS VOICE₁

INSTITUTIONALIZED VIOLENCE OF EMPIRE WITH COLLUSION by religious authorities gives rise to a variety of responses from those who are oppressed. Some choose to cooperate with the ruling authorities and obtain positions of authority in the system. Others organize for resistance through violent uprisings or guerrilla tactics. Many others avoid confrontation by trying to be inconspicuous, doing their best to stay out of the way of the authorities. Still others internalize the violence and withdraw from life. Such appears to be the case for a deaf mute who is brought to Jesus.

People bring a deaf mute to Jesus and plead with him to lay his hands on him for healing.² How will Jesus deal with someone who has no hearing and no speech? Clearly communication must be non-verbal, relying on body language and creative actions.

Mary suggests to Jesus that he use the same approach that was effective with Bartimaeus who became another Adam, son of the Earth.

To avoid further embarrassment for the man, they take him aside from the crowd.

Jesus holds the man's head firmly in his hands, looks compassionately into his eyes, places his forefingers into the man's ears, exerts gentle pressure on his cheeks and the man knows he should open his mouth. There is a deep magnetic resonance between them and powerful Energy is building.

Jesus raises his eyes to the skies for Energy, groans deeply from his soul, gathers saliva in his mouth and spits right onto the man's tongue saying, "Ephphatha!" which means "Open up!"[3]

Immediately his ears open up to hear the "Ephphatha" and his hearing is completely restored. His speech impediment is removed and he starts speaking properly again.[4] His pent up feelings from many years pour out like a torrent of water when a dam is broken. Tears of pain and grief mixed with ecstatic joy flow like sparkling streams in the desert.

Mary and Jesus embrace him and share the "Shalom" a word which means "justice rolled up with peace." Then Mary says to the man "You remind me of Ezekiel, who lost his voice until he was energized by the Spirit to speak truth to power without fear.[4] Now that your fear is gone, your hearing restored and your voice set free, I think you have a new name: may I call you Zeke?"

Startled again, he realizes that just like Ezekiel he was bound and now he is free; he has found his power and his voice. And is able to say with enthusiasm, "Yes, please call me Zeke!"

Then Jesus extends an invitation, "Zeke will you join us in proclaiming the good news to the poor?" And immediately he joins the itinerant band of Jesus, Mary Magdalene, and the other disciples.

A woman in the crowd seeing the amazing change that has occurred in the man who had been deaf and mute, cries out, "Blessed is the womb that bore you and the breasts that fed you." And Jesus replies, "Blessed are those who have heard the word of the Father and have truly kept it."[5]

Now it is time to gather the people again for some teaching.

Jesus says, "What you hear in one of your ears, proclaim from your rooftops."[6]

Mary interjects, "And how many ears do you have?"

Most people respond, "Two." But one thoughtful old man says, "Three."

"Yes," replies Mary. "You are including your Inner Ear, right? It is with the Third Ear that we hear the Voice Within. And which ear do you think Jesus is talking about?"

There is a brief discussion until the group agrees that true hearing includes listening carefully with both outer and inner ears.

Next follows a lively conversation regarding what might happen if one were to proclaim from the rooftops what they hear.

As a caution, Mary adds, "And always remember there is a time for keeping silent and a time for speaking."[7]

practical wisdom

Someone asks "And how do we know when to keep silent and when to speak?"

Mary replies, "Just use your Third Ear and listen to your Inner Voice and you will know!" Smiles and gentle laughter as people begin to understand.

NOTES

1. This chapter is rooted in Gospel of Mark 7:31-37. Compare with Matthew 15:29-31

2. Mark 7:32

3. Mark 7:33-34

4. Ezekiel 3:24-27, "The spirit entered into me, and set me on my feet; and he spoke with me and said to me: Go, shut yourself inside your house. As for you, mortal, cords shall be placed on you, and you shall be bound with them, so that you cannot go out among the people; and I will make your tongue cling to the roof of your mouth, so that you shall be speechless and unable to reprove them; for they are a rebellious house. But when I speak with you, I will open your mouth, and you shall say to them, 'Thus says the Lord God: Let those who will hear, hear; and let those who refuse to hear, refuse; for they are a rebellious house.'"

5. Gospel of Thomas 79

6. Gospel of Thomas 33 (Greek) cf. Q Gospel as found in Luke 12:3 and Matthew 10:27

7. Ecclesiastes 3:7

CHAPTER 19:
AN ARAB WOMAN
GENTLY CONFRONTS JESUS[1]

JESUS AND MARY HAVE BEEN TRAVELING THROUGH villages, towns, farms, and vineyards.

Every where they go, people are being healed, begging Jesus to let them touch the fringe of his cloak. It seems to work because those who come believing are actually cured.[2]

Pharisees and scholars notice that Jesus and Mary are gaining a great deal of attention which they feel is a threat to their authority and control over the people, so they start arguments with Jesus over such minor issues as the rules for washing hands.

Jesus replies that the religious authorities are putting their emphasis in the wrong places by focusing on outer customs while ignoring the issues that originate within the heart: things like arrogance, greed, wickedness, an evil eye, and lack of good sense![3]

After some days of intense demands from people in general and religious leaders in particular, Jesus and Mary say to each other, "Let's take some time out for rest and relaxation." They head up north to Tyre looking for a house where they can stay for awhile and escape notice.

Suddenly an Arab woman comes toward them. "Who is she?" asks

Jesus. "Never seen her before," replies Mary. And Jesus says, "I'm tired, plus she is not one of us, so why do I have to deal with her?"

But there is no way to avoid contact. The woman comes close and says, "Sir, please help me. My daughter is severely possessed."

Jesus does not respond at all.

The other disciples who have tagged along chime in, "Get rid of her because she is badgering us."

Feeling cornered, yet backed up by his disciples, Jesus blurts out, "I was sent only to the lost sheep of the house of Israel. Let the children be fed first, since it isn't good to take bread out of our children's mouths and throw it to the dogs!"

Facing him straight on, the Arab woman says gently, "Sir, even the dogs under the table get to eat scraps dropped by the children."

Taken back by the power of her gentle confrontation, Jesus regains his composure and says, "For that retort, be on your way, the demon has gone out of your daughter. Your trust is enormous! Your wish is as good as fulfilled!"

Returning home, the woman finds her daughter lying quietly on the bed and the demon gone.

Once she is out of earshot, Mary asks, "I know you are tired, but weren't you a little hard on her? Why in the world did you call her a dog? You all but called her a bitch! What's your problem? I know most of our people hate the Arabs, but are you going to perpetuate hatred? Just before we met her you were lecturing the Pharisees about the attitudes of the heart. I notice you didn't include prejudice on your list."

Not willing to admit that Mary has hit a nerve, Jesus yells out, "Enough woman! Leave me alone!"

And Mary replies gently, "Sleep on it: maybe you will feel differently in the morning. How about we go to the beach tomorrow?"

Jesus gives a noncommittal response. She can feel him tossing and turning all night long as though he was wrestling with something.

NOTES

1. This story is rooted in Mark 7:24-30 and Matthew 15:28. The earlier version in Mark places the scene in the region of Tyre; Matthew says, "Tyre and Sidon", two towns about twenty miles apart in Phoenicia so both are in the same general area outside of Galilee. Mark identifies the woman as "A Greek, by race a Phoenician from Syria" and Matthew says she is a Canaanite. These are the people who lived in Syria and Palestine west of the Jordan before the Israelites invaded the area. In the Hebrew Scriptures there are references to Ishmaelites, Midianites, Dedanites, Sabeans, Canaanites, etc., all of whom are later identified simply as "Arabs." "Arab means simply 'Nomad.'" *Interpreter's Dictionary of the Bible*, volume A-D, p. 181. In short, then, the woman is an Arab.

2. Mark 6:56

3. Mark 7:1-23

CHAPTER 20:
A DAY AT THE BEACH₁

AFTER SLEEPING IN LATE, THEY WAKEN TO A NEW DAY
but it is overcast and cloudy.

Jesus asks, "Do you still want to go to the beach this morning?"

Mary replies, "It may burn off. Let's pack a lunch and go." Jesus
says, "Sounds good and I'll bring a bottle of wine, the one the Arab
woman gave us when we left her house last night."

On their way to the beach a young girl with a big smile on her
face runs toward them and says, "Mother says you healed me and
made me well!"

Jesus replies, "We are so happy that you are better, But if the truth
be known, it was your Mother's trust, her faith, the desire of her
heart, that released your healing."

Just then the Arab woman comes out of her house and says,
"Thank you so much!" And Jesus replies, "No, I am the one who
should be thanking you. Will you forgive me for my foul mouth yesterday?"

"Consider yourself forgiven," she replies.

As they leave and walk toward the beach, Mary senses the power
of the encounter, and says gently, "That Arab woman really had an
effect on you, didn't she?"

And Jesus replies, "Yes, I must admit she did. I spoke harshly to her, but there was no resentment on her part! She forgave me! I can't begin to tell you what effect her forgiveness is having on me."

Arriving at the beach, they find a perfect spot to spread a blanket and have a magnificent view of the Mediterranean Sea fading off into the distant horizon.

"There is so much water here: it reminds me of the story of Noah and the Flood," says Jesus. And Mary replies, "Yes, and I like the way in which Philo interprets that story symbolically. He says that the ark represents our human body, that there are holes in the body where each of the senses builds a nest: a pair for the eyes and vision, a pair for the ears and hearing, a pair for the nostrils where the smells make their nest. Plus the larger mouth where the tastes nestle and the tongue finds room for articulating speech.

"Philo says there is a nest inside your skull for the brain and your thinking, there is a pair of nests for your lungs and your breathing plus another pair for your heart and your blood. There are firmer parts like the bones providing nests for the marrow and the softer parts like the flesh where pleasure and pain nestle."[2]

"I like the way Philo's understanding opens up the story in an entirely new way for me," says Jesus.

"And there is more," replies Mary. "Philo says the dimensions of the ark, its length and width, and depth, all correspond to the proportions of the body.[3] Then the entire ark is smeared with pitch, both inside and out, which serves as the glue that bonds the parts of the ark together and keeps it from coming apart. That pitch is the soul."[4]

Jesus ponders these ideas for a moment and then says, "Strange to think of the soul as being pitch, but when it functions as the bonding agent for the entire body, then it makes sense. So without soul, the body cannot hold together, becomes disconnected, and falls apart, like the valley of dry bones in Ezekiel's vision?"[5]

"Yes," says Mary, "and inside the ark are the several decks, the layers, each with its function: food enters at the top, is carried downward and distributed for nourishing the body and eliminating what is no longer needed."[6]

"Noah's ark has many meanings. And it carries many animals

inside: some are tame and easy to control. Others are wild: they can be frightening, but they are also fascinating and powerful."

"Oh, yes, I do understand. Reminds me of right after my baptism when I took time in the wilderness. I was out there with my own inner wild animals who became my friends once I had gotten to know them. I am no longer afraid of my wildness, my naturalness!"[7]

"I like both sides of you, Jesus, your tame animals and your wild ones too, most of the time!"

After a warm embrace, Mary continues, "So Philo teaches that the entire ark, our body, is ready for the storms of life, the outer storms like the rain and the ones that well up from within: both can be very powerful."[7]

"Yes, I know, like what happened yesterday with me and the Arab woman," says Jesus. "I must admit that the real reason my anger flared up from deep inside me was because I felt challenged about my thinking. Until that moment, I had thought that my work is to call our people, the children of Israel, back to our God who will protect us against all others. But when I told her I couldn't take the children's bread and give it to dogs and she asked if the dogs might have the crumbs that fell from the table, well she said it so gently and disarmingly that I was overpowered. During the night it became clear to me that the message of the Kindom of the Father and Mother, the *Way of Mystery,* is for the Jews and the Arabs, for the Greeks and the Romans, and basically, for everybody! Today I realize there is just one humanity to which we all belong."

"Look at the water," says Mary. "When we came down here the waves were dashing against the rocks with tremendous force. Now they are lapping easily with a gentle ebb and flow. I sense the same kind of change in you!"

"Yes, I am calmer now," says Jesus, "and instead of resenting the Arab woman, I am now feeling affection for her. By the way, what is her name? I wonder if she would consider joining up and traveling with us? What would Peter, James, and John, Susanna, and Joanna think? Maybe I should ask them first?"

"Or perhaps you should ask her first?" says Mary. "Who knows whether she would want to travel with us?"

"Good point, Mary!"

"By the way, Jesus, I hear that some people think you walk on water."[8]

"Really? Me walk on water? That's a good joke!"

"Actually, I think the people are right. I see you walking on water right now. Instead of being pulled down into the turbulence of your emotions, you are calmly walking across them to where you need to go."

"Let's have lunch—I'm famished. I'm ready for some of that good Arab wine too!"

They enjoy eating, drinking wine, and laughing together. The winds catch their laughter and carry it into the City where an Arab woman in her home recognizes the voices, understands the laughter, and has a good chuckle herself.

NOTES

1. The scene is a beach outside of Tyre on the Mediterranean Sea. The conversation is rooted in the work of Philo, a Jewish philosopher and contemporary of Jesus and Mary. Philo lived and worked in Alexandria (ca 20 B.C.E. to sometime after 40 C.E.) Intuitively integrating Hebraic and Hellenistic thought, Philo brings out the deeper symbolic and allegorical meaning of stories in Genesis and Exodus. Among the translators of his work are Ralph Marcus, *Philo*, Ten volumes and two supplementary volumes, Harvard University Press, Cambridge, Massachusetts, 1979, and C.D. Younge, *The Works of Philo*, Complete and Unabridged, New Updated Version, Hendrickson Publishers, 1993.

2. Philo, Questions and Answers on Genesis, Book 2, paragraph 3

3. Philo, Questions and Answers on Genesis, Book 2, paragraph 5

4. Philo, Questions and Answers on Genesis, Book 2, paragraph 4

5. Ezekiel 37

6. Philo, Questions and Answers on Genesis, Book 2, paragraph 7

7. Mark 1:13

8. Mark 6:48

CHAPTER 21:
WHO ARE MY FAMILY?[1]

ENERGIZED BY HIS ENCOUNTER WITH THE ARAB WOMAN and his day at the beach discussing Philo, Jesus takes Mary's hand and together they walk with all deliberate speed from Tyre back home to Capernaum. The journey of about thirty five miles takes several days and allows Jesus additional time to ponder what he has experienced: the shattering of his belief in a god for his people alone. His tribal god has died and his energy has been transformed into compassion for all humanity.

Both Jesus and Mary are refreshed and excited about resuming their teaching. Their time away has been very creative, even more than they had hoped for.

Meanwhile, back in Capernaum, their disciples, and others who are curious to hear fresh teaching, are eagerly awaiting their return. When Mary and Jesus reach Peter's house, they find many people gathered to meet them. Entering the house, they have hardly any time to grab a bite to eat.[2] They sit on the floor and disciples gather around while Peter's mother-in-law hands them a snack to tide them over until supper.

Tales of his healings and radical teachings have reached his relatives in Nazareth and even his brother James who has become a Nazarite priest working in Jerusalem. Deciding to investigate what is going on, James comes down from the City, picks up his Mother, brothers, and sisters. When they reach Peter's home, there is such a crowd both inside and outside the house, that they cannot enter.

They send in word and people inside convey the message: "Look, your mother and your brothers and sisters are outside looking for you." And Jesus replies, "My mother and brothers—whoever are they?" And pointing to his disciples he says, "These are my brothers and mother and sisters, those who do the will of my Father."[3]

Someone relays what Jesus has just said to his Mother Mary, brother James, and the rest of the family who are waiting patiently outside. Perhaps after the crowd has dispersed they can talk some sense into him. Mother Mary recognizes a familiar pattern between her sons, Jesus and James: these two have always been so different. They are in greater contrast than any of her children. James is her city boy who has settled in as a Nazarite priest in the Temple in Jerusalem.[4] Jesus is her country boy who has become an itinerant teacher wandering around the Galilean villages. As a Nazarite, James strictly observes the purity laws. Jesus pays scant attention to the purity and ceremonial rules; his attention is focused on one law: Love.

While his family waits patiently outside, Jesus continues his teaching indoors, "Now what do you think? A man had two sons. He went to the first, and said, 'Son, go and work in the vineyard today.' He responded, 'I'm your man, sir,' but he didn't move. Then he went to the second and said the same thing. He responded, 'I don't want to,' but later on he thought better of it and went to work. Which of the two did what the father wanted?"

They said, "The second."[5]

Picking up the dialogue portion of the teaching, Mary asks, "Why do you think the first son agreed to do what his father asked? Why does he say, 'Yes'?"

Responses begin coming from all over the room. One says, "He always wants to please his Father." Another adds, "No way does he want to tangle with the old man."

Mary then asks, "But why does he not do anything about it?"

Responses come quickly, "He just didn't feel like it." "Maybe he resented the old man." "Maybe he feels he always has to do more than his brother."

"And what about the other son?" asks Mary, "Why does he say, 'No' to his father's request?"

"He has been working hard already," says one. "He just doesn't feel like working out in the hot sun all day," says another. "He's got better things to do!" replies a third.

"Then why does he actually go to work?"

"He changed his mind: he actually does respect his father and wants to help out."

"Compare the two sons: notice how the first son's 'Yes' has become a 'No.' And notice how the second son's 'No' becomes a 'Yes.' Whenever you have a choice to make, notice your initial response and then see if there is a second response behind it."

One of the people in the group adds, "It also makes a difference what kind of Father you have: some are kindly and reasonable, others can be mean and overly demanding."

Jesus continues the conversation with another startling teaching, "Whoever does not hate father and mother cannot become my disciple, and whoever does not hate brothers and sisters... will not be worthy of me."[6]

People cry out, "Hate your parents? Are you out of your mind?" Parents are especially upset and an uproar begins. Mary quiets the people down and says,

"What do you think Jesus really means? Might it be that in making a commitment to follow your real Father, you will be in conflict with your father, your mother, your family, even your tribe, your people?"

Everyone becomes silent as they are thinking about the meaning. Into the silence Jesus inserts one more provocative teaching, "Whoever knows the father and the mother will be called the child of a whore."[7]

Bedlam breaks out again and once more Mary calms people down with her penetrating questions, "Which father and mother do you think Jesus is referring to?"

People are mostly quiet until a little light goes on in the mind of one of the women,

"Is Jesus talking about our heavenly Father and Mother? Are you and he saying that when we are doing the will of our heavenly Father and Mother, that others may see us as children of whores?"

Silence resumes in the room for awhile, broken only by another teaching from Jesus, "Whoever does not hate father and mother as I do cannot be my disciple, and whoever does not love father and mother as I do cannot be my disciple. For my mother gave me false-hood, but my true mother gave me life."[8]

A lively discussion ensues as people are sorting out the meaning of the teaching. Gradually people come to see that Jesus is really saying that everyone needs to break with their parents and family, discover who their true parents are, their Mother and Father in heaven, the heaven that resides within each one, and then they will be able to love their parents, their brothers and sisters, and all people in a new way.

Once this new understanding has become clear, Jesus proceeds with one or two more teachings: "Perhaps people think that I have come to cast peace upon the world. They do not know that I have come to cast conflicts upon the earth: fire, sword, war. For there will be five in a house: there'll be three against two and two against three, father against son and son against father, and they will stand alone."[9]

As the meaning begins to sink in, Jesus adds one final teaching for the evening,

"If two make peace with each other in a single house, they will say to the mountain, 'Move from here!' and it will move."[10]

And Mary then asks, "And what kind of mountains might be moved? They can be mountains of mistrust, mountains of anger, mountains of hurt and pain."

Discovering that the true heart of the teachings is reconciliation, people share the peace, offering a heartfelt "Shalom" and warm embrace to one another before leaving for their own homes.

As the last of the visitors are leaving, Peter's mother-in-law says, "So you don't really hate mothers or mothers-in-law after all? If you actually really do love us deep down, then come and eat: supper is ready. And invite your family in."

Jesus invites his Mother Mary, James, and all his brothers and sisters to come into the house for a lively conversation about what Jesus really meant.

Mother Mary says, "Ever since you were little I have thought about what you had to say.[11] I haven't always understood at first. Some things you say still puzzle me."

NOTES

1. This is a chapter on how Jesus sees "family values."

2. Mark 3:20

3. The dynamic of this story is found in Gospel of Thomas 99 with parallels in Mark 3:20-22, Matthew 12:46-50, Luke 8:19-21, and Gospel of the Ebionites 5.

4. Robert Eisenman, *James, the Brother of Jesus*, Viking, New York, 1996, p. 468

5. Matthew 21:28-31

6. Gospel of Thomas 55

7. Gospel of Thomas 105

8. Gospel of Thomas 101

9. Gospel of Thomas 16

10. Gospel of Thomas 48

11. Luke 2:51

CHAPTER 22:
A Toll Collector and a Pharisee[1]

PEASANTS MAKING A BARE SUBSISTENCE LIVING ARE being exploited further by Temple priests who require tithes and offerings that take between 21 and 23 percent of agricultural produce.[2] The Roman occupiers impose a head tax on every person, taxes on all the land, plus duties, tariffs, and tolls. Adding insult to injury, the Romans use the social elite and hirelings from the Jewish people to collect the taxes.

The combined burden of taxes by Temple and Empire is unbearable for the peasants. Yet the Pharisees pay no attention to the oppressive effects on the peasants; they care only for making sure they get what is coming to them.

Check points are set up on roads leading to Jerusalem where tolls are collected from peasants traveling to the temple. Both toll collectors and Pharisees are integral parts of a system engaged in heavy exploitation of working people. In this context, Jesus tells his story:

"Two men went up to the temple to pray, one a Pharisee and the other a toll collector. The Pharisee stood up and prayed silently as follows: 'I thank you, God, that I'm not like everybody else, thieving, unjust, adulterous, and especially not like that toll collector over there. I fast twice a week, I give tithes of everything that I acquire.' But the toll collector stood off by himself and didn't even dare to look up, but struck his chest, and muttered, 'God, have mercy on me, sinner that I am.' Let me tell you, the second man went back to his house acquitted but the first one did not."[2]

Simon reacts quickly and says, "It is time to get rid of all these people: toll collectors, Pharisees, the whole lot."

Levi jumps in and says, "Jesus, are you telling this story about me? Before I met you, I used to collect taxes but because of you I gave that up and changed my ways."[3]

Jesus just smiles and so does Mary who says, "Maybe we can get others to change their ways also!"

Peter adds, "Jesus, if you keep telling stories like this perhaps more toll collectors will change, but Pharisees? Not a chance!"

Mary smiles again and says, "Why rule out the possibility? One of these days we might all be surprised!"

NOTES

1. This chapter is rooted in Luke 18:10-14a. Luke 18:9 is Luke's framing and Luke 18:14b. Most interpreters agree that it is necessary to eliminate the Lukan framing, 18:9 and the generalizing conclusion in 18:14b, which is an independent saying (cf. Matt. 23;12).

2. William R. Herzog, *Parables as Subversive Speech*, p. 181

3. Mark 2:14

CHAPTER 23:
DINNER WITH ZACCHAEUS, THE CHIEF TOLL COLLECTOR[1]

AFTER A LONG JOURNEY MOVING FROM TOWN TO TOWN, Jesus, Mary, and the disciples enter the City of Jericho. Word about Jesus and his followers has preceded their arrival and a large crowd is forming: they are eager to see what he looks like and hear what he has to say.

Scanning the people, Levi notices a short man running ahead of the others: he climbs a sycamore tree to get a better view.[2] Levi says to Jesus, "That man is Zacchaeus, the chief toll collector. He may be short, but he is someone who wields a lot of power. When I was collecting tolls, most of us were afraid of him."

Jesus glances ahead, but right now he has something else on his mind. "Mary, where do you think we will find a place to stay?" "Good question," she replies.

The crowd is calling for Jesus to speak to them. Finding a spot where he can address them, Jesus says, "The Way of the Father is like a shepherd who had a hundred sheep. One of them, the largest, went astray. He left the ninety-nine and looked for the one until he found it After he had gone to this trouble, he said to the sheep, 'I love you more than the ninety-nine.'"[3]

Throughout his message, Jesus realizes that this man in the tree seems especially intent in hearing what he has to say. Whenever speaking to a large group of people, Jesus has discovered that the teaching is more effective when he makes strong eye contact with one person, feels resonance and the exchange of energy. Often the eye contact is with a woman, but this time it is with this man who is up the tree.

Toward the end of his teaching, Jesus feels the impulse of the Spirit, stretches out his hand and shouts loudly, "Zacchaeus, hurry up and come down. I am going to stay at your house today." So Zachaeus scurries down the tree and extends a very warm welcome to Jesus, Mary, Levi, and the others traveling with them.[4]

People in the crowd who had a different set of expectations start complaining and saying, "He is going to spend the day with some sinner!"[5] Most of them lose interest and the crowd disperses which actually works rather well because now Jesus and Mary can focus their conversation directly with Zacchaeus who is eager to respond to what he has heard. "Look, sir, I will give half of what I own to the poor, and if I have extorted anything from anyone, I'll pay back four times as much."[6]

Recognizing his sincerity, Jesus says, "Today wholeness has come to this house."[7]

Levi turns toward Zacchaeus and says, "Remember me? I used to work for you and was afraid of you, but now we are real brothers. As the two men embrace each other with great affection, Mary says with a smile, "Some drop out of toll collecting—others become honest. How much longer will that corrupt system last?" Everyone has a good laugh followed by a great supper and a very good night's rest.

NOTES

1. This chapter is rooted in a story found in the Luke 19:19. There are no parallels in the other Gospels.

2. Luke 19:1-4

3. Gospel of Thomas 107

4. Luke 19:5-6

5. Luke 19:7

6. Luke 19:8

7. Luke 19:9

CHAPTER 24:
A CRIPPLED MAN AT THE POOL₁

EACH SABBATH FINDS JESUS, MARY, AND THE DISCIPLES worshiping with the people in the local synagogue. Most cities and some towns have their own building for synagogue worship; the smaller villages with no synagogue building have an agreed meeting place, even a circle of people under a shady tree.

For the major festivals of the year Passover, Pentecost, and Tabernacles, they make the trip from their homes in Galilee up to the Temple in the City of Jerusalem.

Now they have friends among former toll collectors who help them get through check points with a minimum of hassle.

After arriving unhindered in Jerusalem and participating in the Passover ceremonies led by the priests and Levites, Jesus makes a number of observations. He notices how all the attention seems to be given to outer appearances and not to the inner meaning.

Jesus says to a Pharisee, "Why do you wash the outside of the cup? Don't you understand that the one who made the outside is also the one who made the inside?"2

The Pharisee who has been observing the customs according to the letter of the law appears irritated and annoyed at this question.

So Jesus continues, "You scholars and Pharisees, you impostors! Damn you! You wash the outside of cups and plates, but inside you are full of greed and dissipation. You blind Pharisees, first clean the inside of the cup and then the outside will be clean too."[3]

Realizing that the argument is getting heated and there is likely to be a scene, Mary intervenes and says, "No more now, Jesus." And, cooling off a bit, he agrees, saying, "All right, but later...."

Jesus knows that the religious leaders are cooperating with the Herodians and the authorities of the Roman Empire. They have struck a deal: they can practice their religion and do their ceremonies as long as they do not threaten the Powers that Be or attempt in any way to liberate the people. So Jesus offers as his parting shot, "A person cannot mount two horses or bend two bows. And a slave cannot serve two masters, otherwise that slave will honor the one and offend the other."[3]

They decide to leave the City by way of the Sheep Gate and shortly come to the Pool of Bethzatha (Bethesda) which has five colonnades, among which numerous invalids are usually lying around—blind, lame, paralyzed—waiting for some movement of the water.

According to an old legend the water in this pool has curative powers whenever it is agitated. Angels are presumed to be the cause of the periodic movement of the water.

Located close to a major fault line, springs providing water for these pools are affected by movements of the Earth. Local belief at the time is that when the agitation occurs, the first one into the pool will be cured of whatever disease he or she has.

Jesus observes one man lying there and learns that he has been crippled for thirty-eight years. So Jesus asks him, "Do you want to get well?"

The crippled man replies, "Sir, I don't have anyone to put me in the pool when the water is agitated; while I'm trying to get in someone else beats me to it."

Then Jesus tells him, "Get up, pick up your mat and walk around."

And at once the man recovers; he picks up his mat and starts walking.

Mary invites him to join them and return to Galilee and he replies, "Might as well. I am ready to quit this town and start a new life with you. I'll go wherever you are going."

Now this is a sabbath day. So the Judeans say to the man who has been cured, "It's the sabbath day; you're not permitted to carry your mat around."

But he explains, "The man who cured me told me, 'Pick up your mat and walk around.'"

When the Judeans learn that the one responsible for the crippled man's healing is Jesus from Galilee, they start hounding Jesus for doing things like this on the sabbath day.

Jesus responds, "My Father never stops laboring, and I labor as well."

One of Jesus' disciples seeing the needs of the people, says, "Lord, there are many around the drinking trough, but there is nothing in the well."[4]

"Yes, I agree," says Mary. "These people are dry canals."[5]

Then Jesus, realizing the need for major change in the religion of the time, adds:

"Nobody drinks aged wine and immediately wants to drink young wine. Young wine is not poured into old wineskins, or they might break, and aged wine is not poured into a new wineskin, or it might spoil. An old patch is not sewn onto a new garment, since it would create a tear."[6]

NOTES

1. The story of the crippled man at the pool is from John 5:1-18

2. Gospel of Thomas 89, Luke 11:40

3. Matthew 23:25-26

4. Gospel of Thomas 74

5. "Dry canals" is a phrase from Revelation of Peter 79:46 in the

Nag Hammadi Scriptures, 2007. The text is also known as The Apocalypse of Peter in earlier editions.

6. Gospel of Thomas 47:3-5

CHAPTER 25:
BAPTIZING NICODEMUS₁

THE PEOPLE IN THE TEMPLE ARE GLAD TO HEAR WHAT Jesus has to say, but most of the religious leaders are skeptical, even fearful. Yet among them there is at least one man, Nicodemus, who is very curious and wants to learn more.

Nicodemus comes to Jesus during the night and says, "Rabbi, we know that you've come as a teacher from God; after all, nobody can perform the wonders you do unless God is with him."

Jesus replies to Nicodemus, "No one can experience the power of the Kindom of the Father and Mother, the *Way of Mystery*, without being reborn from above."

Nicodemus says to him, "How can an adult be reborn? Can you re-enter your mother's womb and be born a second time?"

Jesus replies, "No one can enter the Kindom of Father and Mother, the *Way of Mystery*, without being born of water and the spirit. The spirit blows every which way, like the wind: you hear the sound it makes but you cannot tell where it's coming from or where it's going. That's how it is with everyone reborn of the spirit."

"How can that be possible?" Nicodemus retorts.

"Remember the serpent in the Garden? And remember the serpent Moses held high before the people in the desert? The serpent is the Instructor raising eternal questions like:

"Where have you come from?[2]

"Who are you?[3]

"What do you want?[4]

"What is the evidence of the Kindom of Father and Mother, the *Way of Mystery*, in you?[5] When you are ready, you too, can be immersed in the Mystery.

"You will find that baptism is like passing through a narrow passage, a birth canal.[6] You cannot take anything with you: no possessions, no belongings, no clothing, nothing. You go just as you are into the waters and into your deepest Self. Are you ready and willing to go there?"

"I AM!" cries Nicodemus.

In the middle of the night, Jesus, Mary, and Nicodemus slip out of the City and make their journey toward Aenon near Salim,[7] one of their favorite places for baptism since there is plenty of water from hot springs bubbling up freely from Mother Earth. What a perfect place for baptisms![8]

Arriving at the hot springs, they offer prayer together. Then Nicodemus removes his clothing and Jesus immerses him in the water. Nicodemus is baptized, immersed in Mystery, and comes up laughing joyously.

Mary brings chrism and joins Jesus in anointing Nicodemus with oil. Now he knows that he is baptized with Spirit and with Fire.[9]

Because of the responsiveness of Nicodemus, Jesus, Mary, and the disciples extend their stay in the City for teaching, healing, and baptizing. Jesus and Mary work with the Instructing Serpent raising questions and serving as midwives for Nicodemus and all who are open and ready to be reborn of the Spirit.

NOTES

1. John 3:1-22

2. Gospel of Thomas 50

3. Gospel of Thomas 61

4. Matthew 20:21

5. Gospel of Thomas 50

6. Matthew 7:13

7. John 3:20

8. Most springs are cold, but these are hot. Their water is warmed by the fire generated by the movement of the fault line, the one stretching from the East African rift valley and underneath the Dead Sea, the Jordan River Valley, Galilee, and further north. Pressure melts rocks, creates fire, and heats water bursting forth exuberantly from Mother Earth.

9. Matthew 3:17, Luke 4:11

CHAPTER 26:
THE WOMAN AT THE WELL₁

JESUS IS THINKING IT IS TIME TO LEAVE JUDEA AND return to Galilee. He suggests that they travel the shortest route, which means going through Samaria. Judeans normally avoid Samaritans because of ancient differences and feelings of hostility. They each claim to be worshiping the God of Jacob in the right place. Samaritans have their Temple on Mt. Gerizim and Judeans have theirs in Jerusalem. Each claims to have the True Torah Scriptures and the others only a corrupted version. Each says that God is on their side.

Mary recalls the encounter that Jesus had earlier with the Arab woman in Tyre who melted down some of his prejudices. She has just heard him tell his newest parable in which a Samaritan is the hero. Now she is smiling because Jesus is proposing that they travel freely through Samaria. Such an idea would have been out of the question before his attitudes changed.

On their way, they stop at a place none of them has seen before: the famous Jacob's Well located at the foot of Mt. Gerizim.

Jesus, Mary, and the others are feeling exhausted from traveling. The disciples go into town to buy food and drink. As usual, Mary, Joanna, and Susanna pay for the food out of their resources.

Jesus stops at the well to rest. It is about noon, the heat of the day. Most people come to the well in the evening or early in the morning. The open space around the well is deserted. The well is deep and Jesus has no bucket, no way to reach the water so he sits down on the edge of the well and waits. Before long a woman comes to the well with her jar to get water and Jesus strikes up a conversation with her saying, "Give me a drink."

The woman replies to him, "You are a Judean; how can you ask a Samaritan woman for a drink? Judeans do not associate with us."

Jesus answers her, "If you knew what God can give you, and who just said to you, 'Give me a drink,' you would ask him and he would give you lively, life-giving water."

"Mister, you don't have anything to draw water with," she says, "and the well is deep; where will you get this 'lively, life-giving water'? Can you do better than our patriarch Jacob? He left us this well, which used to quench his thirst and that of his family and his livestock."

Jesus responds to her, "Whoever drinks this water will get thirsty again; but all who drink the water I'll provide them will never get thirsty again; it will be a source of water within them, a fountain of real life."

The woman says to him, "Sir, give me some of this water, so I'll never be thirsty or have to keep coming back here for water."

Perhaps Jesus is thinking to himself, "She is missing the point here—I'll try another approach." He says to her, "Go, call your husband and come back."

"I don't have a husband," she answers.

"You're right to say that you don't have a husband," Jesus says. "In fact, you've had five husbands, and the man you are now living with is not your husband; you've told the truth."

Jesus sees into the woman's heart of hearts and hears the longing song of her soul. As her eyes meet his, she feels that he knows her completely. Startled by discovering that Jesus totally understands her, she says, "I can tell you are a prophet."

Stunned and feeling that she needs to make some space before this goes any further, she shifts the subject to something a bit safer saying, "Our ancestors worshipped on this mountain. You people claim Jerusalem is the only place for worship."

Dodging the sidestepping argument, Jesus replies, "Woman, believe me, the time is coming when you won't worship the Father either on this mountain or in Jerusalem. You people worship God-knows-what; we worship what we know—'Judeans are the agents of salvation,' and all that. But the time is coming—in fact, it's already here—for true worshipers to worship the Father as he truly is, without regard to place. It's worshipers of this sort the Father is looking for. The Mystery is not tied to place, and those who worship Mystery must worship in truth, without regard to place."

The woman continues, "All I know is that the Messiah, the one called Anointed, is going to come; when he does he'll tell us everything."

Jesus says to her, "You've been talking to one who is Anointed all along. You, too, can receive the anointing of the free-flowing Spirit, a fountain ready to be released within you, ready to fill you with unspeakable joy and glory!"

The woman feels the infilling of the Spirit rushing through her gently with tremendous power: she is both surprised and delighted to discover that she is now the water jar, the container, the chalice of Mystery.

Just then her ecstasy is interrupted by the disciples returning with provisions. The men are puzzled that Jesus is talking with a woman and are questioning within themselves, "What are you trying to do? Why are you talking with her?" But it is no surprise to Mary: she understands what is happening: no explanation is needed.

Leaving her water jar at the well, the Samaritan woman runs into town, telling everyone. "Come see someone who told me everything I ever did. Could he be the Anointed?"[2]

Wanting to see for themselves, the people of Sychar begin making their way toward Jesus.

Meanwhile the disciples plead with Jesus, "Rabbi, eat something."

And Jesus replies, "I have food to eat, food you know nothing about."

The disciples query each other, "Has someone already brought him food?"

Aware that they are not getting the message, Jesus says even more plainly, "Doing the will of the One who sent me and completing his work—that's my food. You have a saying, 'It's still four months till harvest.' Yet I tell you: look at the fields, they're ripe for harvesting. The harvester is already getting his pay; he is gathering the crop that sustains real life, so planter and harvester can celebrate together. Here the proverb holds true: 'One plants, another harvests.' I sent you to harvest what you haven't labored over; others have labored, and you've benefited from their work.

"Do you see this woman who was just here? She was searching and ready for something new in her life: all it takes is for someone to help her discover that what she needs is already within her: it is time to release the fountain of the Spirit and let it flow. All I did was help her get in touch with her own energies. Whether they realize it or not, the people coming out from town now all desire the same thing: perhaps they, too, will seek and find when they know themselves!"

Many Samaritans from Sychar believed in him because of the woman's testimony, "He told me everything I ever did." They want what she has discovered and beg Jesus to stay with them for awhile.

Jesus, Mary, and the disciples accept hospitality in Sychar for two more days before resuming their journey home to Galilee.

NOTES

1. John 4:1-43

2. John 4:29

CAMEO ESSAY 3:
"SON OF MAN" OR
"SEED OF TRUE HUMANITY"?

ONE OF THE CORE TEACHINGS ASCRIBED TO JESUS IN THE Gospels is embodied in the phrase huios (tou) anthropou which is usually translated as "Son of Man." Scholars have struggled with this phrase and written many volumes on the subject.[1] It remains "one of the most perplexing and challenging in the whole field of Biblical theology."[2]

Exceptionally insightful work on huios (tou) anthropou has been done by Elizabeth Boyden Howes.[3] She carefully identifies and differentiates between the apocalyptic and non-apocalyptic use of this phrase. The scholars of the Jesus Seminar are convinced that the apocalyptic material was added by the Gospel writers and that only the non-apocalyptic uses may have originated with Jesus.[4]

Dr. Howes identifies twelve instances and their parallels of non-apocalyptic use of huios (tou) anthropou in the Gospels of Mark, Matthew, and Luke.[5] The term also appears in the Gospel of Thomas and the Gospel of Mary.[6] Jesus may have known Greek, but his native tongue was Aramaic. So what might have been the Aramaic phrase behind the Greek? Perhaps Jesus said, bar enash,[7] in which case, how might that phrase be best translated into English?

There is a certain urgency to this question because the phrase "Son of Man" contains two masculine nouns which tends to be narrow and exclusive of women. Is there a way to render an accurate translation of the phrase which would be true to the text and true to the Spirit of Jesus which is much more inclusive?

Our only presently known copy of the Gospel of Mary is written in Coptic, but the original text would most likely have been in Greek. The Gospel of Mary 4:5 would have contained *huios (tou) anthropou* which Karen King in her draft translation renders as, "Seed of True Humanity."[8]

When we begin reviewing the non-apocalyptic *huios (tou) anthropou* passages and translating them as "Seed of True Humanity," the teachings of Jesus come alive in a very fresh way. The intent of Jesus is to show us a way of discovering our true humanity. When the phrase is rendered, "Seed of True Humanity," then all of the teachings of Jesus about seeds[9] come freshly alive. Seed stories are about our true humanity within us that is ready to sprout, grow, and bear fruit.

With these insights in mind, I have chosen to render texts with *huios (tou) anthropou* as "Seed of True Humanity" or simply "true humanity." It is my conviction that this translation is closer to what Jesus means and much more accessible to both women and men who are seeking to discover and live out their own true humanity. The Seed of True Humanity within each person carries the potential for trusting one's own true Center, recognizing one's connection with All that is, making more conscious decisions, and living creatively.

NOTES

1. For example, Frederick Houk Borsch, *The Son of Man in Myth and History*, Westminster Press, Philadelphia, 1967; Walter Wink, *The Human Being, Jesus and the Enigma of the Son of Man*, Fortress Press, Minneapolis, 2002; Andrew Harvey, *Son of Man, The Mystical Path to Christ*, Tarcher Putnam, 1998.

2. M. Black as quoted by Frederick H. Borsch, op. cit., p. 15.

3. Elizabeth Boyden Howes, *Intersection and Beyond*, "Son of Man— Expression of the Self" pps. 171-197, Guild for Psychological Studies, San Francisco, 1971.

4. Robert W. Funk, Roy W. Hoover, and the Jesus Seminar, *The Five Gospels, the Search for the Authentic Words of Jesus,* cameo essay p. 76-77, MacMillan Publishing, New York, 1993.

5. Mark 2:23-28, Mark 2:l-12, Matthew 12:31-32, Luke 9:57-58, Matthew 11:11, 16-19, Luke 11:29-30, Matthew 12:38-42, Luke 19:1-10, Mark 8:31, Mark 9:31, Mark 10:33, Mark 14:41.

6. For example, Gospel of Thomas 106 and Gospel of Mary 4:5.

7. Walter Wink, op. cit., p. 20.

8. *The Complete Gospels*, Robert J,. Miller, ed., Polebridge Press 1992. In her *Gospel of Mary*, Polebridge Press, 2003, King replaces the word "seed" with "child," thus rendering the phrase in Gospel of Mary 4:5 as "child of true Humanity." I prefer her first translation.

9. Seed passages from Jesus include the Parable of the Sower, the Parable of the Mustard Seed, the Parable of the Wheat and Tares, all of which point toward the Seed of True Humanity living within us.

CHAPTER 27:
TEACHING IN THE GRAINFIELDS[1]

AFTER WAKING UP EARLY AND GOING OUTSIDE TO TAKE in the fresh air, Mary comes back inside and says to Jesus, "What a beautiful Sabbath this is: the day is sunny and warm, but not too hot and there is a gentle breeze. It is too nice a day to be inside. How would you feel about our skipping synagogue this time and going out in nature to do our teaching?"

"Sounds good to me," says Jesus. "We could start by walking through the grainfields." The disciples agree and off they go. Before long Jesus starts telling stories. He opens with this one:

"Look, the sower went out, took a handful of seeds and scattered them. Some fell on the road, and the birds came and gathered them. Others fell on rock, and they didn't take root in the soil and didn't produce heads of grain. Others fell on thorns, and they choked the seeds and worms ate them. And other seed fell on good soil, and it produced a good crop: it yielded sixty per measure and one hundred twenty per measure."[2]

Mary immediately begins posing some questions, starting with, "What do you think the seed represents?" A variety of responses are given. Then Mary offers some of her own teaching: "I think it is the seed of our true humanity."[3]

Then Mary asks, "And what might the soil represent?" After discussion, everyone comes to agree that the soil refers to the different ways in which the person can respond to the Seed of True Humanity.

One disciple says, "Some people are like the beaten path. Their habits are so well worn, that the Seed of True Humanity just rests on the surface and is quickly snatched away by any bird that comes along!"

Another adds, "And some people are so hardened, that it is impossible for the seed to take any root. I know people like that!"

And a third says, "The thorns are whatever crowds out the good seed; it could be anything that chokes it out before it has a chance."

"And the worms?" asks Mary, "The worms are anything that worms its way into your life and keeps you from living fully!"

Then someone else says, "And the good soil is when we are open and receptive and able to provide a home for the seed of our true humanity, a place within us where the seed can crack open, sprout, send down roots, and sent up shoots that will bear leaves and flowers or fruit!"

"One more question," says Mary, "Do you think the story of the sower and the seed refers to different kinds of people? Or do you think it refers to different ways in which one person might respond to the Seed of True Humanity at different times in that person's life?"

Thomas jumps in and says, "I think the answer to the question is "Yes!" Those who get it smile and laugh a bit. Those who don't look puzzled.

In order to clarify a bit more, Jesus puts the teaching a little bit differently, "The Way of Mystery is like this: Suppose someone sows seed on the ground, and sleeps and rises night and day, and the seed sprouts and matures, although the sower is unaware of it. The earth produces fruit on its own, first a shoot, then a head, then mature grain on the head." But when the grain ripens, all of a sudden that farmer sends for the sickle, because it's harvest time."[4]

"That sounds so effortless! Is that what you mean? Are you saying that we should just let the seed do its work within us?"

Recognizing that the disciples are ready to go even further, Jesus offers another brief teaching, "The Kindom of Father and Mother, the *Way of Mystery*, is like a mustard seed."[5]

One of the disciples who is a farmer says, "A mustard seed? That's just a weed! If you let mustard get into a field of wheat, it will take over completely. What in the world do you mean? Are you saying that the Kindom of Father and Mother, the *Way of Mystery*, grows like a weed?"

"Well, the Romans and the people who work with them think they own the fields and control everything, so if the The Kindom of Father and Mother, the *Way of Mystery*, can grow like a weed, then maybe that would be good for us!" Everyone laughs.

"Now I have a question for you, Jesus. Of what kind is this mustard seed? Is it from heaven or from earth?"

And Jesus replies, "When the Father established the world for himself, he left many things with the Mother of All. Because of this he speaks and acts."[6]

Someone asks, "So are you saying that both the Father and Mother, both the seed and the soil need to be working in harmony with each other? And are you saying that the Kindom and the seed of our true humanity can grow like a weed inside us? I, for one, would be happy to have it take over my life!"

Seeing that his disciples are understanding the teaching and ready to go a little deeper, Jesus adds another, saying, "The Kindom of Father and Mother, the *Way of Mystery*, is like a person who had good seed. His enemy came during the night and sowed weeds among the good seed. The person did not let the workers pull up the weeds, but said to them, 'No, otherwise you might go to pull up the weeds and pull up the wheat along with them. For on the day of the harvest the weeds will be conspicuous, and will be pulled up and burned.'"[7]

"Just a minute, Jesus! I am still trying to figure out what you meant about the Way growing like a weed. Is that why you are saying we should let the weeds and the good seed grow up together? How do you tell the difference between them? Or is that your point?"

The teaching has been deep and the disciples are feeling hungry. Several of them start stripping heads of grain as they walk along, rubbing them in their fingers to remove the hulls, and eating them.[8]

Just then several Pharisees arrive on the scene. They have completed their Sabbath observance and as they come out of the synagogue they notice Jesus and his disciples walking through the grainfields. Wanting to keep a close eye on him and his activities, they catch up with him and try to start an argument. "Jesus, you know the Torah. You know it says that the Sabbath is holy and you should do no work on the sabbath. Your disciples are working by threshing grain in their hands. Why are they doing what is not permitted on the Sabbath day?"[9]

Jesus replies, "Haven't you read what David did when he found it necessary, when both he and his companions were hungry? He went into the house of God, when Abiathar was high priest, and ate the consecrated bread, and even gave some to his men to eat. No one is permitted to eat this bread, except the priests!"[10]

The Pharisees have no answer to the question and Jesus moves in to make yet another point, "The sabbath was created for humankind, and not humankind for the Sabbath."[11] The point is taken, reluctantly, by the Pharisees.

"So, the truly human being takes authority over the Sabbath."

Realizing that they are no match for Jesus this time, they leave angry and subdued and resolve that they will get him next time.

After the Pharisees leave, Jesus says, "The Kindom of Father and Mother, the *Way of Mystery*, is like a person who had a treasure hidden in the field but did not know it. And when he died he left it to his son. The son did not know about it either. He took over the field and sold it. The buyer went plowing, discovered the treasure, and began to lend money at interest to whomever he wished."[12]

One of the tenant farmers speaks up and says, "If we found a treasure hidden in this field, the people who took it away from us and claim to own it now would also claim the treasure as well!"

"Right," says Mary. "And whose field was it originally?" And as a chorus everyone calls out "Ours!"

"One more thing," says Mary, "Do you know that you are the field? Do you know that there is treasure hidden inside you? Look and see what you find!" Feeling a renewed sense of self worth, the people are even more energized than before.

"Just one more thing," says Jesus looking not at the fields but right at the disciples, "The crop is huge but the workers are few, so beg the harvest boss to dispatch workers to the fields."[13]

Everyone has the feeling Jesus is not referring to the fields in which they have been walking, but something else. What is he really trying to tell them? They walk along the rest of the way in silence, each one pondering the teaching. One by one they become aware of the invitation that has just been given. Some keep on walking right out of the grainfields with Jesus and Mary and become the newest members of their group of traveling disciples.

NOTES

1. This chapter is rooted in scenes from the Gospels where Jesus is teaching in grainfields plus wisdom teachings that relate to growing crops.

2. Gospel of Thomas 9, Scholars version

3. Gospel of Mary 4:4, Karen King draft translation

4. Mark 4:26

5. Gospel of Thomas 20

6. Dialogue of the Savior 36:1-3, Scholars Version translation and versification.

7. The earliest form is Gospel of Thomas 57 which is expanded later in Matthew 13:24-30.

8. Mark 2:23

9. Mark 2:24-26

10. Mark 2:25-26

11. Mark 2:27

12. Gospel of Thomas 109

13. Gospel of Thomas 73 and repeated in Matthew 9:37.

CHAPTER 28:
SHARECROPPERS REVOLT

IN THE THINKING OF JESUS AND THE JEWISH PEOPLE OF his time, land is sacred. "The Earth is the Lord's and the fulness thereof," says the Psalmist.[1] A similar understanding is expressed many centuries later by Chief Seattle when he says, "The Earth does not belong to us—we belong to the Earth."[2] The basic understanding is the same: the people of Israel belong to the land which belongs to the Lord: they care for the land and raise their crops as a trust from the Lord until the Roman Empire invades, takes control of the land, and imposes taxes. Farmers find themselves going into debt to pay taxes. The sacred land they have been working for many generations now becomes collateral for loans to pay taxes. Foreclosures come next and the land is now controlled by absentee landlords living in Jerusalem or some other major city.

The peasant farmers find themselves forced into becoming sharecroppers. Now they are farming the land for the owners who take the first cut of the crop with leftovers for the subsistence living of the farmers.

Frustration, anger, and resentments are building among the peasant farmers.

In this volatile context, Jesus offers a simple, open ended story:

"A...person owned a vineyard and rented it to some farmers, so they could work it and he could collect its crop from them. He sent his slave so the farmers would give him the vineyard's crop. They grabbed him, beat him, and almost killed him, and the slave returned and told his master. His master said, 'Perhaps he didn't know them.'

He sent another slave, and the farmers beat that one as well.

Then the master sent his son and said, 'Perhaps they'll show my son some respect.' Because the farmers knew that he was the heir to the vineyard, they grabbed him and killed him."[3]

Jesus pauses and immediately his disciples jump into the conversation voicing their strong opinions. Simon, who has already aligned himself with the Zealots, says, "The only way to get rid of the oppression by landlords and the Romans is to arm ourselves against them. Drive out the landlords, take our land back, then send the Romans back to Rome!"

Judas, who is aligned with the Sicarii, agrees and says, "A few well planned and executed actions can take out the landlords one by one along with anyone else cooperating with the Romans. Do it secretly so no one knows who did it!"

Others offer their opinions until someone finally asks, "Jesus, what do you think?"

And he replies, "Everyone who takes up the sword will be done in by the sword."[4]

"Right," says Simon. "They have already used the sword against us—now it is our turn to take them out!"

"No," says Mary. "We are saying that taking up the sword only brings more bloodshed. There has got to be another Way, like nonviolent resistance!"

NOTES

1. Psalm 24:1

2. Chief Seattle

3. Gospel of Thomas 65 gives us the earliest version of this story. Later Gospels expand the story with allegorical meaning: Mark 12:1-12, Matthew 21:33-46, Luke 20:9-19

4. Matthew 26:52

CHAPTER 29:
FARMERS BECOMING DAY LABORERS[1]

OWNERS OF GREAT ESTATES INCREASE THEIR CONTROL of land through foreclosures on loans and hostile takeovers of peasant farms. Once in control, the landowners switch the agricultural production from grains for local use to vineyards producing wine for export.

The results are a decrease in the food supply for the village peasants and the forcing of subsistence farmers into day laborers competing for employment.

Wages are set by the owners who have power to determine what they think is right. Work is seasonal, primarily at planting and at harvest time. Many workers look for work off-season in the cities. They are less and less able to support families. Often they are reduced to begging before dying of malnutrition. As expendable human beings, their final option is to form outlaw bands. There is increasing strain on the social fabric of village communities. The situation is similar to what happens today when U.S. agribusiness corporations exploit land and peasants in other countries. In this volatile context, Jesus tells his story:

"A proprietor went out the first thing in the morning to hire workers for his vineyard. After agreeing with the workers for a silver coin a day he sends them into his vineyard.

"And coming out around 9 A.M. he sees others loitering in the marketplace and he says to them, 'You go into the vineyard too, and I'll pay whatever is fair.' So they go to work.

"Around noon he goes out again, and also at 3 P.M., and repeats the process. About 5 P.M. he goes out and finds others loitering about and says to them, 'Why do you stand around here idle the whole day?'

"They reply, 'Because no one has hired us.'

"He tells them, 'You go into the vineyard as well.'

"When evening came the owner of the vineyard tells his foreman: 'Call the workers and pay them their wages starting with those hired last and ending with those hired first.'

"Those hired at 5 P.M. came up and received a silver coin apiece. Those hired first approached thinking they would receive more. But they also got a silver coin apiece. They took it and began to grumble against the proprietor: 'These guys hired last worked only an hour but you have made them equal to us who did most of the work during the heat of the day.'

"In response he said to one of them, 'Look, pal, did I wrong you? You did agree with me for a silver coin, didn't you? Take your wage and get out! I intend to treat the one hired last the same way I treat you. Is there some law forbidding me to do with my money as I please? Or is your eye filled with envy because I am generous?'[2]

"Quickly the workers jump into the conversation:

"One says, 'The rich guy is shaming the people who worked all day.' Another adds, 'Yes, and he uses his foreman to do the dirty work!'

"One more adds, 'Right. And he compliments himself for being generous!'

"He rubs it in further by calling him, 'Pal!' 'He thinks the land is his—but we know land belongs to the Lord!'

"Yet another adds, 'The Romans and the land owning Herodians keep trying to divide us and get us fighting among ourselves which makes me even more angry!'

"Yet another adds, 'Reminds me of the saying, "Be angry but do not sin; do not let the sun go down on your wrath."'"[3]

Jesus goes even further with his teaching and says, "Love your enemies, do favors for those who curse you, pray for your abusers. When someone strikes you on the cheek, offer the other as well. If someone takes away your coat don't prevent that person from taking your shirt along with it. Give to everyone who begs from you; and when someone takes your things, don't ask for them back. Treat people the way you want them to treat you."[4]

Many of the workers are confused, but one, having thought about it says, "People with power like to divide and conquer, so is Jesus saying, 'Don't let them divide you'?" Someone else chimes in with, "Maybe he is saying 'Love them—it only confuses them.'" The scene seems to have raised more questions than it has answered... yet somehow a message of solidarity with one another and nonviolent resistance to the Powers that Be is coming through...

Notes

1. Interpretation of this story relies in large measure on the research of William R. Herzog II, *Parables as Subversive Speech*, Chapter 5. This story is found only in Matthew 20:1-15

2. Matthew 20:1-15, Scholars Version

3. Ephesians 4:26

4. Q Gospel 6:27-36

CHAPTER 30:
FORGIVING DEBTS[1]

AS WE HAVE SEEN, MORE AND MORE PEASANTS IN Galilee are being manipulated into debt as a direct result of Roman Empire policies designed to control the land, extract resources, and keep labor costs down. It is a system that runs on force and fear and then, adding insult to injury, calls itself "Peace." In that context, Jesus tells this story:

"The Kindom of Father and Mother, *The Way of Mystery*,[2] should be compared to a provincial official who decided to settle accounts with his slaves. When the process began, this debtor was brought to him who owed him ten million dollars. Since he couldn't pay it back, the ruler ordered him sold, along with his wife and children and everything he had, so he could recover his money.

"At this prospect, the slave fell down and groveled before him: 'Be patient with me, and I'll repay every cent.' Because he was compassionate, the master of that slave let him go and canceled the debt.

"As soon as he got out, that same fellow collared one of his fellow slaves who owed him a hundred dollars, and grabbed him by the neck and demanded: 'Pay back what you owe!'

"His fellow slave fell down and begged him: 'Be patient with me and I'll pay you back.'

"But he wasn't interested; instead, he went out and threw him in prison until he paid the debt.

"When his fellow slaves realized what had happened, they were terribly distressed and went and reported to their master everything that had taken place.

"At that point, his master summoned him: 'You wicked slave,' he says to him, 'I canceled your entire debt because you begged me. Wasn't it only fair for you to treat your fellow slave with the same consideration that I treated you?'"[3]

After Jesus finishes telling his story, the responses begin. Judas says, "Who ever heard of one of these officials forgiving debt, let alone one as large as this?"

Mary says, "I agree, but try and stretch your imagination. Perhaps there could be a merciful one in the lot?"

Simon jumps in and says, "Actually, it is only fair: this slave would never have been in debt if they hadn't taken his land away from him in the first place!"

And Mary adds, "Still the official did wipe out the debt. Why didn't this man show a little mercy on the one who owed him a smaller amount of money? After being forgiven, why doesn't he forgive as well?"

Later on Jesus closes the teaching with a prayer which includes the phrase, "Forgive our debts to the extent that we have forgiven those in debt to us."[4]

Notes

1. This story is told only in Matthew 18:23-33

2. For "Way of the Tao" see Appendix 1.

3. Matthew 18:23-33 in the Scholars Version which translates in terms of dollars. The enormous debt reflects what happens to peasants whose taxes to the Empire have forced them into debt, lose their land, and then exorbitant interest escalates to create enormous debt.

4. Matthew 6:12, Scholars Version

CHAPTER 31:
MORE HANDS NEEDED₁

WORD SPREADS RAPIDLY AND PEOPLE FROM JERUSALEM, Idumea, and across the Jordan from Tyre and Sidon come streaming down to Galilee to see Jesus and hear what he has to say. Huge crowds are following Jesus, Mary, and their disciples.

As they are walking along the road, someone says to Jesus, "I'll follow you wherever you go." And Jesus replies, "Foxes have dens, and birds of the sky have nests, but the truly Human Being has nowhere to lay his head."

To another Jesus says, "Follow me."

But he says, "First, let me go and bury my father."

Jesus says to him, "Leave it to the dead to bury their own dead; but you go and announce The Kindom of Father and Mother, the *Way of Mystery*."[2]

They stop alongside the sea of Galilee to do some teaching. The pushing and shoving of the crowd is about to force Jesus into the water. This is a problem that is easily solved when his fishermen friends provide a small boat. Getting into it with Mary and pushing out just a short way from shore, Jesus sits and teaches from the boat.

There is so much ministry to do—so many people with so many

needs. Mary makes the observation, "We need more hands to do the work, Jesus!" So after dismissing the crowds, Jesus, Mary and the others go up the mountain where they form a group of disciples to be their teaching companions. Once they are instructed, they will be sent out to speak, and to have authority to help people in confronting their inner demons and transforming their chakra energies into creative purposes.[3]

Jesus and Mary assemble their core group which includes Peter and his brother Andrew, James and John, the "Thunder Brothers," Philip, Thomas, Bartholomew, Matthew, James, the son of Alphaeus, Thaddeus, Simon the Zealot, Judas the Sicarii, Joanna, and Suzanna plus additional women.[4]

After giving these companions the teaching and instructions they need, Jesus and Mary send them out in pairs energized for their work.[5] Having modeled the power of working in pairs, Jesus and Mary assist others in finding their partners for this vital ministry.

The instructions from Jesus are simple: "Travel light. Do not take anything on the road except a walking stick: no bread, no backpack, no spending money. Wear sandals and no more than one shirt."[6]

And Mary adds, "Moses had his staff and we have our walking sticks. Mine is made of styrax[7] wood which I prefer because of its lovely scent and healing energy. Find the walking stick that empowers you."

Jesus continues, saying, "And whenever you enter someone's house, stay there until you leave town. And whatever place does not welcome you or listen to you, get out of there and shake the dust off your feet in witness against them."[8]

The core group grows and expands to a total of seventy people who are sent out in pairs[9] announcing that people should turn their lives around. They often help people encounter and transform their inner demons. They anoint many with oil for healing. "The fire is the chrism and the light is the fire."[10]

Mary then says to Jesus, "What are your disciples really like?"

And Jesus says, "They are like little children living in a field that is not theirs. When the owners of the field come, they will say, 'Give us back our field.' They take off their clothes in front of them in order to give it back to them, and they return their field to them."[11]

And someone else asks, "You already told us to go without any extra clothes: now you say strip down entirely? You mean, to go out being open, honest, not hiding anything, no hypocrisy? Am I getting it?"

"Yes," says Jesus, "And there is more. If the owners of a house know that a thief is coming, they will be on guard before the thief arrives, and will not let the thief break into their house and steal their possessions. As for you, then, be on guard against the world. Prepare yourselves with great strength, so the robbers can't find a way to get to you, for the trouble you expect will come. Let there be among you a person who understands. Anyone here with two good ears had better listen!"[12]

Then Jesus adds one word of counsel, "Be wise as serpents and harmless as doves."[13]

NOTES

1. Mark 3:1-6, cf. Matthew 12:9-14, Luke 6:6-11

2. Luke 9:57-60

3. Mark 3:13-19, cf. Matthew 10;1-4, Luke 6:12-16, Gospel of the Ebionites 2:3

4. We do not have the names of the additional women because the male writers of the Gospels have failed to record them. Jesus treats women equal to men, but male writers often have not gotten the message.

5. Gospel of Luke 10:1. Cf. the pattern of pairs in the writings of Paul who says that the apostles have the right to be accompanied by a wife, e.g. I Corinthians 9:5

6. Gospel of Mark 6:7-9, cf. Matthew 10:1, 9-14, Luke 9:1-6. In Mark, the first of the synoptic Gospels, the companions are sent out wearing sandals and carrying a walking stick (staff). Most translations use the word "staff," but I am following the Amplified Bible that uses "walking stick." Curiously, Matthew deletes both the sandals and the walking stick! Are they being asked to travel barefoot? The walking stick is like the staff of

Moses and has great symbolic value: saying, essentially, "Go with energy and power for teaching and healing!" So I follow Mark's version that requires the staff or walking stick.

7. "Since antiquity, styrax resin has been used in perfumes, some kinds of Incense, and medicine... Styrax contains benzoin which today is used in first aid for small injuries as it acts as a disinfectant and local anesthetic and seems to promote healing. It can also be added to boiling water to produce fumes which when inhaled have a soothing effect on the lungs and bronchia, helping to recover from common cold, bronchitis, or asthma." from Wikipedia, the free encyclopedia.

8. Mark 6:7-11

9. Luke 10:1-2

10. Gospel of Philip 66

11 Gospel of Thomas 21

12. Gospel of Thomas 21

13. Gospel of Thomas 39

CHAPTER 32:
GIVING AND RECEIVING HOSPITALITY[1]

IN VILLAGES WITH SUBSISTENCE LIVING, SURVIVAL requires an attitude of "all for one and one for all." Solidarity is the antidote to the "divide and conquer" activities of the Empire and the elites who work for the Empire. Solidarity means that hospitality is the responsibility of the entire village. When unexpected guests arrive in town, they must be shown great hospitality otherwise the honor of the entire village is at stake. In this context, Jesus says,

"Suppose you have a friend who comes to you in the middle of the night and says to you,'Friend, lend me three loaves, for a friend of mine on a trip has just shown up and I have nothing to offer him.' And suppose you reply, 'Stop bothering me. The door is already locked and my children and I are in bed. I can't get up and give you anything'—I tell you, even though you won't get up and give the friend anything out of friendship, yet you will get up and give that person whatever is needed because you'd be ashamed not to."[1]

One disciple replies,"Yes, I would get up and provide bread, even if it was all I had. This goes way beyond friendship."

Another adds, "I agree. After all, I might have an unexpected visitor come to my house when I had little to offer and I would need to ask my friends for help."

And still another replies, "You can't risk the reputation of everyone in town! If you refused to help, what would everyone else think of you?"

Mary smiles and says, "Besides, just think of Sarah and Abraham: they entertained strangers and then discovered that they were angels in disguise, people with a special message for them."

Jesus says, "Whenever you enter a house, first say, 'Peace to this house.' Stay at that one house, eating and drinking whatever they provide. Do not move from house to house. Whenever you enter a town and they welcome you, eat whatever is set before you."[2]

NOTES

1. This chapter is rooted in Luke 11:5-8, a passage that is unique to Luke. Insights for the context come from William R. Herzog, *Parables as Subversive Speech,* chapter 11.

2. Robert Funk, *Gospel of Jesus* 18:6-18 drawn from Thomas 14:4, Luke 10:5, 7, 8; Mark 6:10, Luke 9:4, Matthew 10:11-13.

CHAPTER 33:
TEACHING ON A HILLSIDE[1]

RETURNING FROM JUDEA, JESUS, MARY AND THEIR disciples start touring all over Galilee, teaching in synagogues, proclaiming the Good News of the Kindom of Father and Mother, the *Way of Mystery*, and healing every disease and ailment of the people. Some have followed them back down from Jerusalem and other parts of Judea. Their reputation has been spreading north through the whole of Syria. People are coming down from the Ten Cities and beyond. From all directions huge crowds are coming together everywhere he goes.[2]

Jesus says, "These people are like sheep without a shepherd."[3] And Mary replies, "Yes and I think it is time for a major piece of teaching."

Jesus says, "We need a good spot where everyone can gather and we can see them all in one glance."

"How about our hillside," Mary suggests, "The one with the two smooth rocks to sit on?" Jesus likes the idea and says, "Lead on. The people and I will follow!"

When they get close to the top of the hill with a magnificent view of the sea of Galilee, Jesus and Mary sit down with the other disciples close by[4] and the crowd starts getting comfortable on the grass which is fresh and green from recent rains.

Jesus opens with, "Why have you come out to the countryside? To see a reed shaken by the wind?"[5] The people laugh.

"Have you come out to see a person dressed in soft clothes, like your rulers and your powerful ones? They are dressed in soft clothes, and they cannot understand truth."[6]

Seeing how plainly Jesus is dressed, the people know he is with them and not on the side of oppressive rulers; they are ready to listen attentively as Jesus and Mary begin teaching together:

"Blessed are you poor. The Kindom of Father and Mother belongs to you."[7]

"And Blessed are you poor in spirit, for yours is also the Kindom of Father and Mother![8] Blessed are you who are hungry now, for you will have a feast![9]

"And Blessed are you who hunger and thirst for justice, for you will also have a feast![10]

"Blessed are you who weep now. You will laugh.[11]

"Blessed are you who grieve now. You will be consoled.[12]

"Blessed are you when people hate you, ostracize you, and denounce you and spread malicious gossip about you because of your true humanity. Rejoice and jump for joy! Just remember your compensation is great in heaven![13]

"Blessed are you who have been persecuted within yourselves, for you have come to know your Father and Mother.[14]

"The Kindom of Father and Mother is within you.[15]

"Blessed are you who have toiled and have found life.[16]

"Blessed are the peacemakers.[17]

"Love your enemies.[18]

"Do favors for those who hate you.[19]

"Bless those who curse you.[20]

"And pray for your abusers.[21]

"Blessed are you when you are hated and persecuted."[22]

"Wherever you have been persecuted, they will find no place.[23]

"When someone strikes you on the cheek, offer the other as well.[24]

"If someone takes away your coat, don't prevent that person from taking your shirt along with it.[25]

"Furthermore, when anyone conscripts you for one mile, go along an extra mile."[26]

Mary joins in and says, "I hear some of you scoffing at that idea. Look at it this way: when a Roman soldier forces you to carry his pack he expects you to do what he says. He also expects that you will do it grudgingly, that you resent having to do it and might even try to find a way to get back at him. But suppose you accept his pack cheerfully and strike up a conversation with him, ask him about his family, talk about whatever he is interested in. Then offer to go another mile with him, don't you see how you will surprise him? You might even get him feeling differently. And you may even get him questioning what the Empire is doing to us. In a small way you are helping to undermine the Empire! Just try it and see what happens!"

And Jesus continues, "Give to everyone who begs from you and don't turn away from the one who tries to borrow from you."[27]

"Treat people in ways you want them to treat you."[28]

"If you love those who love you, why should you be commended for that? Even the toll collectors do as much, don't they?[29] And if you greet only your friends, what have you done that is exceptional? Even the Gentiles do as much, don't they?[30]

"Do this and you will become children of your Mother and Father in heaven who cause the sun to rise on both the just and the unjust.[31]

"Be compassionate as your Mother and Father in heaven within you are compassionate.[32]

"And just one more thing: many of you tend sheep so let me tell you that the Kindom of Father and Mother, the Way of Mystery, is like a shepherd who had a hundred sheep. One of them, the largest, went astray. He left the ninety-nine and looked for the one until he found it. After he toiled, he said to the sheep, 'I love you more than the ninety-nine.'"[33]

Mary adds, "I can see from the expressions on your faces that this seems crazy to you. Who would leave ninety nine sheep to go off after one that is lost? Yet within each of us is a lost part. Sometimes the lost part of ourselves is the most important that we need to look for. What part of yourself might be missing? For those of you who have found today's teaching difficult, even ridiculous, perhaps the missing part you need to look for is your own compassion. And the way to cultivate your compassion is through prayer."

Jesus continues, "Ask: it will be given to you; seek: you will find; knock: it will be opened for you.[34] Rest assured: everyone who asks receives; everyone who seeks finds; and for the one who knocks it is opened.[35] When your daughter asks you for bread, who among you would give her a stone?[36] When your son asks you for a fish, who among you would give him a snake?[37] Or if your child asks for an egg, would you give a scorpion?"[38]

"So if you know how to give your children good gifts, isn't it much more likely that the heavenly Father will give holy spirit to those who ask?[39]

"And when you pray, don't act like phonies. They love to stand up and pray in houses of worship and on street corners, so they can show off in public. I swear to you their prayers have been answered![40]

"When you pray, go into your room by yourself and shut the door behind you. Then pray to your Father, the hidden One. And your Mother, with her eye for the hidden, will applaud you.[41]

"And when you pray, you should not babble as the Gentiles do.[42] They imagine that the length of their prayers will command attention. So don't imitate them.[43] After all, your Father knows what you need before you ask.[44]

"Don't be anxious and fret about your life.[45] Don't worry about what you're going to eat.[46] Don't fret, from morning to evening and from evening to morning, about what you're going to wear.[47]

"When you strip without being ashamed, and you take your clothes and put them under your feet like little children and trample them, then you will see the child of the living one and you will not be afraid."[48]

"There is more to living than food and clothing, isn't there?[49] Take a look at the birds of the sky: they don't plant or harvest, or gather into barns. Yet your heavenly Father and Mother feed them.[50] You're worth more than they, aren't you?[51]

"Can any of you add one hour to life by fretting about it?[52] So if you can't do a little thing like that, why worry about the rest?[53]

Notice how the wild lilies are growing over there.[54] They don't slave and they never spin.[55] Yet let me tell you, even Solomon at the height of his glory was never decked out like one of them.[56] If God dresses up the grass in the field, which is here today and tomorrow is thrown into an oven, won't you be cared for even more, you who don't take anything for granted?[57]

"So don't fret. Don't say, 'What am I going to eat?' or 'What am I going to drink?' or 'What and I going to wear?'[58] These are all things Gentiles seek. After all, your heavenly Father is aware that you need them.[59] Instead, seek the Kindom of Father and Mother, the *Way of Mystery*, and their justice first, and all these things will come to you as a bonus.[60]

"Sell your belongings and donate to charity.[61] Don't acquire possessions here on earth where moths and insects eat away and where robbers break in and steal.[62]

"Instead, gather your nest egg in heaven within you where neither moths nor insects eat away and where no robbers break in and steal."[63]

And Mary adds, "As you know, what you treasure is your heart's true measure."[64]

Jesus answered, "When you pray, say something like this:[65] Our Mother and Father, your name be revered.[66] Bring your Way on earth as in heaven.[67] Provide us with the bread we need for the day.[68] Forgive our sins as we forgive others.[69] And please don't subject us to test after test."[70]

After offering the sample of prayer, there is a prolonged silence which is finally broken by a woman in the crowd who says, "Blessed is your Mother: the womb that bore you and the breasts that fed you."[71]

And Jesus replies, "Blessed are those who have heard the word of the Father and Mother and have truly kept it."[72]

Then Jesus and Mary wrap up their hillside teaching: "You are the light of the world."[73] "People do not light a lamp and put it under a bushel basket but rather on a lampstand, where it sheds light for everyone in the house."[74] "That is how your light is to shine in the presence of others, so they can see your good deeds and acclaim your true Father and Mother.[75] Wisdom is a trace of salt.[76] You are the salt of the earth."[77]

NOTES

1. This chapter draws on teaching material in the Gospel of Thomas, the Q Gospel, and the Gospels of Matthew and Luke.

2. Matthew 4:23-25

3. Mark 6:32

4. Matthew 5:1

5. Gospel of Thomas 78:1

6. Gospel of Thomas 78:2-3

7. Gospel of Thomas 54 and Luke 6:20

8. Matthew 5:3

9. Gospel of Thomas 69:2 and Luke 6:21

10. Matthew 5:6

11. Luke 6:21

12. Matthew 5:4

13. Luke 6:22

14. Gospel of Thomas 69:1

15. Matthew 5:9

16. Gospel of Thomas 58

17. Matthew 5:9

18. Luke 6:27 and Matthew 5:44

19. Luke 6:27

20. Luke 6:28

21. Luke 6:28

22. Gospel of Thomas 68:1

23. Gospel of Thomas 68:2

24. Luke 6:29

25. Luke 6:29

26. Luke 6:29

27. Luke 6:30

28. Luke 6:31

29. Matthew 5:46

30. Matthew 5:47

31. Matthew 5:45

32. Luke 6:36

33. Gospel of Thomas 10

34. Luke 11:9

35. Luke 11:10

36. Matthew 7:9

37. Matthew 7:10

38. Luke 11:12

39. Luke 11:13

40. Matthew 6:5

41. Matthew 6:6

42. Matthew 6:7

43. Matthew 6:7-8

44. Matthew 6:8

45. Matthew 6:25

46. Matthew 6:25

47. Gospel of Thomas 36

48. Gospel of Thomas 37

49. Matthew 6:25

50. Matthew 6:26

51. Matthew 6:26

52. Matthew 6:27

53. Luke 12:26

54. Matthew 6:28

55. Matthew 6:28

56. Matthew 6:29

57. Matthew 6:30

58. Matthew 6:32

59. Matthew 6:32

60. Matthew 6:33

61. Luke 12:33

62. Matthew 6:19

63. Matthew 6:20

64. Matthew 6:21

65. Luke 11:2

66. Luke 11:2

67. Matthew 6:10

68. Matthew 6:11

69. Luke 11:4

70. Luke 11:4

71. Gospel of Thomas 79

72. Gospel of Thomas 79

73. Matthew 5:14

74. Matthew 5:15

75. Matthew 5:16

76. Gospel of Philip 36

77. Matthew 5:13

CHAPTER 34:
TEACHING IN THE THEATRE IN SEPPHORIS[1]

"JESUS, I HAVE NOTICED THAT WHEN WE RETURN TO some of the towns and villages where we taught before that many of the people seem to be missing," says Mary one day. And Jesus replies, "Yes, I have noticed the same thing, especially among the carpenters and masons and many of the merchants. I have asked around and found out that many people have been moving to Sepphoris."

Overhearing their conversation, Thomas adds, "Yes. Herod Antipas has a big building program going on in Sepphoris and wages are a little bit better than they are in the villages."

Mary offers a suggestion. "Maybe it is time to go to Sepphoris and do some teaching there. What do you think?" And Jesus replies, "I've always preferred the little places: teaching is so direct and I can feel how people are responding."

"Yes, but many of the people who heard you before are now in Sepphoris and would be happy to hear you again," says Mary.

"Where would we gather people for teaching? I'm not sure that the synagogues would want us there," says Peter.

"So many of the people in Sepphoris speak Greek now. So if we go there, Jesus, how is your Greek?" says Thomas.

Sensing the challenge, Jesus says, "I could do it if I had to." And Mary adds, "And you should. The people in Sepphoris need to hear your message!"

Glancing around the circle of disciples, "Jesus says, "All right, then. Tomorrow we head for Sepphoris and see what happens."

Sepphoris is only four miles from Nazareth, but the feeling of the place is like entering another world. City life is so different from the villages and fields. But the next day as they enter, they are met by large crowds. Many of the faces turn out to be familiar. Just as Jesus and Mary had suspected, here are the people who have been missing.

The crowds are growing in numbers so where can Jesus speak to them and be heard well? Jesus notices an amphitheatre, not yet finished, but far enough along that there is plenty of room for people to sit down. "They say it will seat 3,000 when it is done," says Philip.

Before he knows it, Jesus finds himself in the amphitheatre. The crowds are assembling and calling for him to speak. So he raises his hand for quiet and begins his teaching.

"Everyone hearing my sayings and acting on them is like a person who built one's house on bedrock; and the rain poured down and the flash floods came, and the winds blew and pounded that house, and it did not collapse, for it was founded on bedrock. And everyone who hears my sayings and does not act on them is like a person who built one's house on the sand; and the rain poured down and the flash-floods came, and the winds blew and battered that house, and promptly it collapsed, and its fall was devastating.[2]

"Wisdom says, I will send them prophets and sages, and some of them they will kill and persecute, so that a settling of accounts for the blood of all the prophets poured out from the founding of the world may be required of this generation, from the blood of Abel to the blood of Zechariah, murdered between the sacrificial altar and the House. Yes, I tell you: an accounting will be required of this generation.[3]

"Nothing is covered up that will not be exposed, and hidden that will not be known. What I say to you in the dark, speak in the light; and what you whispered in the ear, proclaim on the housetops."[4]

"And do not be afraid of those who kill the body, but cannot kill the soul. But fear the one who is able to destroy both the soul and body in Gehenna.[5]

"Do not treasure for yourselves treasures on earth, where moth and gnawing deface and where robbers dig through and rob, but treasure for yourselves treasures in heaven within you where neither moth nor gnawing defaces and where robbers do not dig through nor rob. For where your treasure is, there will be your heart.[6]

"When evening has come, you say: Good weather! For the sky is flame red. And at the dawn: Today it's wintry! For the lowering sky is flame red. The face of the sky you know how to interpret, but the time you are not able to?[7]

"Enter through the narrow door, for many will seek to enter and few are those who enter through it. When the householder has arisen and locked the door, and you begin to stand outside and knock on the door saying: Master open for us, and he will answer you: I do not know you, then you will begin saying: We ate in your presence and drank, and it was in our streets you taught. And he will say to you: I do not know you! Get away from me, you who do lawlessness.[8]

"Nobody can serve two masters; for a person will either hate the one and love the other, or be devoted to the one and despise the other. You cannot serve God and money."[9]

Someone in the crowd calls out and asks, "When is the Kindom of God coming?"

And Jesus answers and says, "The Kindom is not coming visibly. Nor will one say, 'Look, here!' or, 'There!' For, look, the Kindom of the Father and Mother is within you!"[10]

Suddenly Jesus is interrupted by a big commotion in the crowd. People are shouting and crying out because Roman soldiers have entered the amphitheater and are breaking up the crowd, arresting people, and dragging them away.

The officer in charge moves directly toward Jesus and attempts to arrest him for assembling a crowd without a permit, but Jesus and Mary skillfully slip through the people and get away. They have avoided arrest and are safe this time.

NOTES

1. Teachings in this chapter ascribed to Jesus are taken from *The Sayings Gospel Q in English* edited by James M. Robinson, Fortress Press, 2002

2. Q Gospel 6:47-49

3. Q Gospel 11:49-51

4. Q Gospel 12:2-3

5. Q Gospel 12:4-5

6. Q Gospel 12:33-34

7. Q Gospel 12:54-56

8. Q Gospel 13:24-27

9. Q Gospel 16:19.

10. Luke 11:20-21

CHAPTER 35:
A LAWYER COMES FOR ADVICE₁

AFTER ESCAPING THE NEAR ARREST IN SEPPHORIS, JESUS
and Mary return to one of the villages where a lawyer stands up and
puts him to the test with a question: "Teacher, what do I have to do
to inherit eternal life?"

Jesus replies, "How do you read what is written in the Law?" And
he answers, "You are to love the Lord your God with all your heart,
with all your soul, with all your energy, and with all your mind; and
your neighbor as yourself."

Jesus replies, "You have given the correct answer; do this and you
will have life."

But with a view to justifying himself, he says to Jesus, "But who is
my neighbor?"

Jesus replies, "This fellow was on his way from Jerusalem down to
Jericho when he fell into the hands of robbers. They stripped him,
beat him up, and went off, leaving him half dead.

"Now by coincidence a priest was going down that road; when he
caught sight of him, he went out of his way to avoid him. In the
same way, when a Levite came to the place, he took one look at him
and crossed the road to avoid him.

"But this Samaritan who was traveling that way came to where he was and was moved with compassion at the sight of him. He went up to him and bandaged his wounds, pouring olive oil and wine on them. He hoisted him onto his own animal, brought him to an inn, and looked after him. The next day he took out two silver coins, which he gave to the innkeeper, and said, 'Look after him, and on my way back I'll reimburse you for any extra expense you have had.'

"Which of these three, in your opinion, acted like a neighbor to the man who fell into the hands of the robbers?"

He said, "The one who showed him compassion."

Jesus said to him, "Then go and be compassionate."[2]

The lawyer has much to think about and goes on his way. Jesus is left alone with Mary who says, "I think that legal expert was asking more than a legal opinion from you; he is really trying to deal with his own questions of how to live his life more fully. And you responded so well: speaking to him in his own terms while helping him to get to the question behind his question.

"When you told the story about the person on journey, I felt I could identify with the traveler just living his life when suddenly he is being beaten and robbed, and then ignored by the priests and Levites who see what is going on, but do nothing about it, not wanting to get involved. They shut their ears to his cries and do not even speak to him.

"What surprised and pleased me was when your story makes the Samaritan as the one who has compassion and is willing to respond to the needs of the wounded person. Before your conversation with the Arab woman and our time at the beach, I felt you didn't care much for Arabs or Samaritans and now it is a Samaritan who is the hero of your story."

And Jesus responds, "Mary, you know me completely and love me devotedly.[3] And yes, the Arabs and the Samaritans are now my neighbors and I love them as myself."

After sharing a warm embrace with Jesus, Mary continues, "In your story, the Samaritan bandages the wounds and pours on oil and wine. Spiritual love is wine and fragrance. All those who anoint themselves with it take pleasure in it. While those who are anointed are present, those who are nearby also benefit from the fragrance. The love in the chrism heals the wounds."[4]

"I am thinking about the Samaritan and why he had compassion. Perhaps he had been wounded himself? Perhaps his wounds had healed? And because of his own healing he was able to understand and have compassion for someone else?"

NOTES

1. The initial part of Conversation between the lawyer and Jesus is found in Luke 10:25-30 which is a reworking of Mark 12:28-34 and Matthew 22:34-40. Luke 10:30-37 adds the story which is known as "The Parable of the Good Samaritan" which might be better named "The story of the One on Journey."

2. Luke 10:

3. Gospel of Mary 10:10

4. Gospel of Philip 111, *Nag Hammadi Library* 77:35-78:10

CHAPTER 36:
STAY OUT OF COURT!

NOTICING THAT JESUS HAS BEEN TALKING WITH ONE OF the legal experts, someone in the crowd comes to him and says, "Tell my brothers to divide my father's possessions with me." Jesus says to the person, "Mister, who made me a divider?" Turning to his disciples, Jesus asks, "I'm not a divider, am I?"[1]

Then he adds, "Why can't you decide for yourselves what is right?"[2]

"If you happen to be offering your gift at the altar and recall that your brother has some claim against you, leave your gift at the altar. First go and be reconciled with your brother, and only then return and offer your gift."[3]

"When you are about to appear with your opponent before the magistrate, do your best to settle with him on the way, or else he might drag you up before the judge, and the judge turn you over to the jailer, and the jailer throws you in prison. I tell you, you'll never get out of there until you've paid the very last penny."[4]

Mary adds, "So here's the message: stay out of court!"

Jesus then addresses the entire crowd and tells this story, "There was a rich man whose fields produced a bumper crop, 'What do I do now?' he asked himself, 'since I don't have any place to store my crops. I know!' he said, 'I'll tear down my barns and build larger ones so I can store all my grain and my goods. Then I'll say to myself, "You have plenty put away for years to come. Take it easy; eat, drink, and enjoy yourself."

But God said to him, 'You fool! This very night your life will be demanded back from you. All this stuff you've collected—whose will it be now?'"[5]

NOTES

1. Gospel of Thomas 72

2. Luke 12:57

3. Matthew 5:23-24

4. Luke 12:58-59

5. Luke 12:16-20

CHAPTER 37:
JESUS AND MARY ATTEND A MERCHANTS LUNCHEON[1]

OVERHEARING THE CONVERSATIONS JESUS IS HAVING ON legal matters, several local merchants invite him to join them for lunch so that they might ask him some questions and hear his teachings. Jesus asks if anyone would mind if Mary joined them as well. Sensing their discomfort at having a woman as part of the discussion, but hearing no objections voiced, Jesus and Mary join the merchants who ask if he has any thoughts on how to build a good business.

Jesus repeats one of his favorite stories, "Everyone who pays attention to these words of mine and acts on them is like a person building a house who dug deep and laid the foundation on bedrock. Later the rain fell and torrents came, and the winds blew and pounded that house, but could not shake it. It did not collapse since its foundation rested on bedrock.

"But the person who listens to these words of mine and doesn't act on them will be like a careless builder who erected a house on the sand. When the rain fell, and the torrents came, and the winds blew and pounded that house, it collapsed. And the ruin of that house was total."[2]

The merchants all agree that Jesus is talking common sense to them when Mary raises a simple and provocative question, "So what is the bedrock of your life?" Some are silent, not wanting to deal with the question, while others become serious and are willing to offer what is really important to them. "And what kind of rains and torrents and winds are you living with in your life?" "And what is the present condition of your house, your life?"

Silence reigns and Jesus allows the questions to sink in.

Sensing that they are ready to go a bit further, Jesus says, "The Way of the Father is like a merchant who had a supply of merchandise and then found a pearl. The merchant was prudent; he sold the merchandise and bought the single pearl for himself. So also, with you, seek his treasure that is unfailing, that is enduring, where no moth comes to eat and no worm destroys."[3]

"What do you mean?" asks one man, "If you tie up all your money in one pearl that you keep for yourself, how can you do any business?"

And another asks, "So what is this pearl that is worth more than anything else in life?"

Jesus does not answer, but allows the merchants to live with the question.

Jesus follows with some one-liners and says, "The one who has become wealthy should reign..." He pauses and sees everyone smiling. Then he completes his thought and says, "and the one who has power should renounce it."[4]

He drives his point home by saying again, "Let one who has found the world, and has become wealthy, renounce the world."[5]

The host, realizing that the conversation is going in directions he had not intended, poses a few practical questions. His first one is, "What do you think is a fair interest rate?"

Jesus says, "If you have money, don't lend it at interest. Rather, give it to someone from whom you won't get it back."[6]

The host tries again to get Jesus back on a practical level and asks, "Do you have any advice about promotions and demotions?"

And Jesus replies, "Those who promote themselves will be demoted, and those who demote themselves will be promoted."[7]

Some come to him and interrogate him as a way of putting him to the test. They ask, "Teacher, Jesus, we know that you are from God, since the things you do put you above all the prophets. Tell us, then, is it permissible to pay rulers what is due them? Should we pay them or not?"

Jesus says to them, "Give the emperor what belongs to the emperor, give God what belongs to God, and give me what is mine."[8]

The lunch meeting breaks up, but as the merchants scatter some of them begin pondering more deeply what Jesus really means. Several ask Mary to explain and she replies, "When Jesus says, 'Give me what is mine,' do you realize he is calling us all to go for what is really ours, the treasure of the pearl within us? Once we find that pearl, no one can take it away."

On the way home, Mary says, "I noticed you told the same story about the house on the rock and the one on sand that you told in Sepphoris. But you got a different response this time."

"Yes," says Jesus. "No Roman soldiers in the audience this time!"

Mary replies, "The Roman Empire will collapse someday: all empires do. Your word will outlast them! The grass withers, the flower falls, but the word of the Lord endures forever."[9]

NOTES

1. This chapter weaves together a number of Jesus teachings and creates as context a businessmen's luncheon.

2. Q Gospel as found in Luke 6:47-49 and Matthew 7:24-27

3. Gospel of Thomas 76

4. Gospel of Thomas 81

5. Gospel of Thomas 110

6. Gospel of Thomas 95

7. Q Gospel as found in Luke 14:11, 18:14, and Matthew 23:12

8. Gospel of Thomas 100

9. Isaiah 40:8

CHAPTER 38:
SIMON'S SYMPOSIUM₁

JESUS AND MARY ARE DISCUSSING PLANS FOR THE evening and Jesus says, "I have been invited to dinner tonight at Simon's."

"Just you? What about me? Simon Peter has always invited both of us before!"

"Not Simon Peter. This is Simon the Pharisee and he has organized a symposium, men only."

"That's all right. Maybe I'll see what Joanna and Suzanna are doing tonight and have dinner with them. But you are telling me that the Pharisees are inviting you to dinner after all you have said about them? You have said, 'They are dogs in the manger: not eating themselves and keeping the cattle from eating'₂ and your remark the other day that 'The Pharisees and scholars have taken the keys of knowledge and have hidden them. They have not entered, nor have they allowed those who want to enter to do so.'₃ And now here you are going to have dinner with them tonight?

"Yes, it is true I said all those things. But the Arab woman surprised me. Perhaps these Pharisees will also. I will try to be on my best behavior, not prejudging anyone. We will see what happens."

155

"Will you tell me all about it when you get home?" Jesus responds with a smile.

Later Jesus enters Simon's house and reclines at table. A local woman, who is known as a sinner, finds out that he was having dinner at the Pharisee's house. She suddenly shows up with an alabaster jar of myrrh and stands behind him weeping at his feet. Her tears wet his feet, and she wipes them dry with her hair; then she kisses his feet, and anoints them with myrrh.[4]

Simon notices what she is doing and says to himself, "If this man were a prophet, he would know who this is and what kind of woman is touching him, since she is a sinner."

Jesus, sensing how his host is feeling, says, "Simon, I have something to tell you."

"Teacher," he says, "Speak up."

"This money lender had two debtors; one owed five hundred silver coins, and the other fifty. Since neither of them could pay, he wrote off both debts. Now which of them will love him more?"

Simon answers, "I would imagine, the one for whom he wrote off the larger debt."

And Jesus answers him, "You're right." Then turning to the woman, he says to Simon, "Do you see this woman? I walked into your house and you didn't offer me water for my feet; yet she has washed my feet with her tears and dried them with her hair. You didn't offer me a kiss, but she hasn't stopped kissing my feet since I arrived. You didn't anoint my head with oil, but she has anointed my feet with myrrh. For this reason, I tell you, her sins, many as they are, have been forgiven, as this outpouring of her love shows. But the one who is forgiven little shows little love." And Jesus says to her, "Your sins have been forgiven."

Then those having dinner with him begin to mutter to themselves, 'Who is this who even forgives sins?'"

And turning to the guests Jesus says, "Why are you bothering this woman? She has done a beautiful thing to me."[5]

Then he says to the woman, "Thank you. Your trust has saved you; go in peace."

The conversation shifts slightly as one of the Pharisees says,

"Some of your disciples are eating without washing their hands. Why do they deviate from the tradition of the elders?"[6]

In response Jesus asks them, "Why do you also break God's commandment because of your tradition? You remember God said, 'Honor your father and your mother' and 'those who curse their father and mother will surely die.' But you say, 'If people say to their father or mother, "Whatever I might have spent to support you has been consecrated to God," they certainly should not honor their father or mother.' So you end up invalidating God's word because of your tradition. You phonies, how accurately Isaiah depicted you when he said, 'This people honors me with their lips, but their heart is far from me. Their worship of me is empty, because they insist on teachings that are human regulations.'"[7]

Before leaving for home Jesus gently offers his final comment, "Those who know all, but are lacking in themselves, are utterly lacking."[8]

NOTES

1. This scene follows Luke 7:36-50. "The incident that Luke relates here concerns a penitent woman who invades a symposium (dinner party for males) given by a Pharisee." *The Five Gospels*, Robert W. Funk, and Roy W. Hoover, MacMillan, 1993, p. 304. There is a similar story in Mark 14:3-9 and Matthew 26:6-13, but in these versions the scene is in the home of Simon the leper. The woman anoints Jesus not with her tears but with expensive ointment in preparation for his burial. There is yet another story in John 12:1-8 where it is Mary of Bethany who anoints Jesus with nard. Often these three separate traditions have been conflated into one, along with the story of the woman taken in adultery told in John 7:53-8:11 and the women in these stories have become merged into just one woman: Mary of Magdalene! The result has been confusion and unwarranted conclusions being applied to her. In this book I am attempting to unsnarl the confusion and let each of the women stand more clearly on her own.

2. Gospel of Thomas 102

3. Gospel of Thomas 39

4. Most translations translate the word as "ointment" but I am following the Scholars Version which is more specific and identifies the ointment as myrrh. "Myrrh was an important ingredient of the sacred anointing oil (Exodus 30:23). As an important ingredient of perfumes, it was used for beauty treatment (Esther 2:13; cf. Song of Songs 5:5) and for scenting clothing (Psalm 45:8, Proverbs 7:17, Song of Songs 1:13; 3:6), and appears in poetic symbolism (Song of Songs 4:6, 14; 5:1, 13; and Ecclesiasticus 24:15. It was among the gifts given to the infant Jesus (Matthew 2:11). On the cross Jesus is offered "wine mingled with myrrh" (as an anodyne; Mark 15:23). Myrrh and aloes were brought by Nicodemus for Jesus' burial (John 19:39' cf. "spices" in Mark 16:1; Luke 24:1)." *The Interpreter's Dictionary of the Bible*, Abingdon Press 1962, volume K-Q, p. 478.

5. Mark 14:6, Matthew 26:10.

6. Mark 7:1-2, Matthew 15:2

7. Matthew 15:1-8

8. Gospel of Thomas 67

CHAPTER 39:
THE MANAGER₁

IF YOU HAVE EVER BEEN A MANAGER, YOU MAY RELATE especially well to this story.

Being in between the boss and the clients, a manager usually feels pressure from both directions. In short, it is a stressful balancing act.

In this context, the manager is caught between the master's greed and excessive demands and the tenant's endless complaints. When loans are made to cover debt, interest is added: normally twenty-five percent for loans of money and fifty percent for goods such as olive oil or wheat. In addition, the manager figures in his own cut, often with deals under the table. He wants to make all the money he can for himself and his family without causing the debtors to rebel while collecting what the master is demanding.

In this scene, the manager is being called to account and is at risk of losing his job.

If his job goes away, he risks falling down the economic ladder to become a day laborer.

With a surplus of day laborers, he is at further risk of having to beg. How will he and his family survive?

Jesus opens his story, "There was this rich man whose manager had been accused of squandering his master's property. He called him in and said, 'What's this I hear about you? Let's have an audit of your management, because your job is being terminated.'

"Then the manager said to himself, 'What am I going to do? My master is firing me. I'm not strong enough to dig ditches and I'm ashamed to beg. I've got it! I know what I'll do so doors will open to me when I'm removed from management.'

"So he called in each of his master's debtors. He said to the first, 'How much do you owe my master?'

"He said, 'Five hundred gallons of olive oil.'

"And he said to him, 'Here is your invoice; sit down right now and make it two hundred and fifty.' Then he said to another, 'And how much do you owe?'

"He said, 'A thousand bushels of wheat.'

"'Here is your invoice' make it eight hundred.' The master praised the dishonest manager because he had acted shrewdly."[2]

After telling his story, Jesus pauses and waits for responses.

The first to speak is Peter who says, "The manager made the debtors happy because he reduced their debt. He made the master happy because he is getting the money in and he makes himself happy by keeping his job. Only problem is he has to absorb the loss! Happens all the time. But what's the point of the story, Jesus?"

John says, "Are you saying that the children of this world exhibit better sense in dealing with their own kind than do the children of light?"[3]

Mary interjects her thinking, "Remember the psalm we sing that says 'the day and the light are both alike'?[4] We are all children of light and darkness: why are you trying to divide people this way?"

James jumps in and says, "I think it means that you should make use of your ill-gotten gain to make friends for yourselves, so that when the bottom drops out they are there to welcome you."[5]

Matthew expands the thinking a little further and adds, "The one who can be trusted in trivial matters can also be trusted with large amounts; and the one who cheats in trivial matters will also cheat where large amounts are concerned. So if you couldn't be trusted with ill-gotten gain, who will trust you with real wealth?"[6]

There is a pause and then, as in one voice, the disciples ask, "So which one of us is right, Jesus? What does your story really mean?"

Jesus remains silent which infuriates the disciples and they start arguing among themselves about the real meaning of the story.

NOTES

1. This chapter is based on Luke 16:1-11 and the research of William R. Herzog II in his *Parables as Subversive Speech*, chapter 13.

2. Luke 15:1-8a

3. Luke 15:8b

4. Psalm 139

5. Luke 15:9

6. Luke 16:11

CHAPTER 40:
EXPOSING EXPLOITATION₁

Empire creates conditions for the rich to get richer and the poor to get poorer.

The economic system rides on the backs of the peasants who are heavily taxed by government and temple. When peasants cannot pay, the rich offer them loans with high interest and their land as collateral. Foreclosures are common.

The idle rich live in Jerusalem and other cities and distance themselves from the peasants by hiring middle men to do their dirty work while they go off on trips for business and pleasure.

In this context, Jesus tells his story of a rich man and three middle men, one of whom becomes the hero of the story:

"A man going on a trip called his slaves and turned his valuables over to them. To the first he gave thirty thousand silver coins, to the second twelve thousand, and to the third six thousand, to each in relation to his ability, and he left.

"Immediately the one who had received thirty thousand silver coins went out and put the money to work; he doubled his investment.

"The second also doubled his money.

"But the third, who had received the smallest amount, went out, dug a hole, and hid his master's silver.

"After a long absence, the slaves' master returned to settle accounts with them. The first, who had received thirty thousand silver coins, came and produced an additional thirty thousand, with this report: 'Master, you handed me thirty thousand silver coins; as you can see, I have made another thirty thousand.'

"His master commended him: 'Well done, you competent and reliable slave! You have been trustworthy in small amounts; I'll put you in charge of large amounts.'

"The one with twelve thousand silver coins also came and reported: 'Master, you handed me twelve thousand silver coins; as you can see, I have made you another twelve thousand.'

"His master commended him: 'Well done, you competent and reliable slave! You have been trustworthy in small amounts; I'll put you in charge of large amounts.'

"The one who had received six thousand silver coins also came and reported: 'Master, I know that you drive a hard bargain, reaping where you didn't sow and gathering where you didn't scatter. Since I was afraid, I went out and buried your money in the ground. Look, here it is!'

"But his master replied to him, 'You incompetent and timid slave! So you knew that I reap where I didn't sow and gather where I didn't scatter, did you? Then you should have taken my money to the bankers. Then when I returned I would have received my capital with interest. So take the money away from this fellow and give it to the one who has the greatest sum.'"[2]

As Jesus is telling the story, the disciples are quiet. Some are even wondering if Jesus is taking sides with the rich man. But when his story shifts to the third man they start to cheer.

Peter says, "It took courage for the last slave to confront the rich man about the way he exploits others: reaping where he didn't sow, gathering where he didn't scatter."

James adds, "That rich man even admits what he has been doing!"

And Matthew says, "What if all three had refused to cooperate with the rich man; what would have happened?"

Peter chimes in, "He might have had to go to work himself!" and everyone laughed.

As the laughter dies down, Mary says gently, "Living in the *Way of Mystery* means speaking truth to power—and being willing to take the consequences!"

NOTES

1. Insights on the context for the story in this chapter are from William R. Herzog II, in *Parables as Subversive Speech*, chapter 9

2. The story is from Matthew 25:14-28 and parallel in Luke 18:11-27 as found in Robert W. Funk's, *The Gospel of Jesus* 4:24-38.

CHAPTER 41:
A WOMAN CONFRONTS AN UNJUST JUDGE[1]

EMPIRES CREATE LEGAL SYSTEMS FOR THE BENEFIT OF the powerful and to control the powerless. Rome allows the Jews to have their own Torah courts which gives the outward appearance of justice being served. The ruling elite remain subservient to Rome while keeping the peasants under control. The oppressed are expected to obey in silence and not make any trouble. Bribes grease the wheels of a system that runs on trickle-down injustice.

Women whose husbands have been worked to death or killed by the soldiers of Empire are especially vulnerable to further exploitation and abuse. Their legal rights, if any, have been swept away. In this context, Jesus says,

"Once there was a judge in this town who neither feared God nor cared about people.

"In that same town was a widow who kept coming to him and demanding: 'Give me a ruling against the person I'm suing.'

"For a while he refused; but eventually he said to himself, 'I'm not afraid of God and I don't care about people, but this widow keeps pestering me. So I'm going to give her a favorable ruling, or else she'll keep coming back until she wears me down.'"

One student says, "The judge has been waiting for the widow's opponent to come up with more money."

Someone else asks, "Where are the men of her family? Will no one go to court for her?"

Joanna says, "She has courage to face this judge in public and expect him to do the right thing even though he admits to not caring about her."

James says, "Usually a woman in her situation has only one remedy left: to give him her body secretly, but here she is exposing him as naked as the emperor with no clothes!

So what is the point of your story, Jesus? Are you saying that when there is injustice we should expose it? If so, that takes courage and is very risky. Are you saying we should do it whether or not it works?"

And Mary adds, "Just persist in seeking justice. Keep knocking on the door and it may finally open."

NOTES

1. This chapter is rooted in a story found only in Luke 18:2-5 which the Jesus Seminar scholars identify as the original story. Luke 18:1 adds a preface: "He told them a parable about the need to pray at all times and never to lose heart." Luke 18:6-8 adds a commentary, "Don't you hear what that corrupt judge says? Do you really think God won't hand out justice to his chosen ones—those who call on him day and night? Do you really think he'll put them off? I'm telling you, he'll give them justice and give it quickly. Still, when the son of Adam comes, will he find trust on the earth?" Eliminate Luke's additions, and you have the powerful message of Jesus about confronting the powers that be.

CHAPTER 42:
ENCOUNTER WITH A ROMAN OFFICER[1]

JESUS AND MARY ARE ACCUSTOMED TO BEING surrounded by occupying forces whose task is to keep the peace for Rome. Centurions, commanders of one hundred soldiers, are required not to be bold and adventurous, so much as to be good leaders with a steady, firm, and prudent mind, not prone to take the offensive or start fighting impulsively.[2]

Roman soldiers are under obedience to their superior officers. As occupying forces they must maintain control over the general populace. They can beat up the men, terrorize the women and children, and call it part of the "Pacification Program." They can catch those who look like troublemakers, torture them, crucify them, and leave their bodies to rot in the blazing sun as examples to others not to attempt any resistance to the power of Rome. The Empire intends to keep the peace through force and fear.

Local people have some choices when they see Roman soldiers on patrol in their neighborhood. The easiest thing to do is to run away or to hide, or simply to keep themselves out of harm's way as much as possible. Resistance forces can hurl rocks at the soldiers whose uniforms make them easy targets.

A Roman centurion approaches Jesus and Mary. This man seems different from most of the other Roman soldiers. There is a look of kindliness in his eyes, plus anxiousness: his body language reveals that he is very distressed about something. As he approaches the couple, someone else close by says, "I know this one, he's all right. He even built our synagogue for us."

"That's interesting. When I began teaching in synagogues, this one here in Capernaum was the first. I'll have to thank the officer for building it!"

The officer speaks in a pleading voice and says, "I have a slave who is very sick, he is running a high fever, is suffering paralysis, and is in terrible pain. It looks like he's not going to make it. I care so much about him and I've heard about you and your healing power...."

Mary and Jesus respond immediately and start walking with the officer toward his home. On the way, the officer says, "Sir, I don't deserve to have you in my house, but only say the word and my slave will be healed. After all, I am under orders myself and I have soldiers under me. I order one to go and he goes; I order another to come, and he comes... But I need your help now to heal my slave: he is like a son to me."

Hearing this, Jesus and Mary stop, look at the officer and say, "Your trust is amazing and brings results. Go on your way." When the officer reaches his house he discovers that his slave has recovered and is in good health. He also learns that the fever broke and the recovery began right when he was having his conversation with Jesus and Mary.

After leaving the officer, Jesus says to Mary, "I've never seen such trust among our people, have you?"

And Mary responds, "Not only that, but he really is a compassionate man after all; his love for his slave has made all the difference. And he has taken some risks: what will the hundred men under him think when they hear that his slave was healed with the help of a couple of Jews from Galilee? And what will his superiors in Rome do when they hear he has been fraternizing with us?"

Jesus smiles with her and says, "Yes, and we also took some risks: this scene could have gone very differently! This man wears the uniform of a centurion, but inside he is not so bad. Reminds me of when Samuel came to the defense of a shepherd boy and said, "People see only the outer appearances, but the Lord looks on the heart."³

And Mary replies, "Yes, and that shepherd boy named David became king of Israel. Sometimes the humble become powerful and sometimes the powerful are actually humble and compassionate inside when you get to know them!"

"You know, Mary, this centurion has gotten me to thinking. We have always heard that 'you are to love your neighbor' and 'you are to hate your enemy.' But suppose we were to risk getting to know our enemies: perhaps we could discover how to love them?"

Speaking from her heart, Mary says, "Love your enemies, even these Romans who occupy our country?"

"Mary, let's think and pray about this some more. You see that hill over there? Let's go up there and take some time out together." Hand in hand they go up the hill, find a couple of comfortable rocks to sit on and gaze out over the Sea of Galilee.

"Feel the sun?"

"Yes, it really warms my back."

"And look all over the valley: the sun is shining down on our people and on the Roman soldiers as well."

The next thing they know dark clouds begin gathering and a storm comes up over the lake as so often happens in this part of the world. Mary and Jesus head for home, but the storm is moving in quickly. Dark clouds open with torrential rain coming down everywhere on everyone. Before they can get indoors, Jesus and Mary are drenched to the skin.

"So the sun rises on the good and the bad," says Jesus. "And the rains come on the just and the unjust," says Mary. "And now that a Roman officer who was our enemy has become our friend, how can you tell which is which?"

"Hard to tell at first glance. Right now, there's only one thing I know for sure: let's get out of these wet clothes."

NOTES

1. Q Gospel 7:1-10, John 4:45-54. "The two versions of this story—the account derived from the Sayings Gospel Q and the report preserved by the Fourth Gospel—differ in almost every detail, yet they agree that Jesus affected a cure at a distance. In the Q version, Jesus is in Capernaum along with the patient; in the Fourth Gospel, Jesus is in Cana of Galilee. John has perhaps moved the location to Canaan in order to link this miracle with the changing of the water into wine which takes place at Cana. The Fellows of the Jesus Seminar were inclined to the view that Jesus was probably in Capernaum along with the petitioner and the patient. In the Q version, the petitioner is a Roman officer (centurion) with soldiers under his command; in the Fourth Gospel, he is an official appointed, presumably, by Herod Antipas.... The three accounts differ on the status of the patient. In Luke, the sufferer is a slave; in Matthew, he is a servant boy; in John he has been elevated to the rank of son. The ailment is also indeterminate. In Matthew, the servant has been struck down with paralysis and is in terrible pain; in Luke, the slave is near death; in John, the son is also near death of a fever. Again, it is impossible to ascertain what particular ailment was involved in the original story... Of the two written versions, the Johannine one is closer to the original form... The Johannine story is derived from the Signs Gospel, a collection of wondrous deeds performed by Jesus underlying the Fourth Gospel." *The Acts of Jesus*, Robert W. Funk and the Jesus Seminar, p. 45.

2. Polybius, History VI.24 as cited in the *Interpreter's Dictionary of the Bible*, volume A-D, p. 548.

3. I Samuel 16:7

CAMEO ESSAY 4:
WERE JESUS AND MARY MAGDALENE MARRIED?

AMIDST ALL THE DISCUSSION AND SPECULATION regarding whether or not Jesus and Mary Magdalene were married, there is one question that needs to be addressed first: What do we mean by "married"?

If we are thinking of contemporary marriage with a couple choosing on their own to apply for a marriage license from the State and making vows together in front of a court official or minister, priest, or rabbi, then the answer is "No." Jesus and Mary never went down to any court house to get a marriage license.

If we are thinking of Jewish marriage in the first century which involved arrangements between parents, then do we have any evidence of Mary's family producing a dowry for her? Being as free spirited as they were and in light of some of the remarks they made about family, would they have submitted to a traditional Jewish marriage of their time? If so, what evidence do we have?

Setting the question aside for a moment, what documentation do we have in regard to the nature of their relationship?

+ Mary Magdalene is the Companion of Jesus and they kissed each other often. (Gospel of Philip 32)

+ Jesus loved her more than any other woman (Gospel of Mary 6:1).

+ Jesus knew her completely and loved her devotedly (Gospel of Mary 10:10).

+ Jesus says, "When you drink from my mouth you will become like me; I myself shall become you, and the hidden things will be revealed to you" (Gospel of Thomas 108).

+ Mary is a woman who fully understood (Dialogue of the Savior 20:2).

The evidence is clear that Mary Magdalene and Jesus are Companions, soulmates, and partners in ministry. But does that mean they were "married"? The question persists: What do we mean by "marriage"?

Jesus and Mary Magdalene have a Sacred Partnership out of which flows their ministry of teaching and healing: they are seeking to assist people in discovering their essential Union with All that Is.

The Gospel of Philip summarizes their work succinctly by saying that Jesus "did everything in a Mystery: a baptism, a chrism, a eucharist, a reconciliation, and a bridal chamber" (Philip 68).

All of their work springs from their own experience with each other and with the Source of Life, that Amazing Mystery, the pulsating Energy of the Universe who is within, between, around, and beyond us, who is our Mother, Father, Teacher, and Lover, who is the TAO of Ten Thousand Names.

They experience and live in Sacred Union. Is there any greater Marriage than that?

CHAPTER 43:
A YOUNG MAN
WHOM JESUS LOVES₁

JESUS, MARY, AND THEIR DISCIPLES KNOW IT IS TIME TO go on the road again. As they set out on their journey, a young man runs up to Jesus, kneels down before him, and starts questioning him. "Good teacher, what do I have to do to really live? I have plenty of assets, but something seems to be missing. I ask myself, is this all there really is?"

Jesus replies, "Why do you call me good? No one is good except for God alone."

As usual, Jesus is pointing beyond himself to the Source of Life. Once that point has been made, Jesus continues to respond by saying, "You know the commandments: 'You must not murder, you are not to commit adultery, you are not to steal, you are not to give false testimony, you are not to defraud, and you are to honor your father and mother.'"

And the young man says, "Teacher, I have observed all these things since I was a child."

Jesus loved him at first sight. He identifies and understands this person's feelings.

Mary and Jesus share a knowing smile with each other: they know what it is like to do everything that is expected, conform to outer expectations, and still feel a sense of emptiness inside. Is this person ready to hear what is really needed?

In a loving tone of voice, Jesus says, "You are missing one thing: make your move, sell whatever you have, give the proceeds to the poor, and you will have treasure in heaven. And then come, follow me!"

The young man is stunned by this advice. He starts scratching his head.[2] He has a fortune and he is expected to give it all up? Jesus is asking too much of him! He had come to Jesus with great expectation and hope, but now he goes away dejected, his hopes shattered by these impossible demands.

Mary and Jesus watch the rich young man go on his way. They feel a sadness for him. He was so close to making his move. What is holding him back? Perhaps he will think it over and return later when he is ready?

Mary recalls the story Jesus tells of a woman who was carrying a jar of meal.[3] While she is walking along a distant road, the handle of the jar breaks and the meal spills behind her along the road. She doesn't know it; she hasn't noticed a problem. When she reaches her house, she puts the jar down and discovers it is empty.

Jesus and Mary agree that the woman in his story and this rich young man have so much in common. Both have been experiencing emptiness inside. The rich young man thinks he will be happy by holding onto his property and possessions, even acquiring more for himself. Jesus and Mary are wondering when this young man will learn that real Life does not work that way.

The disciples of Jesus and Mary are wondering what is going on. What happened to that young man who came with such enthusiasm and is now slinking off, trying to hide himself, looking like he is in great sorrow?

As the young man disappears around the bend in the road, Jesus looks at his disciples and offers some teachings for those who have eyes to see and ears to hear.[4]

Jesus says, "There was a rich man who had a great deal of money. He said, 'I shall invest my money so that I may sow, reap, plant, and fill my storehouses with produce, that I may lack nothing.' These were the things he was thinking in his heart, but that very might he died."[5]

He says, "How difficult it is for those who have money to quit the system, unleash themselves from the shackles of this Empire, commit themselves to the Kindom of Father and Mother and start living in the *Way of Mystery!*"[6]

The disciples are amazed at his teaching: drop out of a corrupt system, go within and find real life, gain perspective, and live creatively in the world!

Jesus continues, "Children, how difficult it is to enter the Way! It is easier for a camel to squeeze through a needle's eye than for a wealthy person to get into the Kindom and live the *Way of Mystery*.

Their disciples are perplexed and astonished by these strange surrealistic metaphors and ask a very simple question, "Well then, who can possibly find the Way and become whole?"

Jesus looks them right in the eye and says, "For people trying to do it alone, it is impossible, but for the Mystery everything is possible."

Mary puts it even more simply and says, "The Seed of True Humanity is within you."[7] Be aware of it! Water it, let it break its shell, sprout, grow to maturity, and bear fruit!"

Peter starts lecturing them, "Look at us, we left everything to follow you!"

Jesus replies forcefully yet gently, "I swear to you, there is no one who has left home, or brothers, or sisters, or mother, or father, or children, or farms on account of the good news, who won't receive a hundred times as much now, in the present time, homes, brothers, and sisters, and mothers, and children, and farms."

Jesus, Mary and their disciples are trading in their old, conventional way of living. They are breaking with restricting relationships and discovering new sacred circles of people that are more amazing and fulfilling. That is the good news.

Then Jesus adds the downside, "Expect persecutions—we are challenging the system of the Empire and of the religious establishment. Expect some reaction on their part! It is risky to live in the Eternal moment!"

Then he adds, "By the way, many of the first will be last, and of the last many will be first."

THE RICH YOUNG MAN RETURNS

Conventional New Testaments publish a version of the Gospel of Mark in which the rich young man leaves and is never heard from again. However, there is more to the story. An earlier edition of Mark's Gospel has been discovered and given the name Secret Gospel of Mark. When the deleted portions are returned to their original place between conventional Mark 10:34 and 10:35 we have the continuation of the spiritual journey of this young man:

And they come into Bethany, and this woman was there whose brother had died.

She kneels down in front of Jesus and says to him, "Son of David, have mercy on me."

But the disciples rebuke her. Jesus gets angry and goes with her into the garden where the tomb is.

Just then a loud voice is heard from inside the tomb. Then Jesus goes up and rolls the stone away from the entrance to the tomb. He goes right in where the young man is, sticks out his hand, grabs him by the hand, and raises him up. The young man looks at Jesus, loves him, and begins to beg him to be with him.

Then they leave the tomb and go into the young man's house. (Incidentally, he is rich.) Six days later Jesus gives him an order; and when evening has come, the young man goes to him, dressed only in a linen cloth. He spends that night with him because Jesus teaches him the mystery of God's domain. From there Jesus gets up and returns to the other side of the Jordan.[8]

AN EXPANSION AND INTERPRETATION
OF THE MEANING OF THIS STORY

How, shall we understand this story? Is it a literal account of a man who actually died and cried out from his tomb? Or is it a vivid account of this young man's experience? Here is someone who was physically alive but feeling dead inside. He is one of the walking dead. His original questions to Jesus, were "Good teacher, what do I have to do to really live? I have plenty of assets, but something seems to be missing. I ask myself, is this all there really is?" But now all his questions and feelings are melded into one last cry.

And what is the name of this man who is crying out? In Mark he is called "a rich young man", but no name is given. The story closely resembles one found in the Gospel of John where the man in the tomb is named Lazarus. Perhaps Mark and John are both relating the experience of the same man. The name Lazarus means "God helps" which applies to the person in both accounts.

Lazarus is in a tomb of his own making where he is feeling very isolated, alone, and disconnected from everyone, everything, and even the depths of his own being. Call it a deep depression. Feel the despair, the disillusionment, the anguish, the unbearable sadness, the deadness. The story of the Young Man whom Jesus loves continues:

His sister has tried to reach him, but nothing seems to work. Perhaps she is feeling it is her fault for failing to reach her brother. Perhaps she is asking herself: "If I had tried a different approach might I have reached him before he cut himself off completely?"

She kneels before Jesus and says, "Have mercy on me."

The disciples rebuke her and wave her off. After all, why should they bother with her and her rich brother who has everything and has come to nothing? Jesus gets angry at the disciples and goes with her toward the tomb in a garden. Like Eden, this garden is a place for re-creation.

Just then they hear a loud voice crying out from Lazarus who is inside the tomb of his own making. At the mouth of the tomb is a stone, a powerful symbol of whatever it is that blocks entrance into the soul of this man and blocks his ability to come out of himself. Jesus knows how to roll the stone away.

Once the blockage is removed, Jesus enters into the deep darkness, grabs Lazarus by the hand and raises him up. As Jesus makes connection and takes hold, Lazarus looks at him and loves him. Just as Jesus had loved him from the first time they met, now Lazarus is able to return that love. He needs whatever it is that Jesus can give him and begs Jesus to stay with him. Asking is all that is needed for him to receive.

Jesus goes with Lazarus into his house, a symbol of his inner and outer life. This is now an open house: everything ready for inspection. Finally, the day has come to sort through the contents and determine what needs to be kept, what needs to be given away, what needs to be transformed.

Jesus says "Lazarus, know what is in front of your face, and what is hidden from you will be disclosed to you. For there is nothing hidden that won't be revealed and exposed and nothing buried that won't be raised."[9]

Jesus says, "Lazarus, when you come to know yourself, then you will become known and you will realize that it is you who are the offspring of the living father. But if you will not know yourself, you dwell in poverty and it is you who are that poverty."[10]

Then Jesus adds an even clearer admonition, "If you bring forth what is within you, what you have will save you. If you do not have that within you, what you do not have within you will kill you."[11]

For six days Jesus and the young man face the contents of his soul: the wounds, the expectations, the dashed hopes, the disillusions, the wasted energy. The six days symbolize the six days of creation, the time needed for a new creation to occur. It is a time of preparation and inner exploration: Like the woman with the jar of meal, he is discovering his emptiness.[12]

Lazarus tells Jesus about the many times he has tried to rid himself of his deep depression, how he has even grabbed the evil spirit of depression by the seat of the pants and the scruff of the neck and thrown him out only to have him return with his cronies: the feelings of guilt, remorse, futility, and so much more. After each episode, his condition seems to have become even worse than before.[13]

Jesus stays with him day after day and night after night, moving him firmly and gently through each of the eternal questions that must be faced if he is to find real life.

And with each eternal question, Jesus asks the necessary follow up questions in order to fully plumb the depths of this man's soul. Gradually Jesus is assisting him in removing everything until he has become core naked, revealing all, hiding nothing. Jesus says, "When you strip without being ashamed, and you take your clothes and put them under your feet like little children and trample them, then you will see the offspring of the living one and you will not be afraid."[14]

Jesus tells Lazarus to close his eyes and go within. After allowing the time needed, Jesus invites him to open his eyes in order to see more clearly. The pattern of closing and opening his eyes repeats over and over as greater awareness is revealed.

After an intense time of preparation, the evening comes when it is time for initiation into the Holy Mysteries. Lazarus comes wearing only a linen cloth which is his baptismal garment.

Jesus spends the night with him. Lazarus is going through the dark night of his soul. Jesus knows when the time is right and the young man is ready to receive full initiation into Holy Mystery.

In the morning Jesus leads Lazarus to the banks of the Jordan River. Lazarus removes his clothes and enters the water, ready for both his outer and inner immersion. Jesus dips Lazarus into the flowing water for his spiritual burial and his spirit filled resurrection.

Lazarus comes out of the water knowing the Mystery in whom he lives and moves and has his being. He is reborn as a child of the Universe.

Now he is ready to receive the full anointing of the Holy Spirit with fire. The opposites of water and fire have come together and he is fully alive for the first time in his life.

Jesus gives thanks for the rebirth of Lazarus and shares a simple meal of bread, water, milk and honey, and wine. The redemption of his body and the reconciling of all that has been separated are coming together. Lazarus now enters into the experience known as the Bridal Chamber: complete holy Union.

Lazarus wakes up to a new awareness. He has direct experience of transcending Mystery and wonder. He feels a renewal of the spirit and an openness to the forces which create and uphold life. He experiences a complete connection with All that Is. Words fail to describe the joy, the ecstasy of knowing directly and simply the Wonder of it all.

After the initiation is completed, Jesus gets up and goes to the other side of the Jordan. Lazarus wants him to stay longer and is reluctant to let Jesus go. But a few days later Lazarus is able to say, "He separated from me and left me. But I did not despair... I rejoiced exceedingly, since I am in a great light and on a blessed path."[15]

Later when Jesus rejoins Mary he says, "I disclose my mysteries to those who are ready for Mystery."[16]

NOTES

1. This chapter is based on Mark 10:17-22 and Secret Mark. Compare it with the story of Lazarus in Gospel of John 11.

2. Gospel of Nazoreans 6

3. Gospel of Thomas 97

4. Mark 10:23-31

5. Gospel of Thomas 63

6. See the cameo essay on "The Kindom of the Father and Mother, the Way of Mystery," p. 35.

7. Gospel of Mary 4:5

8. Secret Gospel of Mark 1:1-13

9. Gospel of Thomas 5

10. Gospel of Thomas 3

11. Gospel of Thomas 70

12. Gospel of Thomas 97

13. Gospel of Matthew 12:43-45

14. Gospel of Thomas 37

15. Allogenes the Stranger 57:25-34

16. Gospel of Thomas 62

CHAPTER 44:
A PEAK EXPERIENCE₁

HAVING SHARED THEIR LIFE AND SACRED PARTNERSHIP working in many different situations with a wide variety of people, Jesus and Mary are ready for some time out. They decide to go up into the mountain on a retreat with their closest friends and disciples. They invite Joanna, Susanna and several other women along with Thomas, Philip, Bartholomew, Peter, James, and John.

As they start up the mountain with walking sticks to steady them, these friends begin recalling similar mountain scenes like the story of Noah and the ark coming to rest on Mt. Ararat and the story of Moses receiving the commandments on Mt. Sinai. They know that mountains are often the settings for peak experiences so their minds are flooding with questions: Why are Mary and Jesus leading us up this mountain? Will they reveal new information for us or give us special teaching?

They pause for a few moments. Jesus looks at them, feels their anticipation, and notices their quizzical looks. He smiles broadly, to the point of gentle laughter, and asks three questions: "What are you thinking about? Why are you perplexed? What are you searching for?"²

Philip ventures his response, "I am searching for the underlying reality and the plan."[3] Several others offer their responses as well.

At periodic intervals, Jesus and Mary stop for rest and invite the others to sit with them in a circle. They pose questions for the disciples to ponder during the next leg of the journey. Just before the final ascent, Jesus asks one probing question, "Compare me to something and tell me what I am like."[4]

Peter says, "You are like a righteous angel."

Matthew says, "You are like a wise philosopher."

Thomas says, "Teacher, my mouth is utterly unable to say what you are like."

Jesus replies, "I am not your teacher. Because you have drunk, you have become intoxicated from the bubbling spring that I have tended." Jesus takes Thomas aside and speaks three sayings to him. When Thomas rejoins the group, they ask him, "What did Jesus say to you?

Thomas replies, "If I tell you one of the sayings Jesus spoke to me, you will pick up rocks and stone me, and fire will come from the rocks and devour you."[5]

Startled by what Thomas has said, everyone falls into a deep Silence as they move toward the summit. Jesus is standing with arms raised praying intensely.[6] The others experience the powerful Energy and feel it may be more than they can face. They are feeling sleepy and having trouble staying awake.[7] Their unconscious is taking over.

Suddenly, everyone comes full awake. All eyes are focused on Jesus as he is transformed in front of them; his face is shining, radiant as the sun. Even his clothes became an intensely brilliant white, whiter than any laundry on earth could make them.[8] Elijah and Moses have appeared and are conversing with Jesus.

The disciples are terrified and awestruck. Only Peter is able to say anything, "Rabbi, it's a good thing we're here. In fact, why not set up three tents, one for you, one for Moses, and one for Elijah!"[9] The Vision is so real that Peter wants to build shrines to contain it, to hold onto it.

A cloud moves in and casts a shadow over them and a Voice comes out of the cloud, saying, "This is my dear son, listen to him!"[10]

Moses and Elijah vanish , and they are alone with Jesus.[11]

This has been a powerful peak experience: too much to grasp all at once. Pondering what has happened and sharing insights, they discover the meaning is becoming clearer. Everyone knows that Moses represents the basic teachings of their faith and Elijah represents the prophetic tradition: putting the teachings into action. As Moses and Elijah fade away, the sense is that somehow Jesus embodies all that they represent and even more: here in Jesus is an amazing vitality going way beyond their traditions.

Coming down the mountain, the implications begin to sink in. In his heart of hearts John hears Jesus saying, "The things I do you will do and even greater."[12] With this Energy, you can do anything!

The friends of Jesus have a basic choice, one that will occur over and over again:

They can admire and stand in awe of the power embodied in Jesus. They can see him as wonderful and can assume that this vitality is his alone.

Or they can begin to become aware of the same Mystery and learn how to tap into the same holy spirit-filled Energy residing within themselves! They have been offered initiation into Holy Mystery.

On the way down, Jesus advises the others not to say anything to anyone about what they have just experienced. Some experiences need to be contained for awhile before attempting to put them into words and tell others what has happened.[13]

NOTES

1. Two traditions are woven together to form this scene: the first is the story of the Transfiguration, told originally in Mark 9:2-8 and retold and expanded in Matthew 17:1-8 and Luke 9:28-36. The second is from the Sophia of Jesus Christ written in Egypt during the latter part of the first century. Scholars debate whether the Transfiguration story is an experience of the disciples with Jesus during his ministry before his death or is it actually a misplaced resurrection narrative? The Sophia of Jesus Christ is written as a resurrection narrative, but perhaps the awareness embodied in the story might have come to the disciples before his death? In this blending of the stories, I have

placed them in the earlier context of the work and ministry of Jesus and Mary.

2. The three questions and Philip's response are from The Sophia of Jesus Christ 92:1-4.

3. Philip's response is from The Sophia of Jesus Christ 92:5

4. Jesus' question is found in Gospel of Thomas 13. A similar question is repeated in the later Gospels of Mark 8:27-30, Matthew 16:13-20, and Luke 9:18-22. In all of the synoptic gospels, the question occurs shortly before the Transfiguration story.

5. All of the responses from the disciples are given in Gospel of Thomas 13

6. Luke 9:29

7. Luke 9:32

8. Mark 9:2-3

9. Mark 9:4-6

10. Mark 9:7 William Tyndale translation, 1526 C.E.

11. Mark 9:8

12. John 14:12

13. Mark 9:9

CHAPTER 45:
AFTER COMING DOWN FROM THE MOUNTAIN₁

COMING DOWN FROM A MOUNTAIN HIGH, JESUS, MARY and their closest friends, are met by the rest of the disciples who have a huge crowd surrounding them. Scholars are arguing with the disciples. Many are asking questions like, "What would Jesus say about this? What would Jesus do about that?"

When the crowd catches sight of Jesus they rush to meet him. Jesus asks his disciples, "Why are you bothering to argue with those scholars?"

Just then one person from the crowd cries out, "Teacher, I brought my son to you because he has a spirit that makes him unable to speak. Whenever it takes him over, it knocks him down. He foams at the mouth and grinds his teeth and stiffens up. I asked your disciples to drive it out, but they couldn't."

In response Jesus says, "You distrustful lot, how long must I associate with you? How long must I put up with you? Bring him over to me!"

And they bring the epileptic over to him. When the spirit notices him, right away it throws the boy into convulsions. The boy falls to the ground, keeps rolling around, and foaming at the mouth.

Jesus asks his father, "How long has he been like this?"

And the father replies, "Ever since he was a child. Frequently it has thrown him into the fire and water to destroy him. So if you can do anything, take pity on us and help us!"

Jesus says to him, "What do you mean, 'If you can'? All things are possible for the one who trusts."

Right away the father of the young man cries out and says, "I do trust! Help my lack of trust!"

When Jesus sees that the crowd is about to mob them, he rebukes the unclean spirit and commands it, "Deaf and mute spirit, I command you, get out of him and don't ever go back inside him!"

After he shrieks and goes into a series of convulsions, the spirit comes out. Now the young man takes on the appearance of a corpse, so the rumor starts going around that he has died. But Jesus takes hold of his hand, raises him up, and there he is standing! The young man heads for home and everyone is amazed at what has happened.

The disciples start questioning Jesus privately, "Why couldn't we drive it out?"

And Jesus replies, "The only thing that can drive this kind out is prayer."

As they head for home in Capernaum, the disciples are arguing with one another.

It is as though the seizures of the young man have spread to everyone else. What has happened to the ecstatic joy that they felt on the mountain?

When they arrive home, Jesus starts questioning them, "What were you arguing about on the road?" They fall completely silent, because on the road they had been bickering about who was the greatest.

Jesus sits down and calls the others to sit with him. Then he says, "If any of you wants to be 'number one', you have to be last of all and servant of all!"

And Mary observes, "With the highs come the lows. The joys are not for you alone, but to empower you to help people like this epileptic boy become free."

NOTES

1. The story follows Mark 9:14-35

CHAPTER 46:
A KISS AND A PLAN CONCEIVED₁

JESUS AND MARY MAGDALENE HAVE COME TOGETHER like two streams creating a single river flowing gently with tremendous Energy. Centered in the *Way of Mystery* together, their companionship and Union manifests even more fully in their shared work of Wisdom teaching and healing.

The Spirit of Mystery is working through them with calm intensity. They are catalysts for transformation. They are bringing good news to the poor. Those who have been living in prisons of their own making are being set free. The blind are seeing with fresh insight. The oppressed are feeling new freedom from the inside out. The fears of so many are fading and they are energized and empowered. For so many people this has been a few years of amnesty.[2]

Some people with a modicum of power like the toll and tax collectors find the courage to face their complicity in oppression and are leaving their occupations. Even an occasional rich person has heard the call to sell all, give to the poor, and become followers of the Way, not knowing what the future holds.

People of every sort and description are following Jesus and Mary from place to place. Some come initially out of curiosity. What is it that radiates so fully through these itinerant teachers? Some choose to become disciples and join their sacred circle.

As the crowds grow larger and the movement keeps spreading throughout most of Galilee, the authorities become increasingly uncomfortable. They see Jesus and Mary and their followers as a potential threat to the status quo. When the crowds get organized, what will they do? Will there be a rebellion?

Scribes and Herodians become uneasy. Local religious leaders become jealous when they see attendance at synagogues declining. Even the priests in Jerusalem are becoming alarmed. Some have come up to Galilee to see for themselves what is going on.

Opposition to Jesus and Mary is growing. It begins with name calling: "Son of the devil,"[3] "drunkard,"[4] and worse. Accusations regarding the sanity of Jesus are next along with attempts to involve his family in taking him away somewhere else.[5]

Heckling becomes more frequent along with attempts to stir up crowds against him. Next come actual attempts on his life. On one occasion there is an attempt to grab Jesus and throw him off a cliff,[6] but Jesus slips away unharmed. Later there is an attempt to stone him,[7] but that also fails.

Rising popularity and organized opposition are both escalating rapidly. Serious conflict is becoming inevitable and Passover, the most important festival of the year is approaching.

One evening about twilight, Jesus and Mary turn, look each other straight in the eye, and begin to speak at once. Jesus says, "I think that..." And Mary begins, "I am feeling that..." Neither completes their sentence but both understand. Their shared intuition springing from the same Spirit provides a deep sensing of knowing what they will do in this pivotal moment.

Together they slip away from the disciples and head up into the hills alone to meditate and pray. As they reach the top of their favorite hill, they sit facing each other on their comfortable rocks where they have prayed so many times before. Twilight fades and yields to darkness. The stars in the sky are twinkling. Soon they are bathed in the light of a full moon. In the moonlight they look deeply into each other's souls.

This is a time for recalling their spiritual journeys, their baptisms,

190 | *John Beverley Butcher*

their deep encounters with the angels, the wild beasts and the Serpent who is their Instructor. This is a time for recalling the first time they met, their attraction to each other, sharing their inner and outer journeys, and choosing to become Companions on the Way.

This is a time for reviewing how their teaching style has evolved, how their healing ministry has developed, and how their disciples increase in numbers and then some start wandering away. Who will be there for the long haul?

Both know that the resistance and opposition to them and their teaching is growing.

Both feel the mounting pressures. Some reactions are out in the open. Others are hidden. They sense that the authorities are increasing their covert activities. No one who is perceived as a threat to the Roman Empire and the Pax Romana will get away with it.

Questions are running through the minds of Jesus and Mary: What will they do next, especially as Passover approaches? Is this a time to cut back on public appearances? Should they go off somewhere and stay out of sight? Will their Instructor, the Serpent, be raising questions and presenting even more choices?

Most years they have gone up to Jerusalem for the festivals. Neither of them can recall a year when they missed Passover. Yet they know that the place for worship is not limited to the Temple in Jerusalem. "God is not tied to place!"[8]

They agree that this is a significant part of their message, especially right now as Passover approaches. Any and all suggestions from the Instructor to hide out for awhile are quickly and resoundingly dismissed.

There are just a few last questions: do they remain in Galilee and attempt to dissuade people from going up to Jerusalem for Passover this year? Or do they go to Jerusalem, expose what the authorities are actually doing, and point people again in a new direction?

They know that the only real kingdom worthy of their allegiance is the Kindom of Father and Mother, the *Way of Mystery*, that lives within them. Will they insist again, this time in the midst of the Temple scene, that what the people are looking for is already hidden inside them?

If they choose to dissuade people from going to Passover, they risk being called subversive. If they go to Jerusalem and proclaim the message that the people themselves are the Temple of the Spirit, they will be seen as even more subversive to the Powers that Be. Now they know what they must do.

Jesus and Mary have been in conversational prayer all night long. At daybreak they come down out of the hills. Their vigil has refreshed, enlightened, and empowered them for taking the next steps in their already risky journey.

They share a kiss and grace flows freely between them. They are united in mind and heart. They are resolute in what they must do next. Out of the kiss their plan has been conceived.[9]

The disciples at the bottom of the hill wake from sleep to see Jesus and Mary kissing as they have done so often before.[10] Feeling jealous and offended, they express their disapproval by asking Jesus, "Why do you love her more than us?" And Jesus replies with a question, "Why do I not love you like her?"[11] Silence reigns. The disciples get the point. Out of the Silence Jesus and Mary announce their intention to go up to Jerusalem for Passover.

NOTES

1. Drawing from Gospel sources, this chapter reports the escalating tensions between Jesus and the religious and imperial Powers that Be.

2. Luke 4:18-19

3. Luke 11:15-20

4. Matthew 11:18-19

5. Mark 3:20-35

6. Luke 4:28-30

7. John 8:59

'8. John 4:23

9. Gospel of of Philip 31, *Nag Hammadi Scriptures* 58, 33-59-6

10. Gospel of Philip 55, *Nag Hammadi Scriptures* 63,30

11. Gospel of Philip 55, *Nag Hammadi Scriptures* 64,1-5

CHAPTER 47:
MARY ANOINTS
AND EMPOWERS JESUS[1]

Over the years Jesus, Mary, their friends, and disciples have been traveling from Galilee down to Jerusalem for Passover and other festivals. But this year things are different. Everyone is very aware that the pressures against Jesus have been building. Peter senses the danger and feels it is much too risky to go into the City. When he tries to get Jesus to change his mind, Jesus becomes angry and says, "Get out of my sight, you Satan, you. You are dangerous to me because you are not thinking in God's terms, but in human terms."[2]

Jesus knows intuitively that the time has come. He is determined to go to the City and his face is "set like flint."[3]

Mary knows that once Jesus has made up his mind and feels empowered by the Spirit, any attempt to convince him otherwise is usually a waste of time. So, despite Peter's warnings, off they go to Jerusalem. They are on the road again, heading straight for the City and ready to face whatever confrontations and dangers await them.

They and the others accompanying them will need a place to stay. Rather than attempting to find lodging in the City itself, they make arrangements to stay with Martha and Lazarus, in Bethany, a small village a little less than two miles east of Jerusalem. This is the home where they have stayed on previous visits for festivals in the City.[4]

When Jesus, Mary, and the others arrive at the house, Martha greets them warmly and says, "Shalom and welcome to my house. Supper is almost ready and I hope you will stay with us through Passover! Your brother, James, is here; he decided to join us tonight also," says Martha. "Yes, come on in, we have been expecting you and please know that you will be safe here," says her brother, Lazarus.

The dinner is a festive "Welcome home" banquet for Jesus and Mary. For many days Martha has been preparing with great care and makes sure to include everyone's favorite dishes.

Mary knows that the coming days may be stressful and difficult, perhaps leading to a confrontation with the authorities. She wants Jesus to be prepared for whatever lies ahead so she has brought with her a pound of expensive perfume made of pure nard, the very best she can find.

When all are relaxing around the table, Mary comes closer to Jesus and begins anointing him lovingly and with great care from his feet on up to his head.[5] Jesus whispers to her, "How sweet is your love, my sister, my bride."[6]

The fragrance of the perfume fills the entire house. In an irritated tone of voice, Judas the Sicarii, says, "Why wasn't this perfume sold? It would bring a year's wages, and the proceeds could have been given to the poor."[7]

"Let her alone; why do you trouble her? She has done a beautiful thing to me," says Jesus.[8]

Mary continues what she is doing in a way that is very sensual, arousing, joyous, and empowering. The loving compassion and warm feeling embodied through touch brings Jesus so much joy.

After the anointing, Jesus and Mary Magdalene embrace each other. Their unspoken feeling is that together in the Spirit they are united and empowered for whatever they must face in the next few days. A fresh and energizing Spirit moves through everyone in the house. There is a sense of calm, as in the eye of an impending storm.

NOTES

1. For the Anointing, see Margaret Starbird, *Mary Magdalene, Bride in Exile*, chapter 3.

2. Mark 8:33, Matthew 16:23, Gospel of Luke 9:51

3. Isaiah 50:7

4. *Interpreter's Dictionary of the Bible*, Abingdon, 1962, volume A-D, pps. 387-388

5. This anointing is grounded in the Gospel of John 12:1-8 and Mark 14:3

6. From the Song of Songs 4:10

7. John 12:4

8. Mark 14:6

CHAPTER 48:
ENTERING THE
CITY OF JERUSALEM₁

THE NEXT MORNING AS THEY WALK TOWARD JERUSALEM from the east, they realize that Pontius Pilate, the Roman Governor is simultaneously arriving in the City from the west at the head of a column of imperial cavalry and soldiers. The standard practice of Roman governors of Judea is to be in Jerusalem for the major festivals, not out of respect for the religious devotion of their Jewish subjects, but for a show of power and readiness in the event of any signs of trouble.[2]

The imperial procession is arriving: cavalry on horses, foot soldiers, leather armor, helmets, weapons, banners, golden eagles mounted on poles, sun glistening on metal and gold. Hear the sounds: the marching of feet, the crackling of leather, the clicking of bridles, the beating of drums, the swirling of dust.[3]

Normally there are about 40,000 people living in Jerusalem, but for a major festival like Passover, 200,000 pilgrims or more would come to the city.[4] Most of the people, residents and pilgrims alike, resent the Romans and if possible stay indoors, out of the way when the Romans are parading through. A few young men hurl stones from rooftops and hide. Most people simply stay clear of Pilate and his Roman entourage. The only welcoming party is put on by the wealthy, the underlings, and the priests of the Temple who are collaborating with the Roman authorities. They know that their own positions of power rest on being on the good side of the Emperor's representatives.

As the Romans are entering the city from the west, someone suggests that Jesus and Mary, their disciples, and friends should also ride into town in style from the east. "Out of the question," says Mary. But then someone brings a donkey and her colt[5] for the couple to ride on.

"Thank you, but we can walk along with everyone else," says Jesus. "I am just a teacher. What are you trying to do: make me out to be a messiah or a king?"

And Mary says, gently, "Rabboni, my little rabbi, if you ride you can see people better and they can see you—perhaps we could do some teaching along the way. Besides, my feet hurt from our long walk down here from Galilee. Today I could use a short ride into the City."

Jesus accedes to her reasoning. People throw cloaks over the donkey and her colt[6] to provide softer rides. Jesus and Mary mount their donkeys and head into town across the Kidron Valley. A geologic fault line runs beneath their feet. Earthshaking events are soon to occur.

Word gets around that Jesus is entering Jerusalem. Many people come out of their houses and spread their cloaks on the road, while others cut down leafy branches from the fields. Those leading the way and those following keep shouting,

"Hosanna! Blessed is the one who comes in the name of the Lord!

"Blessed is the coming kingdom of our father David!"

"Hosanna in the highest!"[7]

As Pilate and his soldiers are approaching the center of Jerusalem, they are informed that another procession headed by a couple of people on donkeys and a motley crowd of people are coming toward them from the east. From the perspective of the Romans the scene is ludicrous, but what if this is some sort of planned political demonstration?[8] Crowds are gathering and tensions are increasing.

As the two processions meet in the center, a centurion near Pilate asks, "Shall we break it up?" "Not yet," replies Pilate, "Wait awhile."

Meanwhile, Jesus and Mary dismount, blend into the crowd, gradually work their way through the people, and enter the Temple. Jesus walks right in, looks around, and sizes up the situation.[9] With soft eyes, he takes in everything.

The religious leadership of the temple is making sure that the observances are done "by the book." They are careful not to be critical of the ruling authorities. Their tactic is to ignore the real plight of the people while keeping themselves focused on the ritual observances. This strategy keeps them from getting into difficulty with the Roman authorities while maintaining their own position, power, and livelihood for themselves and their families. Jesus sees all this and more. We can well imagine what he is feeling, but at this point he does not say or do anything. He simply observes and takes it all in.

The hour is late and they are tired so Jesus, Mary, and the disciples return home to Bethany[10] On the way to Martha's house Jesus pauses for a moment on a hill, looks back at the City, and says, "Jerusalem, Jerusalem, you murder the prophets and those sent to you! How often I wanted to gather your children as a hen gathers her own chicks under her wings, but you wouldn't let me. Can't you see your house is being abandoned?"[11]

He turns toward Mary, their eyes meet. No words are spoken, but he knows she understands. He says to her, "As a lily among thorns, are you, my beloved among women."[12]

During the night Jesus is restless, tossing and turning. Mary says, "You remind me of Jacob wrestling with an angel: who or what are you wrestling with tonight?"

"I have seen what is going on in the Temple. I am feeling the Spirit churning inside me and I know I cannot be silent. Tomorrow I must speak out and take the risks, no matter what the cost!"

NOTES

1. Scholars of the Jesus Seminar have come to the considered opinion that the triumphal entry of Jesus riding a donkey into Jerusalem is a fiction inspired in part by Psalm 118:25-26 and Zechariah 9:9. For a discussion, see *The Acts of Jesus*, page 120.

2. Marcus J. Borg & John Dominic Crossan, *The Last Week,* HarperSan Francisco, 2006, p. 2.

3. *Ibid.,* p. 3

4. *Ibid.,* p. 18

5. Matthew 21:1-6. In Mark's gospel, only one donkey is mentioned; Matthew, in quoting Zechariah 9:9 mentions a donkey and a colt in an effort to make Jesus as the triumphant new king for Jerusalem. Jesus actually makes no claims for being a king or messiah. He just accepts a ride into town. I follow Matthew's version so Mary will have a mount as well.

6. Mark 11:7

7. Mark 11:8-11

8. Marcus J. Borg & John Dominic Crossan, *The Last Week,* HarperSan Francisco, 2006, p. 4, who are quoting George Caird, professor of New Testament at Oxford and author of many books.

9. Mark 11:11

10. John 11:18

11. Luke 13:34-35

12. Song of Songs 2:2

CHAPTER 49:
JESUS TEACHING
IN THE TEMPLE[1]

AFTER A SLEEPLESS NIGHT, JESUS FEELS FRESH RESOLVE. He knows he must get up and go back into the Temple in Jerusalem. He heads out bright and early without any breakfast. Mary barely has time to catch up with him and calls out, "Wait for me!" Several disciples trail behind.

On his way into the City, Jesus sees a fig tree with leaves but no fruit for the simple reason that it is not the season for figs. Jesus would enjoy a fig or two right now, but there are none to be had. In his frustration Jesus curses the tree, "Damn you! May no one ever taste your fruit again!"[2]

Mary has seen him get this way before. She is asking herself, "Why is Jesus taking his frustration out on this little tree?" For the moment Mary decides to remain silent and let it be.

As they are approaching the Temple itself, a man with badly mangled hands comes toward them and says, "I was a stonemason making a living with my hands. I plead with you, Jesus, give me back my health so that I won't have to beg for my food in shame."[3]

Mary asks how his hands had been so badly injured and learns that the stonemason had been working on repairs on the Temple when a large stone landed on his hands and he since then he has not been able to work. She asks, "Where were the Temple officials after this happened? Did they care at all?"

It becomes clear that once injured, he had been discarded to fend for himself. Mary says to him, "Come with us, we care for one another. We all get healthier." The stonemason accepts the invitation and joins the growing band of disciples. The reputation of Jesus has been spreading far and wide. As more and more people come into Jerusalem for Passover, many recognize him with Mary and their companions. A crowd gathers. Some call out and say, "What do you have to tell us, Teacher?"

Jesus moves on into the Temple and finds a place to sit and teach. The crowd quiets down to hear what he has to say. He decides to begin with whatever is on their minds and invites their questions:

Questions come fast and furiously, "Do you want us to fast?" "How should we pray?"

"Should we give to charity?" "What diet should we observe?"[4]

Jesus replies, "Don't lie, and don't do what you hate, because all things are disclosed before heaven. After all, there is nothing that won't be revealed, and there is nothing covered up that will remain undisclosed."[5]

Someone shouts out, "Jesus, you didn't answer the question!"

So Jesus tries again, "If you fast, you will bring sin upon yourselves... After all, what goes into your mouth won't defile you; what comes out of your mouth will."[6] "If you do not fast from the present world order, you will not find the Kindom of Father and Mother, the *Way of Mystery.*[7] So I say again don't lie, and don't do what you hate."

Then, turning toward the Pharisees and scholars in the crowd, Jesus says, "And in regard to paying alms, Damn you Pharisees! You pay tithes on mint and dill and cumin too, but you ignore justice, mercy, and trust."[8]

"Damn you Pharisees! You are like a dog sleeping in the cattle manger: the dog neither eats nor lets the cattle eat."[9]

Before the Pharisees can respond, another question comes from the crowd,

"Is circumcision useful or not?" And Jesus fires back his answer, "If circumcision were useful, their father would produce children already circumcised from their mother. Rather, the true circumcision in spirit has become profitable in every respect."[10]

Jesus is just getting warmed up. Empowered by the Spirit, he continues to call the Pharisees to account: "Damn you, Pharisees! You're so fond of the prominent seats in synagogues and respectful greetings in marketplaces."[11]

"You scholars and Pharisees, you impostors! Damn you! You erect monuments to the prophets and decorate the graves of the righteous and claim, 'If we had lived in the days of our ancestors, we wouldn't have joined them in spilling the prophets' blood.'

So you witness against yourselves: You are the descendants of those who murdered the prophets, and you're the spitting image of your ancestors."[12]

And one more thing, "Damn you legal experts too! You load people down with crushing burdens, but you yourselves don't lift a finger to help carry them."[13]

Right across from where Jesus is teaching he notices the treasury where people are dropping money into a collection box. Many wealthy people are dropping in large amounts. Then one poor widow comes along and puts in two small coins, which is a pittance.

Jesus motions to his disciples and says to them, "I swear to you, this poor widow has contributed more than all those who dropped something into the collection box! After all, they were donating out of their surplus, whereas she, out of her poverty, is contributing all that she has, her entire livelihood."[14]

Mary says to Jesus, "I can feel the intensity of your anger at the way the Temple takes everything from those who can least afford it. I agree with you. But try to be here now and let's just invite this woman to travel with us."

Turning toward the widow, Mary says, "Come with us." The woman's face brightens as she is greeted warmly by the other women as well. Jesus calms down, allows his compassionate energy to flow again, and joins the women in being present to the widow.

They all head back to Martha's house in Bethany for the night, this time with more mouths to feed, including a disabled stonemason and a penniless widow. Martha is ready with yet another meal for everyone. Even though she sees the number of dinner guests has grown, she holds her irritation in check and extends a warm welcome to the stonemason, the widow, and their friends. She knows that they, too, are becoming disciples.

NOTES

1. Teachings in this chapter are rooted mainly in the Gospel of Thomas.

2. See the cameo essay: Jesus Curses a Fig Tree?

3. Gospel of Nazoreans 4 from the *Complete Gospels*, p. 444

4. Gospel of Thomas 6:1

5. Gospel of Thomas 6:2-6

6. Gospel of Thomas 14:1, 5

7. Gospel of Thomas 27

8. Luke 11:42

9. Gospel of Thomas 102

10. Gospel of Thomas 53

11. Luke 11:43

12. Matthew 23:29-32

13. Luke 11:46

14. Mark 12:41-44

CAMEO ESSAY 5:
JESUS CURSES A FIG TREE?

AS THEY WERE LEAVING BETHANY, JESUS GOT HUNGRY. SO when he spotted a fig tree in the distance with some leaves on it, he went up to it expecting to find something on it. But when he got right up to it, he found nothing on it except some leaves. (You see, it wasn't the 'time' for figs.) And he reacted by saying" "May no one so much as taste your fruit again!"[1]

Jesus then goes into the Temple where he turns tables over and clears out the vendors.

Next Mark tells us that "As they were walking early one morning, they saw the fig tree withered from the roots up. And Peter remembered and said to him: "Rabbi, look, the fig tree you cursed has withered up."[2]

The story of Jesus cursing the fig tree originates in Mark. Matthew[3] copies Mark but in his version Jesus curses the fig tree and it withers instantly.

Luke eliminates the story of Jesus cursing the fig tree and replaces it with Jesus telling a parable as follows:

"A man had a fig tree growing in his vineyard; he came looking for fruit on it but didn't find any. So he said to the vine keeper, 'See

204 | *John Beverley Butcher*

here, for three years in a row I have come looking for fruit on this tree, and haven't found any. Cut it down. Why should it suck the nutrients out of the soil?' In response he says to him, 'Let it stand, sir, one more year, until I get a chance to dig around it and work in some manure. Maybe it will produce next year; but if it doesn't, we can go ahead and cut it down.'"[4]

Clearly, the cursing of the fig tree troubled Luke. It also troubles many people, including the Jesus Seminar scholars who say,

"Causing an unproductive fig tree to wither seems uncharacteristic of the historic Jesus. A senseless miracle of retribution, triggered by a petty, even petulant, response, is scarcely a mode of behavior that comports with the Jesus who restored a withered limb, declared a leper clean, ate openly with undesirables, and embraces the poor, hungry, and grieving. What then did the author of the gospel have in mind in recording this story?

In the judgment of many scholars, the story of the tree without figs is an allegory intended to interpret Jesus' pronouncements on and response to the temple cult: since the temple cult no longer "bears fruit," it is to wither and die..."[5]

The allegorical interpretation makes sense to me. And I also see Jesus as being very human, one who can get irritated and angry at injustice to the point of doing something very impulsive and irrational like cursing a tree! Scientific studies have been done with plants showing that plants hearing pleasant music grow well, but plants exposed to harsh metallic acid rock music do poorly. So I have chosen to tell the story from the point of view that Jesus may very well have gotten so angry that he cursed a tree and the energy and velocity of his outrage actually caused the poor little tree to wither and die a bit later.

Thus Mark's version that provides some intervening time makes more sense to me than Matthew's version where the tree withers up instantly.

So now you have a range of opinion from which to choose.

NOTES
1. Gospel of Mark 11:12-14
2. Gospel of Mark 11:20-21
3. Gospel of Matthew 21:18-22
4. Gospel of Luke 13:6-9
5. *Acts of Jesus*, p. 122-123

CHAPTER 50:
AN ATTEMPTED STONING[1]

EACH DAY JESUS AND MARY GO INTO THE TEMPLE AREA for teaching, and then spend the night on the Mount of Olives or in Bethany with Martha and Lazarus. People in Jerusalem would get up early in the morning and go to the Temple to listen to their teaching.[2]

This particular morning the scholars and Pharisees bring him a woman who was caught committing adultery, and they address him, "Teacher, this woman was caught in the act of adultery. The Law of Moses commands us to stone women like this. What do you say?" They are saying this to trap him, so they would have something to accuse him of.

Mary is thinking to herself, "And where is the man? It takes two to commit adultery, doesn't it?" But she keeps silent for the moment.

Jesus remains silent, stoops down and begins drawing on the ground with his finger.

When the scholars and Pharisees keep insisting on an answer, Jesus stands up and says,

"Whoever is sinless in this crowd should go ahead and throw the first stone at her." Once again he squats down and continues writing on the ground.

His audience begins to drift away, one by one—the elders are the first to go—until Jesus and Mary are the only ones left with the woman there in front of them.

Jesus stands up and says to her, "Woman, where is everybody? Hasn't anyone condemned you?"

She replies, "No one, sir." And Jesus says, "I don't condemn you either. You are free to go..."[3]

And Mary adds, "But where will you go? You probably aren't welcome with your husband or your family, or your relatives are you?"

"I have nowhere to go," she replies. Mary and Jesus say in the same breath, "Come with us."

NOTES

1. In many Bibles, the story of the attempted stoning of a woman taken in adultery is found as John 7:53-8:11. "This fascinating little anecdote is an intrusion into the Gospel of John. The earliest manuscripts of John do not have it, and modern scholars are virtually unanimous in concluding that it was not an original part of the Fourth Gospel. It does not match the style of John and it breaks the flow of text from 7:52-8:12. in ancient manuscripts, moreover, its position is not fixed: It sometimes appears in John between 7:52 and 8:12, but it is also found at other locations in John—after 7:36, after 7:44, and at the end of the gospel; it even appears in one group of manuscripts after Luke 21:38. It does not have a fixed canonical home." *Acts of Jesus*, Robert W. Funk and the Jesus Seminar, HarperSan Francisco, 1998, p. 397. I have chosen to place the story as it would be if it were after Luke 21:38, thus making it part of the final conflicts between Jesus and the established religious order.

2. Luke 21:37

3. John 7:53-8:11 or in *The Complete Gospels* on page 453 as an Orphan Saying.

4. Gospel of Thomas 47

CHAPTER 51:
JESUS OVERTURNS THE TABLES OF THE SYSTEM₁

JESUS HAS A PLAN AND IS READY TO PUT IT INTO ACTION: he will upset the system of exploitation and oppression. Jesus begins by chasing the vendors and shoppers out of the temple area. He turns the bankers' tables upside down, along with the chairs of the pigeon merchants. He does not allow anyone carrying a container to pass through the temple area.[2]

Making a whip out of rope, Jesus drives out of the Temple all the money changers, the vendors, along with the sheep and oxen brought to sell for sacrifices.[3]

Having cleared some space, Jesus begins teaching the crowd that is gathering: "Don't the scriptures say, 'My house is to be regarded as a house of prayer for all people'?—but you have turned it into 'a hideout for crooks.'

"You can be free of this corrupt system: Please know that you are the Temple of the Holy. The Kindom of the Father and Mother, the *Way of Mystery*, lives within you. Let your inner Temple be cleansed!"

Jesus then asks, "Is there nowhere in this place that is Holy?" Immediately he knows where he must go. Motioning to the others, he heads right into the Holy Place where the most sacred vessels are to be found.

A Pharisee, a leading priest named Levi, also enters the Holy Place, runs into them, and says to Jesus, "Who gave you permission to wander around in this inner sanctuary and lay eyes on these sacred vessels, when you have not performed your ritual bath, and your disciples have not even washed their feet? Yet in a defiled state you have invaded this sacred place, which is ritually clean. No one walks about in here, or dares lay eyes on these sacred vessels, unless they have bathed themselves and changed clothes."

And Jesus, standing in his true humanity with his disciples replies, "Since you are in the temple, I take it you are clean."

Levi the Pharisee replies, "I am clean. I bathed in the pool of David, you know, by descending into it by one set of steps and coming up out of it by another. I also changed to white and ritually clean clothes. Only then did I come here and lay eyes on these sacred vessels."

In response Jesus says, "Damn the blind who won't see. You bathe in these stagnant waters. You wash and scrub the outer layers of skin... inside you are crawling with scorpions and filled with all sorts of corruption. But my disciples and I—you say we are unbathed—have bathed in lively, life-giving water![4]

"You scholars and Pharisees, you impostors! Damn you! You are like whitewashed tombs: on the outside they look beautiful, but inside they are full of dead bones and every kind of decay. So you too look like decent people on the outside, but on the inside you are doing nothing but posturing and subverting the Law."[5]

His anger has built to the point that Mary feels Jesus might do something that later he might regret. Mary calms him, and say, "Let's go." And Jesus replies, "Fine, but one of these days I am coming back and I will go even further: I will enter the Holy of Holies whether anyone else likes it or not!"

On the way out of the Temple, Jesus calls out to the crowd, "Wisdom says, 'I will send them prophets and apostles, and some of them they are always going to kill and persecute.[6] So I tell you my friends, don't be afraid of those who can kill the body and after that can do no more.[7] The Truth will set you free![8] And when they make you appear in synagogues and haul you up before rulers and authorities, don't worry about how or in what way you should defend yourself or what you should say. The Holy Spirit will teach you in that very moment what you ought to say."9

By his actions, Jesus is pulling out the root of the whole place, while others before him did it only partially.10

Opposition to Jesus is building, especially with his tirade today. When the ranking priests and the scholars hear this they keep looking for a way to get rid of him. They huddle together making plans to have him arrested by trickery and then kill him. They look for the opportune time to execute their plot, saying, "Not during the festival, otherwise people will riot."11

As it is growing dark, Jesus, Mary, and the others make their way out of the City,12 pausing for a few moments on the Mount of Olives.

Turning toward Mary he says, "The Kindom of the Father and Mother, the *Way of Mystery*, is spread out upon the earth and people do not see it..."13 And the words echo in her heart and on her lips, "They do not see it... they do not see it... they do not see it."

And with this mantra of sadness, they resume their walk hand in hand back to Martha's house in Bethany.

NOTES

1. This chapter depicts the last major and rather volatile confrontational between Jesus and the Temple authorities before he is arrested.

2. Mark 11:15-17

3. John 2:15

4. This entire story of the confrontation in the Holy Place is verbatim from the Gospel Oxyrhynchus 840, 2:1-9, found in *The Complete Gospels*, p. 420-421.

5. Matthew 23:27-28

6. Luke 11:49

7. Luke 12:4

8. John 8:32

9. Luke 12:11-12

10. Gospel of Philip 123

11. Mark 14:1-:2

12. Mark 11:11

13. Gospel of Thomas 113

CAMEO ESSAY 6:
THE LAST SUPPER

ARTIST RENDERINGS OF THE SCENE THAT HAS COME TO be known as The Last Supper often show just the male friends of Jesus present. Would Jesus have excluded his Beloved Companion, Mary, and the other women from this meal, especially if he had any intuition that it might be his last?

The tradition of Jesus having a last supper with his disciples in which he takes bread and wine and says, "This is my Body... This is my Blood" is first described by Paul in his letter to the people in Corinth[1] written about 55 C.E., approximately fifteen years before Mark, the first of the synoptic Gospels. "The supper as Paul describes it probably originated in the communities of Asia Minor and Greece where Paul had established churches and not in Jerusalem where Jesus died."[2]

After Jesus died, when his friends gathered, broke bread and shared wine together they discovered his presence with them. Perhaps it is more likely that the practice continued because of their experience and not because Jesus, before his death, commanded that it be done.

This interpretation in no way takes away from the power and

vitality of the sacrament, but seeks to understand its origins in the post crucifixion experiences of the friends of Jesus. It is rather like when a beloved family member or friend dies and is no longer at the dinner table. The place where the Beloved sat is empty. The loss is felt. And then there is the surprise of discovering the presence of the Beloved. People start saying to each other, "We must do this more often!" The friends of Jesus continue meeting in his name, breaking bread, and sharing the cup. In so doing they discover his immediate presence with them. The continuation of the Eucharist comes from people experiencing its energizing vitality.

If the Eucharist had been done only in response to a command, would it have lasted this long?

NOTES
1. I Corinthians 11:23-26

2. *Acts of Jesus*, p. 139

CHAPTER 52:
SUPPER IN THE CITY

JESUS IS OUTRAGED BY THE EXPLOITATION OF PEOPLE BY the religious authorities, but he has transformed his anger into action. Empowered by the full anointing of the Spirit from Mary's hands, Jesus moves deliberately and compassionately into the City of Jerusalem one more time.

As Jesus, Mary, and the others are walking toward the City early in the morning they see the fig tree Jesus had cursed and notice that it has withered from the roots up. Peter remembers what happened a few days before and says to Jesus, "Rabbi, look, the fig tree you cursed has withered up!"[1]

In response Jesus says to Peter, "I swear to you, if you have trust and do not doubt, not only can you do this to a fig tree but you can even say to this mountain, 'Up with you and into the sea!' and that's what will happen; and everything you ask for in prayer you'll get if you trust."[2]

As they are approaching the City, one of the disciples asks Jesus and Mary, "Where do you want us to go and get things ready for you to celebrate Passover?"

Jesus replies by sending two of his disciples on ahead of the others, "Go into the City, and a man carrying a water jar will meet you. Follow him, and whatever place he enters say to the head of the house, 'The teacher asks, "Where is my guest room where I can celebrate Passover with my disciples?"' And he'll show you a large upstairs room that has been arranged. That's the place you're to get ready for us."[3]

One of them answers, "You want us to find a man carrying a water jar? Aren't women the ones who carry the water jars?"

"That's right," says Mary. "That's why you'll have no trouble finding this man; he doesn't mind doing what others think of as women's work."

The two run ahead into the City, find it exactly as Jesus and Mary had told them, and begin getting things ready for Passover.

Jesus, Mary and the rest of the disciples come into Jerusalem and go toward the Temple. As Jesus walks around in the temple area, the ranking priests and scholars and elders come up to him and start questioning him: "By what right are you doing these things?" or, "Who gave you authority to do these things?"

Jesus says to them, "I have one question for you. If you answer me, then I will tell you by what authority I do these things. Tell me, was the baptism of John heaven-sent or was it of human origin? Answer me that."

And they confer among themselves, saying, "If we say 'heaven-sent,' he'll say, 'Then why didn't you trust him?' But if we say 'Of human origin...!'" They are afraid of the crowd since everyone considers John a genuine prophet. So they answer Jesus by saying, "We can't tell."

And Jesus says to them, "I'm not going to tell you by what authority I do these things either!"[4]

Because of the anointing Jesus received from Mary, he is more focused on each immediate situation as he meets and responds to people. Jesus moves with calm intensity even though there is a heaviness of uncertainty lurking in the air.

As evening approaches they go to the room that the two disciples found after following the man with the water jar. It is on the second story of a house and is reached by an outside stairway.

During the meal, Jesus does something that startles everyone.[5] He

216 | *John Beverley Butcher*

stands up and takes off his clothes. Wearing nothing but his loin cloth, Jesus looks like one of the house slaves whose chores include washing the feet of guests.

Jesus wraps a towel around his waist, puts water into a basin, and begins washing the disciples' feet and wiping them dry with a towel.

When he comes to Simon Peter, he says, "Master, are you going to wash my feet?" And Jesus replies, "Right now you do not understand what I'm doing, but later you will."

Peter blurts out, "You will never, ever wash my feet!"

And Jesus answers, "Unless I wash you, you won't have anything in common with me."

"In that case, Master," Peter says, "Wash not only my feet but my hands and my head too." Apparently at the feeling level Peter is beginning to understand.

It is only natural for Jesus to want to give loving attention to his friends in tangible ways such as washing their feet. Having received freely, Jesus is able to give freely.[6] He takes time and care with each person, with Thomas and Philip, with Peter, James, and John, with Joanna, Susanna, and of course with Mary his soulmate, along with all the others who are gathered on that intense evening of energizing and empowering love.

Jesus has received so much love and thus is able to give love to others, no matter what the cost may be. After washing the feet of everyone present, with the exception of Judas who had to leave early, Jesus makes his message very clear: "Just as I have washed your feet; now you go and wash each other's feet. I have given you an example: do to others as I have done to you."

Some of the earlier teachings of Jesus flash into the minds of his friends as he washes their feet, sayings like this one, "Who is the greater, after all: the one reclining at a table or the one who is doing the serving? Isn't it the one who reclines? Among you I am the one doing the serving." "Love one another as I have loved you."

During the meal itself there is an anxious undercurrent, but no one knows exactly what it is. The tone is somber as though great evil and danger were lurking about.

Even so, they are able to conclude their meal by singing a Psalm,

"From the rising of the sun until its going down,
let the Name of the Lord be praised..."[7]

After supper they all go for a walk together and end up in a grove of olive trees where an olive press used to be.

Notes

1. Mark 11:20

2. Matthew 21:21

3. Mark 14:12-15

4. The confrontation with the ranking priests and scholars and elders is from Mark 11:27-33, Scholars version in *The Complete Gospels.*

5. The footwashing story which follows is found in John 13:1-20.

6. Matthew 10:8,

7. Psalm 113:3, anticipating the Hallel, Psalms 113-118 which would normally be sung during a Passover meal.

CHAPTER 53:
JESUS AND MARY
IN THE OLIVE GROVE[1]

A MEDITATION ON THE SCENE
IN CONTEMPORARY LANGUAGE

After supper, Jesus, Mary, and their friends leave the upper room, go down the stairs, and into the narrow streets. They walk to the edge of town and across the Kidron Valley to a low hill where there is a grove of olive trees and an olive press. Even though the Mount of Olives it is only a short distance from the noisy City, it is quieter here. There is a spot here known as Gethsemane where Jesus and Mary have prayed many times before.

The Gospel account is short and I wanted a fuller sense of how it was for them that night so I prayed and this is the dialogue I jotted down:

John: Jesus, what was happening to you that night in Gethsemane?

Jesus: Everything was coming down on me at once: I could feel it. The animosity from the Pharisees is so heavy in the air you can cut it with a knife.

And I felt the Energy and power of the Spirit coming through

Mary, especially at supper. She poured out her unconditional love so freely. During the footwashing our friends seemed to be getting the message in a way they could touch and feel.

Peter warned me about coming into Jerusalem for this Passover and tried to stop me. I felt angry with him, but I knew I had to be here. I'm ambivalent about the festival itself: yet it is good to be celebrating liberation as long as we don't think we have the right to go and take land away from other people. The freedom from slavery, the breaking of bonds both within and without, all that makes enormous sense to me. But the religious authorities are so protective of their own position that they work against liberation for the people. They are helping to keep the people down. Don't they see that they are denying everything that Passover is really proclaiming?

Fighting the Romans is out of the question. Bloodshed is not the answer. An eye for an eye will make everyone blind. There is another way: nonviolence. By being strong inside, being there for one another in the struggle, calling the priests to account like I tried to do the other day by dumping over their money tables in the Temple.

And in all this craziness, what does my Father want from me? What does Mother expect me to do?

There is still time to get out of town and go back to Capernaum or Bethany, or anywhere else in Galilee. The Romans are focused on Jerusalem right now. They won't bother us in the country villages— at least not this week. It sure is tempting to run right now: slip out and go under cover of night.

But there is another part of me that says, "Just stay here. Be here now.'" So I am praying, What do you want from me?

This cup: somebody gave one to Socrates and expected him to drink it. And this one is worse. His cup held hemlock: one swallow and it is all over.

But this cup has endless pain: I see what the soldiers do to other people after they arrest them, beating them to a bloody pulp, making them drag a cross through the streets in front of everyone and then nailing them up!

So they kill me: what good does that do? I've got so much more work to do! Don't take my life now! Don't take me away from Mary or Thomas or Philip or Susanna or Joanna, or Peter and James and

John or any of my friends! Don't take me away from that Arab woman who taught me to include everyone or that centurion who cares so much for his slave, so many people who do get the message, who are living in the Kindom of Heaven now. I've got so much more to teach and to learn!

The whole thing is so crazy—why doesn't the Lord intervene? I've been telling people that the hairs of their heads are numbered, that not even a sparrow falls to the ground without the Father knowing, and all that. I teach what I know and right now I do not know much, so if you care, WHERE ARE YOU NOW?

I'm feeling crushed like olives in the press; this pressure is killing me: and I am feeling the fresh anointing of the oil of the Spirit!

So what do You want from me?

(Silence)

I see Mary over there—she is praying and so are some of the other women; I've gone about as far as I can with my prayer. I could go over to Peter and James and John, but they are asleep, they can't handle it, they can't take it, so they drop unconscious.

Go ahead, sleep on—it doesn't matter now.

All right, so it is just You and me!

So what do You want from me?

(Silence)

I pray, I pour out my heart. I try to get through to You and there is no God damn answer! We are not getting anywhere: I cry out and I don't hear anything coming back except my own echo! I am sweating it out, not just sweat but blood as well. To hell with this!

I feel like Job, "Though You slay me, yet will I trust You!

But I will defend my ways to Your Face."[2]

So what do You want from me?

(Silence)

Now I understand—You are in this craziness with me. Your Silence speaks louder than words..."

MARY IN GETHSEMANE

Meanwhile, Mary is praying in the same olive grove, just a short distance from where Jesus is having his encounter with Mystery. I ask her a question and jot down her response:

John: And what is going on for you, Mary?

Mary: I'm beside myself—I am so scared about what may happen any minute now. They could come and get him: I feel the heaviness in my heart. Jesus is a good man. I do not want to lose him. We have a good teaching ministry going together. I do not want to lose him.

He is stubborn: he's staying with his convictions. I respect that and in a strange way I agree with him, but the stakes are so high. I know what the Roman soldiers are doing to other people. I could not bear to see what they might do to him.

Why the torture, the unremitting pain, the cruel death that takes so long? One thing I know: these bastards can kill Jesus, but they'll never kill the message he is teaching. This is trial by fire—and fire will ignite in other people: I can see it now!

It is all so stupid, so futile, so crazy.

DON'T TOUCH MY JESUS!

I want to run to him but he needs his own time of prayer now and I'll let that be.

I would rather be praying with him—we can do this better together.

We can go back to my place or anywhere else in Galilee. Or we can face these Romans head on. Or do whatever we have to do, but it will be TOGETHER!

What do You want from us?

(Silence)

Why don't You speak up?

I'm not going to be like Job's wife: I'm not going to tell Jesus to curse God and die.[3]

We will praise You no matter what happens, but what do YOU have to say?

I am listening... I am quiet... Speak for Your servant hears..."

(Silence)

NOTES

1. The Gethsemane story is told in the Gospel of Mark 14:26-42 with parallels in Matthew, Luke, and John. In this telling, I am attempting to relate the scene from the perspective of Jesus and Mary. The dialogue originated as I prayed the scene with them. At core, it resembles my own prayer when the United States started bombing the people of Iraq in March 2003. I cried out, "Where are YOU?" There was no verbal answer, but I did have the deep feeling that the Mystery, the Source of Life was right in the midst of this horror with us.

2. Job 13:15, King James Version

3. Job 2:9, King James Version

CHAPTER 54:

ARREST, TRIALS, AND DEATH OF JESUS[1]

A FEW OF THE CLOSEST FRIENDS AND DISCIPLES OF JESUS and Mary are with them in the olive grove, with one notable exception: Judas. He left the supper early and disappeared into the night. Now he is back with a detachment of Roman soldiers and a crowd of people.

Judas comes up to Jesus and kisses him. Immediately the soldiers step forward and arrest Jesus. Most of the friends scatter into the night.

Things happen very quickly. The men friends of Jesus go into hiding. Mary and the other women are excluded from the proceedings. Jesus is brought alone before Caiaphas, the High Priest, who hands him over to Pilate, the Empire's Governor of Judea. The primary charge against Jesus is this one: "We found this man perverting our nation, and forbidding us to give tribute to Caesar... He stirs up the people, teaching throughout all Judea from Galilee even to this City of Jerusalem."[2]

After the secret trials, Jesus is flogged and turned over to be crucified. The soldiers keep pushing Jesus along saying, "Let's drag the son of God along, since we have him in our power." And they throw a purple robe around him and sit him upon a mock judgment seat and say, "Judge justly, king of Israel." One of the soldiers brings a crown of thorns and sets it on his head. Some standing around spit in his eyes. Others slap him in the face, and others poke him with a rod. Some keep flogging him as they say, "Let's pay proper respect to the son of God."[3]

And the Roman soldiers bring him to the place Golgotha, which means "Place of the skull," and the soldiers crucify him. Observing his crucifixion from a distance are Mary and his mother, plus many other women.[4]

They are close enough to hear what may be his very last words, "My power, my power, you have abandoned me."[5]

There is no answer and the Silence is deafening.

Jesus breathes his last and is gone.

NOTES

1. This scene is rooted in *The Gospel of Jesus According to the Jesus Seminar* 21, Mark 14:43-52, John 18:1-12, and Gospel of Peter 3.

2. Luke 23:2, 5

3. Gospel of Peter 3

4. *The Gospel of Jesus According to the Jesus Seminar*, chapter 21

5. Gospel of Peter 5:5

CAMEO ESSAY 7:
LIFE AFTER DEATH OR RESURRECTION NOW?

CHILDREN OFTEN GROW UP THINKING THAT IF YOU ARE good, then you will be rewarded and if your are bad you will be punished. But listen to them on a playground and sooner or later you will hear a child cry out, "That's Not Fair!" A bully is being mean to other children and gets away with it. A beloved pet dies and there is nothing anyone can do about it.

As adults we see diligent workers suddenly laid off. The rich get richer and the poor get poorer. And across the planet huge numbers of people are starving while the resources of their land are exploited and exported to other countries. Adults echo the feelings of children when we ask, "Why do bad things happen to good people?"

Sooner or later we all come face to face with the inconvenient truth that Life is not fair. We become keenly aware of all the undeserved suffering and yearn to find meaning. Why do these things happen? Will the day come when everything will be made right?

A classic example of an inquiring mind wrestling with the problem of evil can be seen in the Book of Job. Another is in the Book of 2 Esdras,[1] probably written by a Jew about the year 100 C.E., several decades after the total destruction of the Temple and City of

Jerusalem by the Romans in 70 C.E. The writer is wrestling with an essential problem that boils down to this: he cries out to the Lord saying, "You are our God and we are your people. We have obeyed you and we believe you will save us: that is our agreement, our covenant. Why then, has the Temple and all of Jerusalem been destroyed? Why are our people suffering?" During the course of the telling of the story, the writer of 2 Esdras imagines an afterlife where all will be made right. He attempts to resolve the problem of evil by creating a life after death.

Many religions have teachings about heaven and hell. In the days of a three story universe, heaven was above and hell was below. By teaching that there will be a system of rewards and punishments in the next life, religious leaders have often attempted to control the behavior of people in this life. Things are tough now, but everything will be fine in the sweet bye and bye.

But then along comes a perceptive person like John Lennon inviting us in his song "Imagine" to envision a world with no heaven or hell. For many, the notions of an afterlife complete with heaven, hell, and perhaps purgatory no longer make any sense. These ideas have vanished like a puff of smoke.

Yet the problem of evil persists.

Some embrace the notion of Reincarnation: you keep coming back until you get it right! There are so many attempts to create a theory that resolves the problem of evil by making everything come out right in the end.

In the crucifixion of Jesus we see the prime example of a good person suffering and dying with his final words, "My power, my power, why have you abandoned me?"

Then comes the resurrection of Jesus with the crucial question: which body rose?

Was it the same tortured, beaten, and crucified body that had hung on a rough wooden cross? Or is it the body of his friends who experience his Spirit living within them?

Perhaps the problem of evil will continue to persist. With it comes the responsibility of the living to put their energies into working for justice and reconciliation with one another, and discovering how to live in harmony with our Mother the Earth and all sentient beings, human, animal, plants, even microorganisms and plankton. The issues are systemic and require the transformation of social and political structures based on the recognition that there is One Planet and One Humanity so why can't we learn how to live and love creatively together?

Life is not fair. We cry out to "God" or the Universe "What are you going to do about it?" And back comes the echo, "What are you going to do about it?"

NOTES

1. 2 Esdras is not found in many Bibles, but is included in the *New Revised Standard Version with Apocrypha*. See *The Access Bible*, Apocrypha p. 286ff, Oxford University Press, 1999.

CHAPTER 55:
MARY'S VISION OF JESUS IN A GARDEN,

IN THEIR OVERWHELMING GRIEF, MARY AND THE OTHER women know they must prepare the body of Jesus for a proper burial. But Rome has a strict policy that the soldiers are required to enforce: leave all crucified bodies on their crosses for the people to see that this is what will happen to them if they do not cooperate with Roman rule. Let them watch the vultures come and feast on the bodies of anyone who challenges the Empire.[2] Fear and terror are the ruling policy.

Having executed Jesus, the Roman authorities continue their operation by searching for his friends and followers. No one close to Jesus wants to wait around in Jerusalem to be arrested and crucified. Clearly there is nothing left to do but to leave the City quickly and return to Galilee: go back to their familiar home towns of Capernaum, Bethsaida, and Nazareth.

The return trip takes even longer because of the heaviness of their grief. They try not to be noticed by anyone. Deeply troubling questions consume their minds and tear at their hearts: What in the world will they do now? How can they reconstruct their shattered lives?

On the way back home, Mary says to herself, "I must first take some time alone visiting the places where Jesus and I were together. I will walk the paths we walked, go to the beaches where we relaxed, shared our thoughts and feelings from our hearts. I will go up into the hills and find again the pair of comfortable rocks where we felt the warmth of the sun and then the wetness of the rain, when we knew clearly that the sun shines and the rain falls on the just and the unjust alike."

And it is there, on this hillside that Mary has her first intense vision: "I am in a beautiful garden, luxuriant as the garden of Eden. It feels as sensual as the one in the Song of Songs.[3] Everything is vibrantly alive. I must explore this garden fully and move toward the Center to the Tree of Life and taste its fruits. I must be as close to the Center as I can now. But over there in this beautiful place is a cave, the kind often used for burials. Strange, but this lovely garden now feels like the burial place of my beloved, Jesus.

"I see a large stone rolled off to one side of the cave: it must have been used to close the entrance and keep wild animals from further desecrating the body. The cave is open and it is inviting me to come inside. I am looking all around and his body is missing! There is nothing but his burial shroud left behind! It reminds me of a chrysalis that remains after the butterfly has emerged. Where is his body? What have they done with him?

"I look inside the cave and see two angels sitting where the body would have been before: one at the head and the other at the feet. I hear them asking me, 'Woman, why are you weeping?' Somehow I find the words to reply, 'Because they have taken away my Jesus and I do not know where they have laid him.'

"I hear a sound and as I turn around with my back to the cave of death, I see someone standing there who speaks to me and asks, 'Woman, why are you crying? Who are you looking for?'

"I imagine he must be the gardener, so I say to him, 'Please, mister, if you've moved him, tell me where you've put him so I can take him away.'

"The gardener speaks my name, 'Mary,' and I recognize the voice; it is the same one I have heard speaking my name for so many years in so many places. The same resonance, the same strong, loving, gentleness. The Voice coming up from within the depths of my own soul is the Voice of my Beloved, Jesus. And I reply, 'Rabboni, my little rabbi!'⁴

"And I hear him saying, 'Don't try to hold onto me because I am returning to the Father. I need you to go and tell my mother, my brothers and sisters, our friends and disciples, that I am returning to the One who gives life and takes it back again, to the One in whom we live and move and have our being.'

"Then, in even further amazement, I watch as Jesus moves away from me to the top of the hill where a chariot of fire sweeps down and whisks him away like a whirlwind. And as he ascends into the furthest reaches of outer space, something falls from the chariot and lands softly right at my feet: it is his mantle, the cloak I have seen him wear so many times before.

"In my mind and heart I know what this vision means: just as Elijah ascended into the heavens and his mantle dropped to Elisha,⁵ so the mission, work, and Energy of Jesus have passed to me. So I cry out saying, 'Give me a double portion of your Spirit!' And from the deepest places within me I know that my desire for fullness of Energizing Spirit is already fulfilled. My heart says, 'I know what I must do. I will continue our ministry of teaching and healing that Jesus and I shared before he died.'

"Now I have a double spirit: my own and the Spirit of Jesus. We will continue to live and work together, for Jesus is so vibrantly alive within me. On the one hand our sacred partnership has ended; on the other hand it is revitalized, more vibrant than ever! I have seen him. I have heard his Voice. He lives completely within me now; we are One."

The vision is over and the lasting effects remain. Mary pauses for a few moments to allow the vision to sink in more fully and then runs down the hill to share the good news with family friends, students, everyone in the world: "I have seen him: Jesus lives!"

Returning home that evening Mary discovers, much to her surprise, that Jesus had left his cloak behind when he made his last trip up to Jerusalem. It is hers now. She will take over where Jesus left off; she knows she will continue their shared work of teaching, healing, and gathering students together to form communities in every town where the Spirit directs her to go.

NOTES

1. "Many scholars have concluded that the earliest resurrection appearances were located in Galilee." Robert W. Funk and the Jesus Seminar, *The Acts of Jesus*, p. 453. The Gospel of Peter "may contain, in an embedded source document, the primary material for the passion and resurrection stories in the canonical gospels." *The Complete Gospels*, p. 5. In all the Gospels, Mary Magdalene is the first person to experience the resurrected Jesus, the Reality that even after his death he lives vibrantly within her. This story is drawn from the gospels, especially Gospel of John 20.

2. Martin Hengel, *Crucifixion in the Ancient World and the Folly of the Message of the Cross* as quoted by John Dominic Crossan in *Jesus, A Revolutionary*, HarperSan Francisco, 1994, p.124.

3. The Song of Songs, also known as the Song of Solomon, is in the Hebrew Scriptures.

4. "Rabboni" is "my little rabbi", a pet name of endearment. See Jane Schaberg in her book, *The Resurrection of Mary Magdalene*, Continuum, 2004, p. 328

5. The story of Elijah passing his energy to Elisha is found in 2 Kings 2:1-18. The connection of Mary's experience with the Elijah-Elisha story is made convincingly clear by Jane Schaberg in her book, *The Resurrection of Mary Magdalene*, Continuum, 2004.

CHAPTER 56:

PETER'S VISION ON
THE SEA OF GALILEE,

FOR SAFETY'S SAKE, PETER AND HIS BROTHER, ANDREW, go into hiding along with Thomas, Philip, Nathanael, and James and John, the Sons of Thunder. Before long they make plans to slip out of the City at night hoping to be unnoticed under the cover of darkness. They realize that Mary Magdalene and the other women have already left during the day and are way ahead of them.

After a hard day's journey, the weary travelers are relaxing around their campfire when Peter says, "I warned Jesus not to go up to Jerusalem,² but there was no stopping him. Now look at what has happened. Why wouldn't he listen to me? Now Jesus is dead! I can't stand it—so cruel and so sad!"

They continue sharing their pain and grief over what has just happened along with recollections of their travels with Jesus. As they talk around the fire, they disturb the ashes with their sticks, hoping new meanings will be uncovered. As the stars brighten with the increasing darkness in the sky and in their souls, Jesus does not fade into the shadows of their minds despite the fact that he has died.³

After several nights and days, Peter and the others finally reach Capernaum. They go home to greet the family, and then down to the lake to retrieve Peter's old boat, still abandoned close to where he left it. After making repairs on the boat and mending their nets, Peter sets out with Thomas, Nathanael, the Thunder boys and several others.

Mary Magdalene, who has been wondering when they would show up, sees that they have returned. She decides to join them in the boat: there are seven in all.

They fish all night and catch nothing. Then as the morning light dawns Peter has an amazing vision: he sees someone on the shore calling out, "Friends, you haven't caught any fish have you?" "No," they reply. Then he tells them, "Cast your net on the right side of the boat and you'll have better luck."

In his vision Peter sees them following the stranger's instructions and now they can't haul the net in for the huge number of fish. Mary, the disciple Jesus loved most,[4] exclaims to Peter, "It's the Teacher!" When Simon Peter hears her say, "It's the Teacher," he ties his cloak around himself, since he was stripped for work, and throws himself into the water. The rest of them come in the boat, dragging the net full of fish. They are not far from land, only about a hundred yards offshore.

In the vision, Peter sees them returning to shore where a charcoal fire is going with fish cooking and bread warming. He hears Jesus saying to them, "Bring some of the fish you've just caught."

Simon Peter sees himself going aboard and hauling the net full of large fish ashore—one hundred fifty-three of them. Even though there are so many fish, the net does not tear.

He hears Jesus saying to them, "Come and eat." None of the disciples dares to ask, "Who are you?" They know it is the Teacher. Jesus comes, takes the bread and gives it to them, and passes fish around as well.

In his vision, Peter sees everyone sharing the bread and fish together. All are astonished and trying to understand what has just happened.

Peter asks, "What do you think my vision means?" One replies, "Jesus is alive!" And another agrees, saying, "Yes, he is alive and telling us to try fishing off the right side of the boat."

The fishermen and Mary share a meal together and Peter says,

"Jesus is here with us." And Mary adds, "He is in us now. We are all his body now. This is what I was trying to tell you when I spoke of my vision in the Garden."

"But I have one question," says Nathanael. "In the vision why are there exactly one hundred and fifty-three fish in the net? Peter replies, "If you did more fishing, Nathanael, and spent more time with fishermen, you would know that there are one hundred fifty-three kinds of fish."[5]

Thomas adds, "And that means we are supposed to resume fishing for people as when Jesus first called us! All kinds of fish means all kinds of people. No one is excluded!"

And Mary adds, "The number also means reclaiming the Feminine from the deep. That is our task."[6]

Everyone falls silent as together they continue sorting out the meaning of the vision and deciding what they must do next.

NOTES

1. "Many scholars have concluded that the earliest resurrection appearances were located in Galilee." Robert W. Funk and the Jesus Seminar, *The Acts of Jesus*, p. 453. The story in this chapter is rooted in John 21:1-14.

2. Mark 8:31-33

3. Thanks to Norman McMullen, a visionary from Northumberland, for imagining this campfire scene.

4. See the Cameo Essay 8: Who is the "Beloved Disciple"?

5. In the first century there was a common belief that there were 153 species of fish. Today we know that there are, in fact, many more species than 153—but the symbolism speaks says clearly that all kinds of people are to be included, none excluded.

6. In her research, Margaret Starbird has found that in gematria the Magdalene's sacred number is 153, "the sum of h Magdalhnh, was associated with the womb, the matrix, the cauldron of creativity, and the 'vessel of fish.'" So the 153 fish may also mean reclaiming the Feminine embodied in Mary Magdalene. See

Margaret Starbird's book *Bride in Exile*, p. 66 and her book, *Magdalene's Lost legacy, Symbolic Numbers and the Sacred Union in Christianity*.

CAMEO ESSAY 8:
WHO IS THE
"BELOVED DISCIPLE"?

"THE DISCIPLE WHOM JESUS LOVED" IS A PHRASE THAT occurs several times in the Gospel of John.[1] Scholars have long struggled with the question: who is the "Beloved Disciple"?

Raymond E. Brown explores the question rather thoroughly:

"First, it has been proposed that the Beloved Disciple is not a real figure but a symbol...

Second, Lazarus is the one male figure in the Gospel of who it is specifically said that Jesus loved him...

Third, John Mark is another possible candidate for the role of Beloved Disciple.

Fourth, John son of Zebedee seems to meet many of the basic requirements for identification of the Beloved Disciple. He was not only one of the Twelve, but, along with Peter and James one of the three disciples constantly selected by Jesus to be with him...

There are, then quite clearly, difficulties to be faced if one identifies the Beloved Disciple as John son of Zebedee. However, in our personal opinion, there are even more serious difficulties if he is to be identified as John Mark, as Lazarus, or as some unknown. When all is said and done, the combination of external and internal evidence associating the Fourth Gospel with John son of Zebedee makes this the strongest hypothesis, if one is prepared to give credence to the Gospel's claim of an eyewitness source."[2]

Ray Brown devotes his attention only to male disciples and his careful scholarship is still inconclusive. But when we notice that the same phrase occurs in the Gospel of Mary we realize that perhaps the "Beloved Disciple" is Mary Magdalene. Perhaps the original pronouns have been changed from "she" to "he" in order to hide her identity?

Hans Martin Schenke has combed the Nag Hammadi texts for other figures who resemble the Beloved Disciple, and he proposes that Mary Magdalene, James the Just, and Judas Thomas also function as beloved disciples in one way or another in gnostic texts.[3]

Marvin Meyer proposes that the prototype or "historical model" of the Beloved Disciple may best be understood to be the paradigmatic youth in Secret Mark and Lazarus in John.[4] The story is clear that Jesus loved this young man[5] and that the young man loved him back.[6]

We have many texts that support Mary Magdalene being the Beloved Disciple. For example, the Gospel of Mary tells us that Jesus "loved her more than any other woman"[7] and that he "knew her completely and loved her devotedly."[8] Can it be said any more clearly that she is a Beloved Disciple? Scholars like Jane Schaberg are building a strong case for Mary being the Beloved Disciple.[9]

Some scholars offer the possibility that Mary Magdalene may be the author of the Gospel of John.[10] Sandra M. Schneiders presents an argument that is more open-ended and explores a variety of possibilities.[11] Some say that Mary Magdalene is both the Beloved Disciple and the author of the Gospel of John.[12]

Whether or not Mary Magdalene is the author of this Gospel, it appears that many of the experiences described in John actually originated with her visions of the Resurrected Jesus who has come alive in her and in many of the friends and disciples of Jesus. In other words, Mary had the Visions and someone else transcribed them and included them in the Gospel of John.

Who, then is the Beloved Disciple really? The question assumes that there is one and only one such person. Is it John Mark, John the

Evangelist, Thomas, James the brother of Jesus, Lazarus, the Young Man in the Gospel of Mark, Mary Magdalene, or someone else?

Examine all the evidence, the sacred texts, and careful scholarship, and come to your own conclusion. When you do, you may wish to include one more possibility: perhaps Jesus has more than one Beloved Disciple?

NOTES

1. John: 13:23, 19:26, 20:02, 21:07, 21:20.

2. *The Gospel According to John,* (Volumes 29 and 29A in the Anchor Bible series) Doubleday & Company 1966, see the Introduction, p. XCII-XCVIII.

3. Marvin Meyer, *Secret Gospels,* Trinity Press International, 2003, p. 144

4. Marvin Meyer, *Secret Gospels,* Trinity Press International, 2003, p. 146

5. Mark 10:21

6. Secret Gospel of Mark 1:8

7. Gospel of Mary 6:1

8. Gospel of Mary 10:10

9. See Jane Schaberg, *The Resurrection of Mary Magdalene,* Continuum, 2002, especially her chapter seven, "Mary Magdalene as Successor to Jesus."

10. See Ramon K. Jusino, M.A. www.BelovedDisciple.org.

11. Dr. Schneiders' article, "Because of the Woman's testimony: Reexamining the Issue of the Authorship in the Fourth Gospel" was published in *New Testament Studies* #44, October, 1998, pages 513-535.

12. For a brief discussion of Mary being the Beloved Disciple and possibly the author of the Gospel of John, see Dan Burstein and Arne J. De Keijzer, *Secrets of Mary Magdalene,* CDS Books, 2006, p. 164-165.

CHAPTER 57:
MARY BECOMES THE LEADING TEACHER[1]

ON YET ANOTHER OCCASION IN GALILEE, A GROUP OF friends of Jesus is gathered together in a home. Most notable among them are Mary Magdalene, Peter, Andrew, and Levi. They are sharing food and recalling everything that has been happening since the death of Jesus.[2] Suddenly and unexpectedly the group has a shared experience in which they are hearing the Voice of Jesus saying to them, "Peace be with you!" This familiar greeting of "Shalom" resonates deeply as they hear Jesus add, "Acquire my peace within yourselves![3]

"Be on your guard so that no one deceives you by saying 'Look over here!' or 'Look over there!' For the Seed of True Humanity exists within you. Follow it! Those who search for it will find it.[4]

"Go then, preach the good news of the Kindom. Do not lay down any rule beyond what I ordained for you, nor promulgate law like the lawgiver, or else it will dominate you."

After he said these things, he left them.[5]

The disciples are grieved and weep greatly, saying, "How are we going to go out to the rest of the world to preach the good news about the Kindom of Father and Mother, the Way of Mystery, and the Seed of True Humanity?"[6]

Then comes their real concern and fear: "If they did not spare him, how will they spare us?"[7]

Mary stands up, greets them all, tenderly kisses each one, and says, "Brothers and sisters, do not weep and be distressed nor let your hearts be irresolute. For his grace will be with you and will shelter you. Rather we should praise his greatness, for he has joined us together and made us true human beings."[8]

Jesus is alive in Mary. His clear Voice resonates through her. Mary's touch and her message are beginning to transform fearful individuals into one spirit-filled Body, a New Humanity.

As Mary says these things, she turns their minds toward the Good and they begin to ask about the words of the Teacher.[9] Peter says to Mary, "Sister, we know that the Teacher loved you more than any other woman. Tell us the words of the Teacher that you know, but which we haven't heard."

Mary responds, "I will report to you as much as I remember that you don't know. And she begins speaking these words to them.[10] "I saw the Teacher in a vision and I said to him, 'Lord I see you now in this vision.' He said to me, 'How wonderful you are because you are not wavering when you see me. For where the mind is, there is the treasure.'

I said to him, 'Lord, how does a person who sees a vision see it—with the soul or with the spirit?'

The Teacher answered, 'The visionary does not see with the soul or with the spirit, but with the mind which exists between the two."[11]

Mary relates the wisdom teachings she has been receiving from the Resurrected Jesus. She relates the inner journey of her soul. After many struggles with conflicting inner powers, she is able to say, "What binds me has been slain, and what surrounds me has been destroyed, and my desire has been brought to an end, and my ignorance has died. In a world, I was set loose from a world and in a type, from a type which is above, and from the chain of forgetfulness that exists in time. From now on, for the rest of the course of the due measure of the time of the age, I will rest in silence."

After pouring out her heart freely to others, Mary falls silent.

Andrew is the next to speak. "Brothers, what is your opinion of what has been said? I for one do not believe that the Teacher said these things, for these teachings are strange ideas. What she said appears to give views that are different from his thought."[12]

After reflecting on these matters, Peter says, "Has the Teacher spoken secretly to a woman and not openly so that we would all hear? Surely he did not wish to indicate that she is more worthy than we are?"[13]

Mary weeps and says to Peter, "Peter, my brother, what are you imagining about this? Do you think that I've made all this up secretly by myself or that I am telling lies about the Teacher?"[14]

Levi jumps into the conversation and says, "Peter, you have a constant inclination to anger and you are always ready to give way to it. And even now you are doing exactly that by questioning the woman as if you're her adversary. If the Teacher considered her to be worthy, who are you to disregard her? For he knew her completely and loved her devotedly."[15]

"Instead, we should be ashamed and, once we clothe ourselves with perfect humanity, we should do what we were commanded. We should announce the good news as the Teacher ordered, and not be laying down any rules or making laws."[16]

Levi, who seems most sensitive to understanding Mary and what she is revealing, shifts the message into mission.

After saying these things, Levi leaves and begins announcing the good news.[17]

NOTES

1. This chapter is rooted in the Gospel of Mary.

2. Gospel of Mary 4-10

3. Gospel of Mary 4:1-2

4. Gospel of Mary 4:3-7

5. Gospel of Mary 4:8-11

6. Gospel of Mary 5:1-2

7. Gospel of Mary 5:3

8. Gospel of Mary 5:4-8 Mary tenderly kissing each one is found in

an earlier Greek fragment known as Papyrus Oxyrhynchus 3525. The later Coptic text omits the kisses!

9. Gospel of Mary 5:9-10

10. Gospel of Mary 6:1-4

11. Gospel of Mary 7:1-6

12. Gospel of Mary 10:1-2 The phrase "for what she said appears to give views that are different from his thought" is in a Greek fragment known as Papyrus Rhylands 463.

13. Gospel of Mary 10:3-4

14. Gospel of Mary 10:5-6

15. Gospel of Mary 10:7-10

16. Gospel of Mary 10:11-13

17. Gospel of Mary 10:14

CHAPTER 58:
DISCIPLES
BECOMING ONE BODY[1]

AMONG THE DISCIPLES RETURNING TO GALILEE AFTER the crucifixion of Jesus are Cleopas and his unnamed companion. They have a vivid experience to share with Mary and the others. They know it is dangerous to remain in Jerusalem, so they are heading back home, planning to make their first stop in Emmaus, a village about seven miles west of the city.

Cleopas says, "We were engaged in conversation about all that had taken place. And it so happened, that during the course of our discussion, another traveler approached us and began to walk along with us. He asked, 'What are you talking about so intently?'

We paused for a moment. We were feeling depressed and also wondering why this stranger was asking this question. So I replied, 'Are you the only visitor to Jerusalem who doesn't know what's happened there these last few days?'

And he said to us, 'What are you talking about?'

And we replied, 'About Jesus of Nazareth, who was a prophet powerful in word and deed in the eyes of God and all the people, and about how our ranking priests and rulers turned him in to be sentenced to death, and crucified him. We were hoping that he would be the one who was going to ransom Israel. And as if this weren't enough, it's been three days now since this all happened. Meanwhile, some women from our group gave us quite a shock. They say they were at the tomb early this morning and didn't find his body. They came back claiming to have seen a vision of heavenly messengers, who said that he was alive."

Then this stranger had the sheer gall to say to us, 'You people are so slow witted, so reluctant to trust everything the prophets have said! Wasn't the Anointed One destined to undergo these things and enter into his glory?'

Then, starting with Moses and all the prophets, he interpreted for us every passage of scripture that referred to Jesus.

It had been a long conversation and we were getting close to Emmaus where we were going. He acted as if he were going on further. But we strongly urged him to stay with us. We told him, 'Look, it's almost evening. The day is practically over.' So he came into the house and stayed with us.

We were hungry and ready to eat. As soon as he took his place at table with us, he took a loaf of bread, gave a blessing, broke it, and started passing it out to us and others around the table.

Our eyes of perception were opened and we recognized that Jesus was really with us. The stranger vanished, leaving us trying to understand what had just happened. My companion said, 'Weren't our hearts burning within us while he was talking to us on the road, and explaining the scriptures to us?' We were so amazed that when we were breaking and sharing the bread we became aware of Jesus."

Hearing their story, Mary and the others embraced and kissed them and said, "Yes, we understand! The same things have been happening here with us! Whenever we gather together and discuss the scriptures and especially when we recall the teachings of Jesus, break bread and share a meal together, we discover he is here with us.

And looking around the room, Mary Magdalene says to Cleopas and his companion, "There is something of Jesus in every one of us. We all listened to his teachings before he was arrested and crucified. Many here experienced healing. Practically everyone would say that in one way or another their eyes have been opened and their ears have actually heard his Voice. Everyone here has stories to tell. All of us have felt the pain of his cruel death by the Romans. We thought everything was lost. Now we keep discovering that Jesus is alive with us, especially when we meet together and talk to each other. Most amazingly, it is when we share our meals with bread, water, milk and honey, and wine. Jesus is here looking at us and we hear him saying, 'This is my Body!' We are his Body now! Cleopas, you and your companion are part of the same Resurrected Body of Jesus with us! It is so amazing, so wondrous!"

Everyone joins in spontaneous prayer and song and dancing!

The transformation of a roomful of mourners into ecstatic celebrants experiencing their simultaneous coming together as One Body elicits in Mary a vision with tremendous power and energy.

Mary looks and sees as her vision: the people are all celebrants of a wedding where Jesus is the groom and she is the bride. In her heart she hears Jesus saying to her, "How fine you are my love, your eyes like doves..." and feels her heart responding, "How fine you are my Lover, what joy we have together...."[2]

Jesus is saying to her again, "When you drink from my mouth you will become like me; I myself shall become you and the hidden things will be revealed to you."[3] They are kissing long and deeply, the way they have so many times before. She knows in the very depths of her soul that even in death she is eternally united with Jesus.

All the guests are celebrating with them and the wedding feast is underway. The people in the room and the vision are blended into one. Mary is feeling that all the people have become more than guests: they, too, are married to him. The vision seems strange on the one hand, yet very real on the other. Her doubts fade and she embraces Jesus even more fully. She hears him saying to her, "Come with me, my love, come away."[4] Yet this is a vision she must keep to herself for awhile.

NOTES

1. This chapter is rooted in the Emmaus story found in Gospel of Luke 24:13-32

2. Song of Songs, Marcia Falk translation

3. Gospel of Thomas 108

4. Song of Songs, Marcia Falk translation

CHAPTER 59:
MARY'S VISION OF
A WEDDING IN CANA₁

FEELING DEEPLY HER UNION WITH THE RESURRECTED
Jesus and energized by her most recent vision, Mary knows she must
continue sharing the Good News of the Seed of True Humanity and
continue her journey through the villages of Galilee. She prays and
asks, "Where are You leading me next?"

Just then, Nathanael, who has been with Mary since their visit to
Capernaum, invites her to travel west with him to his home town of
Cana.² Word has already spread ahead of them that Nathanael is
coming home and when they arrive in Cana, they are met and greeted by family, friends, and disciples of Jesus.

Many had been in Jerusalem just before Passover and knew the
horror of Jesus being arrested, tortured, and crucified. They had fled
the City with so many others, fearing for their own lives at the hands
of the Roman authorities. They had also heard rumors that Jesus had
risen from the dead which was wondrous on the one hand and pre-
posterous on the other. They hope that Nathanael whom they trusted and Mary Magdalene who had been the Companion of Jesus
would provide some reliable information.

Mary and Nathanael had planned to gather people in his home, but clearly that space would be much too small. It is the evening of the Sabbath when they arrive and no one can wait any longer to hear what they have to say. The obvious place to gather on the Sabbath is in the synagogue.

Nathanael is known and respected, so he has an easy entree to speak that evening. Nathanael is welcome to speak, but not Mary. Some of the elders do not want a woman to speak in synagogue. "Either she speaks or I am silent as well," says Nathanael. Mounting pressure from the crowd along with their own curiosity causes the elders to yield and allow both Nathanael and Mary to speak.

They relate some of the amazing things that have been happening since the death of Jesus. Nathanael opens by saying that several women had told them that they had received the clear message to return to Galilee and there they would see Jesus. Mary then begins sharing her own vision of being with the Resurrected Jesus who had come to her in the garden. Nathanael retells the story of Peter, Andrew, and the others returning to their boats on the lake. Then he tells the story of Cleopas and his companion on the road to Emmaus and how they had joined with others a few nights ago and Jesus was known to them in the breaking of the bread.

She proclaims the central message "The Seed of True Humanity is within you." She tells again some of the teachings of Jesus about seeds and invites them to allow that seed of new Life to open up, take root, grow to maturity, and produce flowers and fruit of Spirit-filled living within them.

Mary Magdalene is still feeling the intensity of her own most recent vision of her union with Jesus. He is so real to her that she feels she can reach out and touch him. Mary decides not to reveal everything in her vision but she chooses to reveal parts of it now, hoping that the hearers will have ears to hear and eyes to see.

"I was given a vision. And in my vision there was a wedding right here in Cana of Galilee. Jesus and I, Mother Mary, his brothers and sisters, and a number of our friends and disciples were here.

The wine had run out, so Jesus' mother says to the servants, 'Whatever he tells you, do it.' Six stone water-jars were standing there, and each could hold twenty or thirty gallons. 'Fill the jars with water," Jesus tells them. So they fill the jars to the brim. Then he tells them, 'Now dip some out and take it to the caterer.' And they do so. When the caterer tastes the water, now changed into wine, he calls the groom aside and says to him, 'Everyone serves the best wine and only later, when people are drunk, the cheaper wine. But you have held back the good wine until now.'"

Mary then asks the people assembled, "Do you understand this vision?"

"Great party!" says one man. "A good magic trick," says another. A third calls out, "I know how to turn wine into water!" Laughter runs throughout the synagogue.

Mary enjoys the joke and then says, "Now that the vision has your attention, what do you think it really means? Start with the jars of water, what do they remind you of?"

Some reply, "They are like the large containers used for purification rites."

"They hold all our traditions and customs."

"Are you saying that these traditions and customs are being transformed by Jesus?"

Mary remains silent and allows the meaning to sink in. After a long pause, she asks, "And whose wedding might this be?"

And someone replies, "Well, you said it happened right here in Cana, so this could be a wedding for any of us!"

"Yes," replies, Mary. "Now hear what Jesus has said to me and is also saying to each of you, "Whoever drinks from my mouth will become like me; I myself shall become that person, and the hidden things will be revealed to him."³

Many are scoffing because the Vision makes no sense to them. But Mary can see from the expressions on their faces that there are others who have understood and are ready to experience their own union with Jesus. Through him they become One with the Mystery and with All that is.

The message is too strange for many and they begin leaving. But others remain. Mary and Nathanael stay with them, praying with them, inviting them to open their hearts and release the Spirit already within them.

In their midst is Jesus who is saying, "There are many standing at the door, but only those who are alone, the single or solitary, will enter the bridal chamber."[4]

Nathanael and Mary remain all night with several who are ready to enter more deeply into the Mystery.

The next day Nathanael and Mary are reflecting on what happened the night before.

Nathanael says, "Sometimes I feel we are casting pearls before swine as Jesus used to say."[5] "Yes, so do I," replies Mary. "Yet he never stops offering the pearls!"

"I know," says Nathanael. "It is the same old problem of 'ears to hear' and 'eyes to see'. We might as well get used to it!"

NOTES

1. This chapter is rooted in the story of the wedding at Cana in the John 2:1-11

2. John 21:2

3. Gospel of Thomas 108

4. Gospel of Thomas 75

5. Matthew 7:6

CHAPTER 60:
MARY'S VISION OF THE BREAD OF LIFE₁

RETURNING TO MAGDALA, MARY GOES DIRECTLY TO THE home of her parents and greets them warmly. They are glad to see her and relieved to know that she is safe after everything that has happened recently in Jerusalem. Her father says, "You have been traveling with Jesus for several years and we rarely saw you. Now that Jesus has died, we thought we might see you more often, but here you are still traveling. Is this never going to end?"

Then her mother adds, "Besides, when you do come home, you bring so many other people with you. What do you think we have here, some sort of inn? Who do you have with you this time?"

Mary feels their irritation with her. Simultaneously the words of Jesus flash through her mind again, "Foxes have holes, the birds of the air have nests, but the truly human being has nowhere to lay his head and rest."² But she keeps the thought to herself. Nathanael speaks gently and says, "Thank you for your warm hospitality, be assured we won't be staying long. As Jesus says, 'Be passersby.'"³

"So who do you have with you this time, Mary?" asks her younger brother. Mary replies, "Peter, Andrew, James, and John have continued on to Capernaum so all I have with me at the moment is

Nathanael, Philip, Thomas, Joanna, and Susanna." "All right,' says her mother," I suppose we can make do."

Feeling the need to pitch in and help as much as she can, Mary begins immediately to prepare and make bread for everyone. While she is waiting for the bread to finish baking she has the warm sensation that Jesus is right there with her: she looks and has a vision much like the others: Jesus is so real! Mary feels she can reach out and touch him. It is the Voice of Jesus echoing in her soul that comes through so clearly:

"Don't work for food that goes to waste, but for food that lasts— food for real life...

I am the bread of life. Your ancestors ate the manna in the desert, but they still died.

This is the bread that comes down from heaven: anyone who eats it never dies.

I am the life-giving bread. Anyone who eats this bread will live forever..."[4]

She repeats to herself over and over again, "I am the Bread of Life." The more she repeats this mantra, the more she realizes that the Great I AM is manifesting nourishment in Jesus. This is the same I AM who spoke from the Burning Bush to Moses, the I AM present everywhere and in everything who lives not only in Jesus but also in her, and in all who take and eat this wondrous Holy Bread.

Mary prepares this evening's bread with even greater care than usual because she knows that when all gather round the table and eat this bread together they may very well experience the Presence of Jesus who manifests the great I AM, the Mystery whose true Name cannot be uttered, but whose presence can be deeply felt and known.

Later in the evening as they share the meal and eat the bread, the Reality of Jesus comes through gently and forcefully again. And this time Mary's parents share in the experience. Words fail to express what they are feeling, but this time both her father and her mother say in one voice, "This is so amazing: please stay as long as you can..."

That night during her sleep Mary has a dream: she sees Jesus crossing over to the far side of Galilee. A huge crowd is following him because they want to see him performing miracles for the sick.

She sees Jesus climbing up a mountain. He sits down with his disciples. It is about the time for the Jewish celebration of Passover. Jesus looks up and sees a big crowd approaching him. Jesus says to Philip, "Where are we going to get enough bread to feed this crowd?" And Philip replies, "Half a year's wages wouldn't buy enough for everyone to have a bite."

Andrew says, "There's a boy here with five loaves of barley bread and two fish; but what does that amount to for so many?"

As her dream continues Mary hears Jesus saying, "Have the people sit down."

As they begin sitting down on the grass, it is easier to get an overview of the crowd: it looks like about five thousand people have come.

Jesus takes the loaves, gives thanks, and passes them around to the people along with the fish. And when they have eaten their fill, Jesus says to his disciples, "Gather up the leftovers so that nothing goes to waste."

So they gather up the scraps and fill twelve baskets![5]

In the morning when Mary wakes up she remembers all the details of her dream. She recalls a story she heard as a child in synagogue: the one about the prophet Elisha feeding a hundred people with only twenty loaves of barley bread. After everyone eats, there is some bread left over.[6]

Mary understands immediately: what happened with Elisha is occurring again. This time there is even less bread in hand and much larger multitudes to feed. Even so, there is plenty to feed even more people. The message is clear. We think we only have a little at hand, but we have the Bread of Life to share with thousands and this is what we must do: feed everyone.

NOTES

1. This chapter is rooted in John 6

2. Gospel of Thomas 86

3. Gospel of Thomas 42

4. John 6:27, 48-51

5. John 6:1-13

6. 2 Kings 4:42-44

CHAPTER 61:
MARY AND PHILIP TEACHING IN THE VINEYARDS AND FIELDS₁

ON ANOTHER DAY, MARY AND PHILIP DECIDE TO GO INTO the vineyards and fields on the fertile plain of Genneserat. Word of their coming has preceded their arrival. People are gathering and eager to hear whatever they have to tell them.

Mary and Philip tell the story plainly: Jesus was arrested, tortured, and crucified by the Roman authorities. In returning to Galilee and all the familiar places, they and so many others have discovered that Jesus is resurrected from the dead! He is alive and well and living within them and among them as they gather together! They themselves are becoming the risen body of Jesus!

The people listen attentively. Some scoff calling it all just crazy talk. Others are taking the reports to heart, wondering what it all means. Mary recalls when Jesus was in the very same vineyards and the fields nearby. Among this crowd are many who heard the wisdom teachings of Jesus and experienced healing right here in this place.²

One by one they speak up and ask questions. "Jesus always understood the oppression we live under. We felt he was empowering us, but what do we do now?"

Another adds, "Here we are: still working as sharecroppers for the owners in the City! Nothing has changed!" And a third says, "Just to add insult to injury, all we produce is shipped off to Rome for Caesar and all his drunken bastards! So what do you have to say about your Jesus now?"

Hearing their intense anger and taking it into her heart, Mary pauses and centers herself. In a moment she has a Vision of the Vine and gives immediate voice to what she sees and hears. She pauses after each phrase to allow the meaning to sink in.

You see only these vines, but listen to what I hear Jesus saying to us now:

"I am the authentic vine and my Father does the cultivating...
He prunes every branch of mine that does not bear fruit...
and every branch that does bear fruit he dresses
so it will bear even more fruit...
You have already been 'dressed up' by things I have told you...
Just as a branch cannot bear fruit in and of itself
so you cannot bear fruit unless you are attached to me...
I am the trunk, you are the branches.
Those who stay attached to me—and I to them—
produce a lot of fruit;
You are not able to achieve anything apart from me...
Those who don't remain attached to me
are thrown away like dead branches;
they are collected, tossed into the fire, and burned...
If you stay attached to me and my words lodge in you,
ask whatever you want and it will happen to you.
My Father's honor consists of this:
the great quantity of fruit you produce in being my disciples."[3]

A profound silence settles in as people begin to understand that they are part of something much greater than these vines they are working. Mary invites everyone to join hands, form a circle, and feel the connection: the Energy running through them, the new life filling them and making them one living and loving vine.

Looking round the circle into the eyes of each person, Mary continues speaking lovingly in the Way that goes right to the heart, "I hear Jesus saying to us: 'I loved you in the same way the Father loved me. Live in my love. If you observe my instructions, you will live in my love, just as I have observed my Father's instructions and live in his love.'"[4]

Some have hearts so hardened, minds so frozen in time, that they can neither hear nor understand. But others do have ears to hear and eyes to see the Vision. These are the ones who leave their tools and join Mary and Philip as they move on into fields where another crowd of farm workers is eager to hear what they have to say.

As in the vineyard, Mary and Philip begin sharing more of their experiences of the Resurrected Jesus here in Galilee. This time it is Philip who has a visionary experience that he relates with great care, phrase by phrase, allowing the meaning to sink in and touch hearts.

"Farming in the world requires the cooperation of four essential elements. A harvest is gathered into the barn only as a result of the natural action of earth, water, air, and light."

Everyone nods in agreement. Philip is simply stating the obvious. Then he continues.

"God's farming likewise has four elements—faith, hope, love, and knowledge...

Faith is our earth, that in which we take root...

And hope is the water through which we are nourished...

Love is the air through which we grow...

Knowledge is the light through which we ripen."[5]

It has been a long day and soft twilight is settling over the land and shining in their faces with a lovely glow. Mary and Philip lead the way into the village and find a home where those who are ready for more teaching can gather.

Mary is keenly aware that a division is occurring between those who are ready for the message and others who are still resisting. The division is breaking her heart and she yearns, like Jesus, to bring them all together. So she adds a teaching that she hopes will bring healing, "The Kindom of Father and Mother, the *Way of Mystery,* is like a person who has good seed. His enemy comes during the night and sows weeds among the good seed. The person does not let the workers pull up the weeds, but says to them, 'No, otherwise you might pull up the weeds and pull up the wheat along with them.'[6]

So let us love one another!"

Someone blurts out, "Yes, let us love one another! I'm hungry: how about something to eat?" Mary and Philip smile and with their hosts begin sharing a simple meal with everyone.

As they share bread, Mary invites the people to say to one another, "I am the Bread of Life." Taking a cup of water into her hands, she says, "I am the Water of Life...." And everyone shares. Then a cup of milk and honey is passed. And then comes a cup of wine, this time with deeper meaning than ever: someone cries out, "You are the Vine and we are the branches!" Others pick up the phrase and say together as a mantra. Then another mantra breaks out spontaneously, "Jesus is alive in us!" When it is time to leave, the people move unafraid through the darkness toward their homes.

Mary and Philip remain a few more days to share wisdom teachings. The people join in recalling teachings they heard from Jesus before his fateful trip to Jerusalem. To these they add their own visions and insights from the Spirit moving freely within and among them.

Philip remains in the village teaching and encouraging the disciples. Mary knows it is time for her to move along to other towns and villages.

NOTES

1. The Gospel of John records Mary Magdalene's visionary experience of being with the resurrected Jesus in a Garden. And how and through whom did the other visionary teachings originate? Perhaps Mary is also the primary source for others like the Vision of the Vine and Branches?

2. Mark 6:53 and Matthew 14:34

3. John 15:1-8

4. John 15:9-10

5. Gospel of Philip 115 (Nag Hammadi Scriptures notation is Philip 79:18-31)

6. Gospel of Thomas 57:1-3

CHAPTER 62:
PETER'S VISION OF
THE PEARL MERCHANT₁

MOVING ON TO CAPERNAUM, MARY AND THE OTHERS GO
directly to Peter's house where a large crowd is already gathered. She
slips into the room as unobtrusively as possible, just in time to see
the light on Peter's face as he relates his latest Vision of the
Resurrected Jesus:

"Several of us were praying together and this vivid scene came to
me: We were of one mind, and we decided to complete the ministry
to which the Teacher appointed us. We came to an agreement with
each other, and we went down to the sea at the right time, which we
learned from the Teacher.

We discovered a ship moored at the shore, ready to sail, and we
spoke with the sailors of the ship about whether we could come
aboard with them. They were very friendly with us, as was arranged
by the Teacher.

It happened that after we put out to sea, we sailed for a day and
a night. Then a wind blew the ship and brought us to a small city in
the middle of the sea.

I, Peter, asked residents standing on the dock about the name of
this city. One of them answered and said, 'The name of this city is

Abide'—that is to say, establish yourself in endurance. Your leader within you will guide you...

Now, when we went ashore with the baggage, I entered the city to inquire about lodging. A man came out wearing a linen cloth bound around his waist with a gold belt, and a shawl was tied on his chest, going over his shoulders and covering his head and hands.

I was staring at the man, because he was good-looking in appearance and demeanor. I saw four parts of his body: the soles of his feet, a portion of his chest, the palms of his hands, and his face. That was all I could see.

There was a bound book like that of an official in his left hand and a staff of styrax wood in his right hand, He spoke slowly, with a resonating voice, and called out in the city, 'Pearls! Pearls!'

The wealthy people of that city heard his voice and came out of their hidden chambers. Some were peering out of the rooms of their houses; others looked from their upper windows. They saw nothing in him, for there was no bag over his shoulder and no bundle within his linen cloth or shawl. In their arrogance they did not even ask who he was, and he in turn did not make himself known to them. They went back to their rooms and said, 'Is this man mocking us?'

The poor of that city also heard his voice, and they approached the man who offered to sell this pearl and said to him, 'Please show us the pearl so that we at least can see it. We are poor and don't have money to buy it. But show it to us, and then we can tell our friends that we saw a pearl with our own eyes.'

He answered and said to them, 'If you can, come to my city, so that I may not only show it to you but may give it to you free of charge.'

When the poor of that city heard this, they said, 'We are beggars, and we know that nobody gives a pearl to a beggar. Beggars usually get bread and money. So we ask you this favor, that you show us the pearl, and then we can brag to our friends that we saw a pearl with our own eyes. For this does not happen among poor people, especially beggars like us.'

He answered and said to them, 'If you can, you should come to my city, that I may not only show it to you but may give it to you free of charge.'

The poor and the beggars rejoiced because of the man who gives free of charge.

Some people asked about hardships. I, Peter, replied and told them what I heard on the way, for we had endured hardships in our ministry.

I said to the man who offered to sell the pearl, 'I would like to know your name and what hardships there are on the way to your city. We are strangers and servants of God, and we must be obedient and spread God's word in every city.'

The man answered me and said, 'Since you ask, my name is Lithargoel, which means "light bright stone." And concerning the way to this city, which you also have asked about, I shall tell you. None can travel that road unless they renounce all their possessions and fast daily from one night's stay to the next. There are many robbers and wild beasts on that road. If people take bread on the road, black dogs kill them because of the bread.

If they carry expensive garments of this world, robbers kill them because of the garments.

If they are concerned about meat and vegetables, lions eat them because of the meat, and if they get away from the lions, bulls devour them because of the vegetables.'

When he said this to me, I groaned within and said, 'What great hardships are on the Way! May Jesus give us strength to walk this path.'

He saw that my face was downcast and that I was groaning, and he said to me, 'Why are you groaning if you know the name of Jesus and believe in him? He is a power great enough to give you strength. For I also believe in the Father who has sent him.'

I asked him again, 'What is the name of the city you are going to?'

He said to me, 'This is the name of my city: In nine gates let us praise God, and consider that the tenth gate is the main gate.'

After this I left him in peace and went to call my friends."

Having completed the retelling of his vision, Peter becomes silent and all in the room join him in a period of profound silence.

Mary allows enough time for people to reflect on the meaning of Peter's vision. When the time feels right to her, Mary asks questions to help the people go deeper into the heart of the story. She opens

262 | *John Beverley Butcher*

with, "Is there anything about this man that reminds you of Jesus?"

"Yes, of course," cried out one man. "He had the five wounds in his hands, his feet, and his side, yet he was healed, healthy, and handsome. Surely this man in the vision is Jesus who has risen from the dead!"

Someone else adds, "I remember when Jesus told his story about the pearl merchant who looked everywhere until he found the pearl of greatest value and how he then sold all that he had to obtain that pearl!"

"And what might that pearl be?" asks Mary. A woman in the group replies, "I think it is wisdom! It is the wisdom we receive through hearing the teachings you and Jesus have been giving us and learning what they really mean."

"Yes," replies Mary, "And as you gain wisdom you will discover more of your true humanity!"

A man jumps into the conversation with another response, "Now I understand why Jesus sent us out in pairs to minister to people. He told us not to take anything on the road, except a staff: no bread, no knapsack, no spending money, but to wear sandals, and to wear no more than one shirt.[2] Now I get it: when you have nothing, no one can take it away from you. Jesus wants us to be safe! Not only that: he wants us to go and be pearl merchants now, offering his wisdom to others. Some are ready to receive it. Others are not interested. Like Jesus, we are expected to make the offer!"

"Now I have a question for you Peter," asks a woman in the back. "You said that in your vision the man's name was 'Lithargoel.' So was this Jesus or was it Lithargoel? Or is Lithargoel another name for Jesus? Who is he really?"

Mary smiles and in her heart knows the answer and says to herself, "Jesus, you are always my pearl…" She looks around and sees that many are also smiling, especially those who knew Jesus before he was executed know that Jesus is their pearl who gives them the pearl of wisdom.

Mary asks one final question, "So what do you think is the point of the Vision? What does Jesus expect us to do now?"

Peter and Andrew, Philip and Thomas, Joanna and Susanna all reply as one chorus,

"To go on the road again!"

"First thing in the morning," says Mary. But now it is getting dark, time to eat and get some rest. People begin sharing bread and the cup and experience once again their coming together as One Body, the living Body of the Resurrected Jesus.

NOTES

1. This chapter is rooted in a resurrection story recorded in The Acts of Peter and the Twelve Apostles, found in *The Nag Hammadi Scriptures*.

2. Mark 6:7-9

CHAPTER 63:
PETER'S VISION
OF THE DOCTOR[1]

In the morning Mary is about to pray with the disciples and send them out in pairs. She hears Peter and John say, "We must tell you about the vision we had late last night:

"A man named Lithargoel[2] appeared to us again and he looked different from before. This time he took the form of a doctor with a medicine case under his arm, and there was a young student following him with a bag of medicine. We did not recognize him at first.

"I, Peter, spoke up and said, 'We wish you to do us a favor, since we are strangers. Take us to the house of Lithargoel before evening comes.'

"He said, 'With an upright heart I shall show it to you. But I wonder how you know this fine man. He does not reveal himself to everyone, because he is the son of a great king. Rest a little while, and I shall go and treat this patient and then return.'

"He hurried off, and he returned soon.

"He said to me, 'Peter!'

"I was startled that he knew my name was Peter so I responded, 'How do you know me, for you called me by name?'

264

"Lithargoel answered, 'I want to ask you who gave you the name Peter?'

"I said to him, 'It was Jesus... He gave me this name.'

"He answered and said, 'It is I. Recognize me, Peter.'

"He loosened the garment he was wearing, the one he had put on so that we did not recognize him.

"When he revealed to us that this really was he, we fell down and worshipped him... He reached out his hand and made us stand up. We spoke with him in a humble manner, and with our heads bowed down in modesty we said, 'We shall do whatever you wish. Just give us the strength always to do what you wish.'

He gave us the medicine case and the bag that was in the student's hand, and he offered these instructions and said, 'Return to the city you came from, called Abide-and-remain-in-endurance, and teach all who have believed in my name that I too have endured adversities of faith. I shall grant you your reward. To the poor of the city give what they need to live, until I present to them what is better, about which I told them, "I shall give it to you free of charge."'

"I answered and said to him, 'Master, you have taught us to renounce the world and everything in it. We have forsaken these things for your sake. Now we are concerned only about food for a single day. Where can we find what the poor need, which you ask us to give to them?'

"The teacher answered and said, 'Peter, it was necessary for you to understand the parable I told you. Don't you know that my name, which you teach, is worth more than all riches, and the wisdom of God is worth more than silver and gold and precious stones?'

"He gave us the bag of medicine and said, 'Heal all the people of the city who are sick and believe in my name.'

"I was afraid to take issue with the Teacher a second time, so I motioned to John, who was next to me, and said, 'John, you say something this time.'

"John answered and said, 'We are afraid to say too much in your presence, but you have asked us to practice this art. We have not been taught to be doctors. How, then, shall we know how to heal bodies, as you have told us?'

"Lithargoel answered, 'You have said it well, John: "I know that

266 | John Beverley Butcher

the doctors of this world heal what is of the world, but the doctors of souls heal the heart." So, first heal bodies, that through the real powers of healing their bodies, with no medicine of this world, they may come to believe in you, that you also have the power to heal sicknesses of the heart.'"

After Peter finishes sharing his vision with them, silence reigns. The assembled disciples realize that just as Jesus had sent them out to the villages to teach and to heal before he was crucified, so the Resurrected Jesus is continuing to empower them for ministry.

Mary then gives the disciples some additional instructions that she had received from the Resurrected Jesus, "This is why you get sick and die: you love what deceives you. Anyone with a mind should use it to think! Attachment to matter gives rise to passion against nature. Thus trouble arises in the whole body. This is why I tell you 'Be in harmony...' If you are out of balance, take inspiration from manifestations of your true nature. Become content of heart. Those who have two ears capable of hearing should listen!"

Mary continues her teaching, "As the Blessed One says, "Peace be with you! May my Peace arise and be fulfilled within you! Be on your guard so that no one deceives you by saying, 'Look over here!' or 'Look over there!' For the Seed of True Humanity exists within you. Follow it! Those who search for it will find it."[3]

Peter and John had prepared walking sticks of styrax wood for each of the disciples along with a flask of aromatic oil that had come from that tree.

As disciples come to them in pairs, Peter and John hand them walking sticks. With Mary they lay their hands on the disciples and pray, "Go then and proclaim the good news of the Kindom of the Father and Mother, the *Way of Mystery*. Do not lay down any rule beyond what I ordained for you, nor promulgate law like the law-giver, or else it will dominate you.[4]

"First heal bodies, that through the real power of healing their bodies, with no medicine of this world, they may come to believe in you, that you also have the power to heal sicknesses of the heart."[5]

Empowered by the Spirit within them, they set off from Capernaum to Chorazin, Bethsaida, Gergesa, and several other near-by villages and towns proclaiming the Good News of true humanity. In each place they find disciples who had known Jesus before his death. They are eager to hear the news of his resurrection among them. Communities of Spirit-filled people begin forming in each place, meeting regularly to share their experiences of Jesus and his wisdom teachings, to break bread together, to pray, and to share the Good News with everyone they meet.

The number of disciples grows, many are baptized, and the power of the Spirit is released freely among them.

NOTES

1. This chapter is rooted in a resurrection story recorded in The Acts of Peter and the Twelve Apostles, a second century document in *The Nag Hammadi Scriptures.*

2. The name Lithargoel is composed of two Greek words: *lithos*, "stone," and *argos*, "shining," followed by the Semitic honorific suffix *el*, which refers to God and appears often in angelic names. Lithargoel is the Pearl of God, another name for the resurrected Jesus who is seen as not only a pearl merchant by the Pearl itself, and now is a doctor.

3. Gospel of Mary 3:7-4:7.

4. Gospel of Mary 4:8-10

5. Acts of Peter and the Twelve Apostles

CHAPTER 64:
JAMES EXPERIENCES HIS BROTHER, JESUS,

AFTER THE DEATH OF JESUS, MOST OF HIS FAMILY, friends, and disciples, fearing for their own lives, flee Jerusalem and return to their homes in the villages of Galilee. But there is at least one notable exception: James, the blood brother of Jesus, who remains in the City. He has been in Jerusalem for many years as a Temple priest and member of the Zealots who are plotting and preparing for a revolt against the Roman occupiers of their land.[2] It is most likely that in addition to his own personal grief, James is becoming even more angry toward Roman power and is redoubling his underground revolutionary efforts. It is also quite likely that he will make occasional trips to Galilee to visit with the rest of his family and with friends of his deceased brother, Jesus. One such visit is described in the Secret Book of James[3] as occurring five hundred fifty days after Jesus rises from the dead.[4]

James becomes aware of the presence of the Spirit of his brother and blurts out angrily and resentfully, "You went away and left us."[4] James and the others hear the Voice of Jesus replying, "No, but I shall go to the place from which I have come. If you wish to come with me, come on!"

They all reply, "If you bid us, we'll come." And Jesus says, "I swear to you, no one will enter the Kindom of Heaven at my bidding, but rather because you yourselves are full. Let me have James and Peter, so that I may fill them..."

The Voice of Jesus speaks directly to James and Peter, "So don't you want to be filled? And is your heart drunk? So don't you want to be sober?... Yours is life!.. Become full and leave no place within you empty... Become full of the spirit but lacking in reason. For reason is of the soul; indeed, it is soul."

Then follows a conversation about feeling empty and then being filled.

The conversation shifts to other topics as they hear the Voice of the Resurrected Jesus saying to them, "If you think about the world, about how long it existed before you and how long it will exist after you, you will discover that your life is but a single day, and your sufferings but a single hour. Accordingly, since what is good will not enter this world, you should scorn death and be concerned about life. Remember my cross and my death, and you will live!"[5]

Next they hear a rather startling statement, "Become better than I; be like the child of the Holy Spirit."[6]

Then they hear a clear warning, "Don't let the Kindom of Father and Mother, the *Way of Mystery*, wither away. For it is like a date palm shoot whose fruit fell down around it. It put forth buds, and when it blossomed, its productivity was caused to dry up. So it also is with the fruit that came forth from this singular root: when it was picked, fruit was gathered by many. Truly, this was good. Isn't it possible to produce new growth now? Can't you discover how?"[7]

The new teachings from the Resurrected Jesus prompt recollections of his earlier ones so familiar that a single word or two brings them to mind. It is enough for some people to hear a phrase and recall the rest: they mention Jesus' stories of "The Shepherds," and "The Seed," and "The Building," and "The Lamps of the Virgins," and "The Wage of the Workers," and "The Silver Coins and the Woman."

They hear the Voice of Jesus expressed through them saying, "Become eager for instruction. For the first prerequisite for instruction is faith, the second is love, the third is works and from these comes life. For instruction is like a grain of wheat. When someone sowed it, he had faith in it, and when it sprouted he loved it, because he saw many grains instead of just one. And after he worked, he was saved because he prepared it as food and he still kept some out to sow.

This is also how you can receive for yourselves the Kindom of Heaven, the *Way of Mystery*. Unless you receive it through knowledge, you will not be able to discover it…[8]

"Pay attention to instruction, understand knowledge, love life…. You are the beloved; it is you who will become the cause of life for many…. Yours is life!"[9]

"Heaven's Kindom, the *Way of Mystery*, is like a head of grain that sprouted in a field. And when it was ripe, it scattered its seed, and again it filled the field with heads of grain for another year. So with you, be eager to harvest for yourselves a head of the grain of life that you may be filled with the Kindom.

And as long as I am with you, pay attention to me and trust in me because I was with you and you did not know me.

Blessed are those who have known me.

Woe to those who have heard and have not trusted.

Blessed are those who have not seen but yet have trust.

Once again I appeal to you. I am disclosed to you as I am building a house useful to you when you find shelter in it, and it will support your neighbor's house when theirs is in danger of collapsing….

Do not let Heaven's Kindom, the *Way of Mystery* become a desert within you."[10]

A profound Silence falls over everyone. And out of the Silence, Mary speaks, "That final warning is the most important of all, 'Do not let the Way become a desert within you.'"

James has been present, hearing again the heart of his brother's teaching which stands in stark contrast to his own efforts of aligning himself with those who choose force to rid themselves of the Roman occupiers. James and Jesus have always seen life quite differently.

James has heard the men and has been even more moved by the women who have spoken from their hearts as well as their minds. Speaking to the men, he says, "Encourage these four: Salome, Mary, Martha, and Arsinoe."[11]

James has been with Mary Magdalene, Peter, and the others who are becoming knit together in One Living Body. He has much to ponder as he returns to Jerusalem.

NOTES

1. This chapter is rooted in excerpts from the Secret Book of James found at Nag Hammadi. "The most ancient of the sayings absorbed into Secret James may well belong to the earliest period of collected sayings traditions." *Complete Gospels,* p. 334.

2. For documentation and thorough discussion of James as a Zealot priest in the Temple of Jerusalem, see Robert M. Eisenman, *James the Brother of Jesus,* Viking, 1996.

3. The Secret Book of James, known as the Apocryphon of James in earlier translations of Nag Hammadi texts, is an early second century text attributed to James as the author. James died ca. 66 C.E. during a major revolt so someone else is writing in his name. However, the content is primarily first century material.

4. The Secret Book of James 2:3 Why is the context mentioned as being 550 Days after the resurrection? This story follows the symbolism in the Ascension of Isaiah, a Jewish apocryphal text with Christian interpolations, which speaks of a period of 18 months, or 540 days, before Isaiah ascended. The story of Jesus recapitulates the story of prophets like Isaiah who lived before him.

5. The Secret Book of James 4:8-11

6. The Secret Book of James 5:6

7. The Secret Book of James 6:9-12

8. The Secret Book of James 6:15-18

9. The Secret Book of James 6:27, 36, 38b

10. The Secret Book of James 8:3-5, 7, 11

11. First Apocalypse of James 40:24-25 in *The Nag Hammadi Library,* revised edition 1988, p. 267.

CHAPTER 65:
WHO WILL LEAD US?[1]

MORE AND MORE PEOPLE ARE EXPERIENCING THE Resurrected Jesus within themselves and one another. The communities of friends of Jesus are asking themselves many questions: Who will lead us? What does the future hold? When will the new order come? Will we ever have peace? In their anxious moments, the people turn to Mary with their questions and she invites people to sit down, express how they feel, and listen to one another.

One man opens up a conversation by saying, "I was praying and asked Jesus, 'Who will be our leader?' And I heard him reply, 'No matter where you are, you are to go to James the Just, for whose sake heaven and earth came into being.'"[2]

Another man responds saying, "Yes, I agree. James is the oldest brother. By right he should be our leader now!"

"But he is up in Jerusalem and we are here in Galilee!" adds another. "Let him lead the few disciples who are there—we need someone to lead us right here!"

"How about Simon Peter?"[3] asks someone else. "Jesus named him 'Rock' so we can rely on him."

Everyone seems to be speaking at once. Finally, it is Mary who brings a bit of calm when she says, "I hear Jesus saying, 'Show me the stone that the builders rejected: that is the keystone.'[4] Jesus is still our keystone, the One who holds all the stones of the entire arch together." The response is Deep Silence.

But before long other anxious questions about the future begin erupting, "When will the new world come?"[5] And Mary replies, "Jesus says, 'What you are looking for has already come, but you don't know it.'"[6]

And Thomas adds, I remember when we asked Jesus, "When will the Kindom of Father and Mother come?" and he replied, "It will not come by watching for it. It will not be said, 'Look, here!' or 'Look, there!' Rather, the Kindom of the Father and Mother is spread out upon the earth and people do not see it.'"[7]

Mary expands the teaching further and says, "Jesus says, 'There are many standing at the door, but those who are alone will enter the bridal chamber.'"[8]

Some understand because they have already experienced the inner Union. Mary can tell quickly who they are because of the expressions on their faces.

She also notices the quizzical expressions of others who clearly do not yet understand. She speaks directly to those who are puzzled, "Jesus says, You examine the face of heaven and earth, but you have not come to know who is in your presence, and you do not know how to examine the present moment."[9]

Mary pauses, scans the room making eye contact especially with those who do understand, and adds, "Jesus says, 'When you are in the light, what will you do? On the day when you were one, you became two. But when you become two, what will you do?"[10] Mary repeats the saying over and over as a mantra and feels its energy coursing through her body. In her heart she is asking, "What will emerge from the Oneness I know? Jesus and I became one. Now we are two. What will I do?"

Her inner meditation is interrupted as people begin dispersing to return to their homes. Several women and a few men stop to speak with Mary saying, "You are our Teacher. You are our Leader now."

When all the others have gone and Mary is alone, reclining and ready for rest, she feels Jesus even more deeply within her. She hears his gentle strong Voice saying to her, "I am the light that is over all things. I am all: from me all came forth, and to me all attains."[11]

The room itself has become dark, but Mary is basking in warm, embracing Light.

NOTES

1. The evidence now shows that Mary Magdalene is one of the primary teachers and leaders in the emerging communities of the Resurrected Jesus.

2. Gospel of Thomas 12

3. Matthew 16:18

4. Gospel of Thomas 66

5. Gospel of Thomas 51

6. Gospel of Thomas 51

7. Gospel of Thomas 113

8. Gospel of Thomas 75

9. Gospel of Thomas 91

10. Gospel of Thomas 11:3

11. Gospel of Thomas 77

CHAPTER 66:
DÉJÀ VU IN DAMASCUS₁

RECALLING HER EARLIER JOURNEYS TO DAMASCUS WITH Jesus, Mary knows she must go there again quite soon to visit with friends and disciples who live there. Some of them had traveled to Jerusalem for the Passover and knew about the arrest and crucifixion. Those who had not made the trip are well aware of the tragedy. She knows she must continue the work of proclaiming the Gospel of the Seed of True Humanity, the same teachings she and Jesus offered before plus whatever new teachings come welling up from deep within her.

Mary sets out with John, Susanna and Joanna, Philip and Thomas. Everywhere she looks, every turn of the road, and every scene reminds her vividly of Jesus. Fresh meanings flash vividly before her: a shepherd crosses the road with his sheep and she hears a resonant Voice within her saying, "I am the Good Shepherd. The good shepherd gives his life for his sheep. A hired hand, who isn't a shepherd and doesn't own the sheep, sees the wolf coming and runs off, abandoning the sheep; then the wolf attacks the sheep and scatters them. He runs off because he's a hired hand and the sheep don't matter to him. I am the good shepherd; I know my sheep and my sheep know me, just as the Father knows me and I know the Father: so I give my life for my sheep. Yet I have sheep from another fold, and I must lead them too. They'll recognize my voice, and there'll be one flock, one shepherd."[2]

Mary keeps pondering this insight and knows in her heart that she and the others who knew Jesus before his death now share in caring for the sheep they already know and those they will be meeting from another fold: she will find out their names and then call them by name. She shares this vision with her companions.

Mount Hermon comes into view on their left. As she views the beautiful mountain she recalls so many peak experiences especially their shared teaching on the mount and the day when the inner transformation of Jesus was manifested in the transfiguration of his outer appearance for all to see. She is recalling so many moments of insight and awareness.

And the Voice within her keeps repeating,

"I am the Light of the world..."[3]

"I am the Resurrection and the Life..."[4]

"I am the Way, the Truth, and the Life..."[5]

"I am... I am... I am..."

The day is coming to a close and there is no village for miles and miles so it is time to make a campsite, build a fire and cook a simple meal. Thomas gathers a few stones to form a circle and splits wood for the fire. In everything he does he, too, is feeling the presence of Jesus. A Voice within Thomas says, "Split a piece of wood; I am there. Lift the stone, and you will find me there."[6]

Gathering around the campfire and sharing their simple meal of bread and dried fish that Mary has brought along, Thomas gives expression to the Voice of Jesus welling up from within him, "Whoever is near me is near the fire, and whoever is far from me is far from the Kindom of Father and Mother, the *Way of Mystery*."[7]

They pour and pass a cup of wine around the circle from Mary to Thomas, Joanna, Philip and Susanna. As the circle is completed, one of them says, "I feel Jesus saying to us, 'Whoever drinks from my mouth will become like me; I myself shall become that person.'"[8] There is a profound Silence and then they say spontaneously and together, "We are One!"

They share the "Shalom" with warm embrace and turn in for the night.

A few days later they approach the bustling City of Damascus. All sorts and conditions of people come into view. Mary now sees something of the Mystery in every person as she hears the Voice within her saying,

"For I am the first and the last.
I am the honored one and the scorned one.
I am the whore and the holy one.
I am the wife and the virgin.
I am the mother and the daughter.
I am the barren one and many are my sons.
I am she whose wedding is great,
and I have not taken a husband.
I am the midwife,
and I am she who does not bear.
I am the solace,
and I am the labor pains.
I am the bride,
and I am the bridegroom.
I am begotten by my husband.
and I am the mother of my father.
I am the sister of my husband,
and he is my offspring.
I am the slave of him who prepared me.
and I am the ruler of my offspring
I am the staff of his power in his youth,
and he is my rod of my old age."[9]

Everywhere she turns, everyone she sees, is filled with the Great I AM. Mary is filled to overflowing in amazement. She shares her wonder with her companions and learns that they, too, have been entering into the same mystical awareness of All That Is.

Reaching their destination, Mary and her companions are welcomed into the home of friends she has known for many years. There is so much to share, so many tears, both of sorrow over the death of Jesus and tears of joy in discovering his presence within themselves and one another.

The repeating "I am" mantra keeps running through Mary's mind as it has throughout the journey. All day, all night, and into her sleeping the "I ams" reverberate through her soul:

"I am the Silence that is incomprehensible.
I am the Idea whose remembrance is frequent.
I am the Voice whose sound is manifold.
I am the Word whose appearance is multiple.
I am the Utterance of my name.
I am the Name of the Sound and the Sound of the Name."[10]

The next day they waken to the clamor of a large crowd outside wanting to see them and hear what they have to say. The house is much too small, so they find an open space on a small hill with several nice size rocks, just the right size to sit on for teaching.

Mary greets the people assembled with "Shalom!" and her core teaching, "The Seed of True Humanity is within you! Follow it!"[11] She invites people to remember the teachings from Jesus when they were in Damascus together several years ago.

Then she motions toward John who continues the teaching by relating his own experience from a few days before. "On our way here I was feeling distressed because our Teacher had been taken from us, so I went into a desert place below Mount Hermon and was surprised by the joy of seeing the heavens opening, all creatures under heaven lit up, and the world felt like it was shaking. I was afraid and I saw within this great Light someone standing by me. As I was looking, it seemed to be an elderly person. Again it changed its appearance to be a youth. Not that there were several figures before me. Rather there was one figure with several forms within the light. These forms were visible through each other, and the figure had three forms.

"The figure said to me, 'John, John, why are you doubting? Why are you afraid? Aren't you familiar with this figure? Then do not be fainthearted. I am with you always. I am the Father, I am the Mother, I am the Child. I am the incorruptible and the undefiled one.

Now I have come to teach you what is, what was, and what is

going to come, that you may understand what is invisible and what is visible; and to teach you about the unshakable generation of true humanity.

So now, lift up your heads that you may hear the things we shall tell you today, and that you may relate them to your spiritual friends who are grounded in their own true humanity."[12]

After John finishes sharing his vision, others open their hearts and tell about their own peak experiences.

Mary waits until she feels the Spirit urging her to begin teaching from familiar stories, give them fresh meaning, and invite people to choose a new Way of Living.

"As in the Garden of Eden story, you will be able to face the Serpent, the Instructor, who raises questions so you can make decisions and experience healing. As Moses led the people into the wilderness and held up the serpent before them, seek to be wise as serpents and harmless as doves. Know that now you will be able to pick up serpents and they will not hurt you."[13]

Empowered by the pulsating Energy of the I AM's, Mary radiates a Presence that permeates the crowd. They discover that they, too, are becoming living members of One Body. Many respond and are ready for the inner journey so they move down the hill with Mary, John, and their companions to the Abana River for baptism in the flowing waters of the Holy Spirit.

Notes

1. Damascus, "The region of Damascus is an oasis watered by a system of rivers.... Damascus itself is situated on the Nahr Barada (River Abana).... Damascus has always played an important role as a center of commerce and religion because of its situation where, since time immemorial, the most important military and commercial routes have met." *Interpreter's Dictionary of the Bible,* Abingdon 1962, Volume A-D, p. 757. "There was in Damascus a large Jewish community which may in some way have been affiliated with the Qumran Community," *Anchor Bible Dictionary,* volume 2, page 8, Doubleday, 1992.

2. John 10:11-16

3. John 8:12

4. John 11:25

5. John 14:6

6. Gospel of Thomas 77

7. Gospel of Thomas 82

8. Gospel of Thomas 108

9. Excerpts from The Thunder, Perfect Mind, George W. MacRae translation in *The Nag Hammadi Library,* third edition

10. Excerpts from The Thunder, Perfect Mind, George W. MacRae translation in *The Nag Hammadi Library*, third edition

11. Gospel of Mary 4:5

12. Excerpts from the beginning of The Secret Book of John, a second century document reflecting first century experiences.

13. Mark 16:18

CHAPTER 67:

SAUL BECOMES PAUL₁

MARY AND HER COMPANIONS LIVE AND TEACH IN Damascus for awhile. A new community is forming and leadership is emerging.

Among the more spiritually alive people is Ananias who, since his baptism in the Spirit, has been developing his own intense daily practice of prayer. One morning as Ananias is praying he sees a vision and hears his name being called, "Ananias!" He replies, "Here I am, Lord." And the Lord says to him, "Get up and go to Straight Street and at the house of Judas look for a man of Tarsus named Saul. At this moment he is praying, and he has seen in a vision a man named Ananias coming in and laying hands on him so that he may regain his sight."

Ananias answers, "Lord, I have heard from many about this man, how much evil he has done to your saints in Jerusalem and here he has authority from the chief priests to bind all who invoke your name."

But the Lord says to him, "Go, for he is an instrument whom I have chosen to bring my name before Gentiles and kings and before the people of Israel; I myself will show him how much he must suffer for the sake of my name." So Ananias goes over to Straight Street and enters the house of Judas Thomas where he finds Saul, lays his hands on him, and says, "Brother Saul, the Lord Jesus, who appeared to you on your way here, has sent me so that you may regain your sight and be filled with the Holy Spirit."

And immediately something like scales fall from Saul's eyes, and his sight is restored. Ananias takes him down to the Abana River and baptizes him. As a new convert, Saul is filled with enthusiasm.[2] He takes a new name and asks people to call him "Paul." Mary is impressed with Saul's conversion but is concerned that he does not know the teachings of Jesus. She invites Paul to remain in Damascus for instruction in the wisdom teachings of Jesus, but he insists on leaving immediately for the desert of Arabia.[3]

Mary says, "I can understand your need for time in the desert, Paul. Jesus needed to be in the wilderness after his baptism and so did I after mine. But be sure to return here so that we can tell you more about the wisdom teachings of Jesus."

After his sojourn in the desert, Paul does return to Damascus and remains there for three years,[4] living in the community of faith, and listening to the stories of so many others who have experienced the resurrected Jesus within themselves and one another.

Then comes the day when Paul feels impelled to move out on his own, to begin proclaiming the Gospel as he understands it. Paul's primary focus is on the resurrection and his deeply felt experience of the living Christ within him, along with other teachings that he has been developing on his own.

Even though Mary and the others have done their best to share the wisdom teachings of Jesus, Paul turns a deaf ear toward them and does not include those teachings in his own preaching. Paul is replacing Jesus as Teacher with Christ as a savior.

Mary says to herself, "Paul is a joy because he has given up persecuting followers of the Way and become a proclaimer of the Gospel. But he has gone off on his own without incorporating the wisdom teachings of Jesus. How can this man be such a joy and such a disappointment at the same time?"

NOTES

1. This chapter is rooted in Damascus.

2. The story of Saul's conversion is found in Acts 9.

3. Galatians 1:17

4. Galatians 1:17-18

CHAPTER 68:
MARY'S VISION OF JESUS PRAYING FOR UNITY₁

FEELING BOTH HAPPY AND DISAPPOINTED WITH PAUL, Mary goes into deep meditation and prayer, out of which comes yet another Vision:

She sees Jesus and the disciples seated at table as they were during the last meal they shared before his arrest. Jesus looks up and prays, "Father, the time has come. Honor your son so your son may honor you. Just as you have given him authority over all humankind, so he can award real life to everyone you have given him. This is real life: to know you as the one true God. I honor you on earth by completing the labors you gave me to do. Now, Father, honor me with your own presence, the presence I enjoyed before the world began.

"I have made your name known to all those you gave me out of the world of humankind. They were yours, you gave them to me, and they have kept your word. They now recognize that everything you gave me is really from you. I passed on to them the things you gave me to say, and they have been receptive to those things and have come to know truly that I have come from your presence; they have also come to believe you sent me.

"I plead on their behalf; I am not pleading for the world but for those you turned over to me because they are yours. Everything that belongs to me is yours, and everything that belongs to you is mine; so I have been honored by them. I am no longer in the world, but they are to remain in the world, while I am going to return to you.

Holy Father, keep under your protection all those whom you have given me, so they may be one just as we are one."

Mary knows that the Resurrected Jesus manifests in many different ways. Now she is feeling even more of the unity in the diversity. She is able to pray, "Bless Paul, wherever he goes, whatever he teaches, whatever he chooses to do. Meanwhile I will continue to teach what Jesus and I know is real."

NOTES

1. This chapter is a retelling of John 17.

CHAPTER 69:
PETER'S VISION:
A SHEET FROM HEAVEN₁

Peter, Paul, and Mary separate and go in different directions as led by the Spirit. Once in awhile their paths converge and they have an opportunity to catch up with one another, pray together, and share their visions of the Resurrected Jesus.

Peter relates one especially intense vision and says, "I was down on the coast at Joppa. Right in the middle of the day I went up on the rooftop of the house where we were staying. I was feeling hungry and wanted something to eat; while it was being prepared, I fell into a trance and saw the heavens opened and something like a large sheet coming down, being lowered to the ground by its four corners.

In it were all kinds of four-footed creatures and reptiles and birds of the air. Then I heard a voice saying to me, 'Get up, Peter; kill and eat.' But I replied, 'By no means, Lord; for I have never eaten anything that is profane or unclean.'

The voice said to me again, a second time, 'What God has made clean, you must not call profane.'

This happened three times, and the thing was suddenly taken up to heaven.

Now while I was greatly puzzled about what to make of the vision that I had seen, men sent by Cornelius from Caesarea suddenly appeared and were standing at the gate.

While I was still thinking about the vision, the Spirit said to me, "Look, Peter, three men are searching for you. Now get up, go down, and go with them without hesitation; for I have sent them.

So I went down to the men and said, 'I am the one you are looking for; what is the reason for your coming?'

They answered, 'Cornelius, a centurion, an upright and God-fearing man, who is well spoken of by the whole Jewish nation, was directed by a holy angel to send for you to come to his house and to hear what you have to say.'

So I invited them in and gave them lodging.

The next day I got up and went with them, and some of the believers from Joppa accompanied me. The following day we came to Caesarea. Cornelius was expecting us and had called together his relatives and close friends.

When we arrived, Cornelius met us, and falling at my feet, worshipped me! Imagine that: here is this Gentile Roman soldier kneeling before me!

But I made him get up and told him, 'Stand up; I am only a mortal.'

And as I talked with him, I went into his house and found that many had assembled; and I said to them, 'You yourselves know that it is unlawful for a Jew to associate with or to visit a Gentile; but God has shown me that I should not call anyone profane or unclean. So when I was sent for, I came without objection. Now may I ask why you sent for me?'

So Cornelius replied, 'Four days ago at this very hour, at three o'clock, I was praying in my house when suddenly a man in dazzling clothes stood before me. He said, 'Cornelius, your prayer has been heard and your alms have been remembered before God. Send therefore to Joppa and ask for Simon, who is called Peter; he is staying in the house of Simon, a tanner, by the sea.' Therefore I sent for you immediately, and you have been kind enough to come. So now all of us are here in the presence of God to listen to all that the Lord has commanded you to say.'

Then I began to speak to them: 'I truly understand that God

shows no partiality, but in every nation anyone who fears him and does what is right is acceptable to him.

You know the message he sent to the people of Israel, preaching peace by Jesus the Anointed. This message spread throughout Judea, beginning in Galilee after the baptism that John announced: how God anointed Jesus of Nazareth with the Holy Spirit and with power; how he went about doing good and healing all who were oppressed by the devil, for God was with him. We are witnesses to all that he did both in Judea and in Jerusalem.

They put him to death by hanging him on a tree; but God raised him on the third day and allowed him to appear, not to all the people but to us who were chosen by God as witnesses, and who ate and drank with him after he rose from the dead. All the prophets testify about him that everyone who believes in him receives forgiveness of sins through his name.'

While I was still speaking, the Holy Spirit fell upon all who heard the word. The believers who had come with me were astounded that the gift of the Holy Spirit had been poured out even on the Gentiles, for we heard them speaking in tongues and extolling God.

Then I said, 'Can anyone withhold the water for baptizing these people who have received the Holy Spirit just as we have?'

So we baptized them and stayed on a few days longer."

After hearing Peter's story about his vision and how it had changed his attitude toward Gentiles, Mary smiled a great all-embracing smile, saying, "It reminds me of the day Jesus and I were with the Arab woman in Tyre and how his attitude changed right there on the spot. Instead of limiting his message to Jews only, he opened himself fully to everyone. Peter, your vision of the sheet coming down from heaven is also like a vision I had not long ago of Jesus at table with us praying that we might all be One! We are all One Body!"

NOTES

1. This chapter is rooted in Peter's Vision recorded in Acts 10 & 11.

CAMEO ESSAY 9:
THE CITY OF SEPPHORIS

THE HOMETOWN OF JESUS WAS NAZARETH, A SMALL insignificant village located just a few miles from Sepphoris, a major city. Even though there is no specific mention of Sepphoris in the conventional New Testament, it is very likely that Jesus went into that City from time to time. One logical route from Nazareth to Cana of Galilee ran through Sepphoris. Jesus may very well have done some teaching there.

Sepphoris is the most likely candidate for being the place where people assembled to compose the first written Gospel, known by scholars as Q. Because of its importance, here is some background information from the *Anchor Bible Dictionary*:

> The rabbis believed that Sepphoris was founded by Joshua the son of Nun... The name of the city means 'bird', and one rabbi explained that it got its name because it perched on a hill like a bird....
>
> Sepphoris entered recorded history for the first time in 103 B.C.E. when Ptolemy Lathers, the King of Cyprus, was at war with King Alexander Jennies of Israel.... Ptolemy

besieged Sepphoris on a Sabbath, but with no success (Ant 13.12.5).

If Sepphoris was already a secure, walled city at this period, then it was likely Greek in character, as was Ptolemais, Shikmoras, Dora, Strato's Tower, Joppa, Azotus (Ashdod), and other coastal cities. Since Ptolemy besieged Sepphoris on a Sabbath in order to gain advantage, it is likely that it had a large Jewish population.

There is no historical information about the city at the coming of Rome in 63 B.C.E. However in 55 B.C.E. Gabinus, proconsul in Syria, recognized the strategic importance of Sepphoris and located one of the five Roman Synedria or Councils there, and the only one for Galilee. During the winter of 39/38 B.C.E. Herod the Great took Sepphoris during a snowstorm immediately after Antigonus abandoned it. Herod retained the city as his Northern headquarters for the remainder of his reign.

Judah the son of Hezekiah led the Sepphoreans in revolt immediately upon the death of Herod the Great in 4 B.C.E. The Roman Governor of Syria, Varus, responded swiftly. He dispatched to Sepphoris a portion of his legions and auxiliary troops under his son and under Caius, a friend, while Varus marched on to Sebaste. His legions sacked Sepphoris, reduced the city to ashes, and sold its inhabitants as slaves (Ant 17.10.9.)

Herod Antipas, son of Herod the Great by the Samaritan wife Malthace, inherited Galilee and Perea (Transjordan) at the death of his father. Antipas immediately set to work to rebuild Sepphoris and its wall, employing craftsmen from villages all over Galilee. It was Sepphoris that Josephus called the "ornament of all Galilee" and the strongest city in Galilee." Evidently it surpassed Tiberias and Julias in beauty and opulence. (Ant 18.2.1) Antipas probably granted Sepphoris the rank of capital of Galilee (Ant 18.2.1).

The works of Herod Antipas at Sepphoris included a theatre that seated 3000, a palace, and an upper and lower city with an upper and lower market. The upper city was pre-

dominantly Jewish by the time of the Second revolt and likely earlier....

The destruction of Sepphoris by Varus and its rebuilding
by Antipas seems to mark its transition from a Greek city to
a loyalist Roman city of Jewish and Gentile population...

Pharisaic families are scarcely mentioned in the first century in Sepphoris. Instead we find references to those with
some sort of priestly connection. Sepphoris was therefore
likely a priestly or Sadducean city... It is important that, after
70 C.E. and the destruction of the Second Temple, the second priestly course of Jedediah settled at Sepphoris....[1]

Jesus grew up in the village of Nazareth, just four miles from
Sephoris, so it is most likely he went there sometimes and may have
taught there as well, even though there is no specific mention of
Sepphoris in the New Testament Gospels.

NOTES
1. *The Anchor Bible Dictionary,* Doubleday, 1992, Volume 5, pps.
   1090-1091.

CHAPTER 70:
SEPPHORIS COMMUNITY WRITES Q GOSPEL[1]

Time passes. It has been almost two decades since the death of Jesus. During this time Mary has gone many places, revisiting some, always moving in the impulse and Spirit of Jesus.

Mary decides to revisit Sepphoris, the city on the hill just four miles north of Nazareth. As a result of Roman city planning under Herod Antipas, Sepphoris is neat and orderly and serves as a center for governing Galilee. The government buildings and houses are built by working people skilled in the trades. Administrative jobs are readily available; literate people have a leg up for employment. More and more people are working there. Some are moving to Sepphoris or living in nearby villages. The community of followers of the Way keeps growing. Relative prosperity prevails at the expense of oppression of the people.

On this visit, Mary is warmly welcomed into the congregation in Sepphoris and quickly learns that there is a lively discussion over whether or not to write down the teachings of Jesus. Many of the people who knew Jesus during his ministry before his crucifixion are getting older. Quite a number have died. How can his teachings be preserved and transmitted to future generations?

Some argue that word of mouth is just fine, that stories have always been transmitted orally from generation to generation: who needs to write it all down? Those with this opinion are mainly unable to read or write themselves and feel a little on the defensive about "books."

However, an increasing number of people in the Sepphoris congregation are literate and have discovered the value of written material. Just about everyone is bilingual with Aramaic as the language learned at home and Greek as a necessity for communicating for work and business transactions in the city of Sepphoris. Even though the Romans are the dominant force, Greek remains the main language used for writing. Even Roman officers giving orders to lower rank soldiers serving in Galilee would normally use Greek.

Jesus was bilingual using both Aramaic and some Greek in his teachings and communications with people. Some of his sayings may very well have been spoken first in Greek. Thus for many reasons, the language of choice for what is about to become one of the first Gospels will be Greek.

Those who feel it is time to write down what they remember of the teachings of Jesus have already received word that Mary Magdalene is coming to visit with them. They have organized an initial meeting with her. Even those who are of the opinion that oral tradition is enough have been invited to be part of the gathering: their memories need to be included.

Mary appreciates the warm welcome she is given and realizes that perhaps her presence is helping people get started on creating a written collection of the teachings of Jesus. She eagerly takes her place in the circle and offers prayer for the Spirit of Jesus to guide the work.

"Where shall we begin the story?" asks one of the scribes eager to get started. "Might as well start from the beginning," says Mary. Write about John the Baptizer, his message, and his baptizing us down at the Jordan. If it weren't for John, perhaps neither Jesus nor I or many of you would have been baptized into the depths of Mystery! Write about Jesus going into the wilderness to spend forty days with the angels, the wild beasts, and the Serpent, the Instructor, who raises the questions that take us deeply within. Write about

Jesus coming out of the wilderness empowered by the Spirit and ready to begin his teaching."

Everyone agrees that the story of his baptism is the place to begin and once that is done to start recording his teachings. People begin calling out their favorite sayings from Jesus. "Blessed are the poor..."[2] and "Damn you rich!"[3] "Blessed are the hungry..."[4] "Damn you who are well fed now!"[5] "Blessed are you when people hate you and when they ostracize you and denounce you and scorn your name as evil."[6]

And someone else says, "Be sure to include what he says about 'loving your enemies,'[7] 'praying for your abusers,'[8] being 'peacemakers.'"[9] Another person interjects, "Some of that I would just as soon forget—it is too hard to do!" People laugh in recognition of the difficulty of living these things, but all agree they must be included if the collection is going to be true to what Jesus actually taught.

In a lighter moment, someone says, "Don't forget his camel jokes: how he said, 'It is easier for a camel to squeeze through a needle's eye than for a wealthy person to get into the Kindom of Father and Mother.'[10] And 'You blind leaders! You strain out a gnat and gulp down a camel.'"[11]

The conversation turns to people recalling the stories that Jesus tells: like the one about two men building houses, one on sand, the other on rock.[12] Once in awhile an argument breaks out regarding just exactly how it should be written, but usually a consensus is reached as people agree, "Yes, that's how I heard it, right from Jesus himself."

Scenes flash to mind as people recall Jesus with a Roman officer and his sick slave,[13] children in the marketplace,[14] John's arrest, and the one about foxes with holes, birds having nests, but the truly human one having nowhere to rest his head.[15]

Memories are triggered and the lively conversation outpaces the ability of the scribe to keep up. On into the night the room reverberates with the sounds of people calling out their favorite stories of Jesus. Finally, when people are tired and ready to go home, one person calls out, "Be sure to mention what Jesus said about the City on the hill that cannot be hidden[16] and your readers will know where we did this work: right here in Sepphoris!"

Little do Mary, the scribes, or any of the people assembled know that the Gospel they are composing would eventually be incorporated into the Gospels of Matthew and Luke and that two thousand years later scholars would be struggling to determine what their original document looked like and that they would give it the name "Q."[17]

NOTES

1. The community that produced "Q" the Source Gospel has been located by reliable scholars in Galilee, most likely in Sepphoris or possibly Caesarea. From a lecture by Jonathan L. Reed during the Fall 2006 Meeting of the Westar Institute in Santa Rosa, California.

2. Luke 6:20

3. Luke 6:24

4. Luke 6:21

5. Luke 6:25

6. Luke 6:22

7. Luke 6:27

8. Luke 6:28

9. Matthew 5:9

10. Luke 18:25

11. Matthew 23:24

12. Luke 6:46-49

13. Luke 7:2-10

14. Luke 7:31-35

15. Luke 9:57-58

16. Matthew 5:14, Thomas 32

17. "Q" stands for "*Quelle*," the German word for "Source." It is the source gospel behind the almost identical passages found in both Matthew and Luke. If the scholars who first began identifying

this source gospel had been English speakers, the document might very well have been called "S" for source.

CHAPTER 71:
GOSPEL OF THOMAS COMPILED IN EDESSA₁

INSPIRED BY THE PEOPLE IN SEPPHORIS WHO ARE working on a collection of Jesus wisdom teachings, Mary feels impelled by the Spirit to set off on a journey up north to Edessa in Syria. She does not know exactly why she should go there, but intuitively she knows that Edessa is where she needs to be next. Perhaps she will discover why after she arrives in town.

Before making the trip, Mary gathers the others in her sacred circle and tells them that she feels the Spirit is telling her to go to Edessa. When she went there with Thomas he had remained there. More recently she has received word that a vibrant community of followers of the Way gathers regularly in Edessa. Questions flood her mind: How is Thomas now? How is the congregation doing? Even though it is a long trip, does anyone else feel led by the Spirit to travel with her?

After a time of prayer with her immediate circle, Mary discovers that several others are ready, willing, and able to accompany her up to Edessa. They make preparations and set off together.

When they finally arrive in Edessa, they find that the community has indeed grown and is meeting in a larger space than before. A most unexpected surprise follows: Thomas has moved on, some say to India. But his memory is very strong and continues to energize the community even from a distance.

When the community of the Way gathers, Mary shares with them what is going on in Sepphoris with the collecting of wisdom teachings of Jesus. Scribes are putting them in written form. She is pleasantly surprised to learn that the Edessa community has also started work on a collection of wisdom teachings from Jesus given to them by Thomas. They have already decided to name the book the Gospel of Thomas.

The opening lines have already been penned, "These are the secret sayings that the living Jesus spoke and Didymos Judas Thomas recorded. And he said, 'Whoever discovers the interpretation of these sayings will not taste death.'"[2]

Mary replies, "You call these secret sayings? Jesus always taught openly, never trying to hide anything or keep things secret. Those with ears to hear and eyes to see understand. For those unable to hear or see, the meaning remains hidden. Is that what you mean? And sometimes people did not like what they hear which is why Jesus would say sometimes, 'No prophet is welcome on his home turf; doctors don't cure those who know them.'[3] Sometimes later on people would become more ready to hear. I recall Jesus saying, 'Often you have desired to hear these sayings that I am speaking to you, and you have no one else from whom to hear them. There will be days when you will seek me and you will not find me.'[4]

"One other thing you should know. Jesus has his own sense of timing regarding when he is ready to offer certain teachings. He says, 'Seek and you will find. In the past, however, I did not tell you the things about which you asked me then. Now I am willing to tell them, but you are not seeking them.'[5]

"Jesus also says, 'The one who seeks is also the one who reveals.'[6]

"Sometimes Jesus says, 'Those who have something in hand will be given more, and those who have nothing will be deprived of even the little they have,'[7] which often feels unfair. Yet when a person has received some of the teachings, they are ready for more. Those who resist them lose whatever they might have had. Very paradoxical!

"Jesus is always ready to encourage and applaud those who are willing to go within themselves and find. Jesus says, 'Blessed are those who are alone and chosen,[8] for you will find the Way of the Father. For you have come from it, and you will return there again.'"[9]

With these understandings, the community continues recalling the teachings of the living Jesus so that the scribes can write them down. They decide to include all the teachings that Mary remembers. What an exciting Gospel this will be!

NOTES

1. "Most likely the Gospel of Thomas was composed in Greek, probably in Syria, perhaps at Edessa, where Thomas was revered and his bones venerated." *Nag Hammadi Scriptures*, International Edition, HarperSan Francisco, 2007, p. 137. Edessa is the same as present day Urfa in East Turkey. *Anchor Bible*, volume D-G, p. 284.

2. Prologue and first saying in the Gospel of Thomas.

3. Gospel of Thomas 31

4. Gospel of Thomas 38

5. Gospel of Thomas 92

6. Dialogue of the Savior 7:2

7. Gospel of Thomas 41

8. The term "chosen" has been problematic throughout history whenever one tribe or group of people have the idea that their "God" has chosen them and excluded other people: they consider themselves to be superior to everyone else. Out of this kind of thinking comes the very dangerous "God on our side" mentality. However, Jesus uses the term "chosen" in an entirely different way, usually in connection with the broader phrase, "Many are called but few are chosen." Matthew 22:14. Essentially, the call is issued broadly to everyone. Those who have eyes to see and ears to hear, those who are open to receive the message and respond, are chosen. This process is actually one of self-selection

based not on exclusion, but on an openness and readiness to receive. Everyone is invited: will you come?

9. Gospel of Thomas 49

CHAPTER 72:
THE DEATH AND RESURRECTION OF MARY MAGDALENE[1]

WHEN, WHERE AND UNDER WHAT CIRCUMSTANCES DID Mary Magdalene die? How old was she and who was by her side?

One tradition says that she retired to Ephesus with John and Mary the Mother of Jesus.[2] This possibility lends credence to the thesis that she and her experiences of the Resurrected Jesus were major contributors to the book that came to be known as the Gospel According to St. John.

Another very strong tradition is that Mary Magdalene and her companions made their way to the south of France where she proclaimed the Gospel and lived the ministry of teaching and healing, eventually retiring to a cave where she lived in prayer until she died.

On July 5, 1995, I was in the south of France and visited St. Maximum where my daughter, Marie, and I saw what is reputed to be Mary Magdalene's skull with gold veil covering the top and back of the head. As I viewed it I said to myself: "This is the actual skull of Mary Magdalene—or it isn't." I realized that it really did not matter. Either way, this skull held symbolic value for me. I had a fresh appreciation for holy relics. Whether or not they are literally true, they serve the purpose of constellating our own thinking and energies.

Yet another tradition says that she traveled north, crossed the English Channel, and into the land of the Druids, the Tor, and Glastonbury. And later that she retired in Wales.[3]

With so many traditions, both fanciful and plausible, will we ever know for certain where and with whom Mary Magdalene spent her later years?

This one fact we know for certain: Mary Magdalene died as do all human beings. More important than her death is her resurrection which has been occurring in a variety of manifestations for two thousand years thus far. As with Jesus, her resurrection is what is most important. Her resurrection occurs in a wide variety of ways.

Of particular note is the way in which she has carried the archetype of the reformed sinner. Her name has been often used for homes for women who are ready to leave their work performing sexual services for men and find alternative ways of living and surviving economically.

Interestingly, she was never labeled as a prostitute in the thinking of the eastern Orthodox Churches where she is more often known as "the apostle to the apostles."[4]

The way she is revealed in art over the centuries provides amazing insight into her persistent power to evoke deep archetypal interest.[5]

More recently she has been resurrecting as a very strong figure, particularly in the feminist movement. As a person in her own right, she is being seen as intelligent, strong, a leader and teacher of both men and women.

We are experiencing an explosion of interest in Mary Magdalene both in scholarly research and in popular writing, movies, and television specials. She insists on being resurrected right here and now in our midst. Her archetypal energies will have their Way.

St. Mary Magdalene Day[6] on July 22 is celebrated more and more in ever widening circles of people, often with very creative energizing festivals.[7]

As with all archetypes, her energies originate in the eyes and soul of the beholder.

Her resurrection which is occurring these days with tremendous vitality and power has the potential of doing several things:

+ Help restore full humanity to our view of Jesus

+ Reclaim the feminine archetype for the Ultimate Source of Life and Death whom some name as "God" or the Mystery.

+ Assist men in activating their anima more creatively

+ Assist women in discovering more of their own potential.

+ Help us all to discover more of our own True Humanity.

In conclusion, I will say that my dearest hope for you, the reader of this book, is that Mary Magdalene and Jesus her Companion may be resurrected and fully embodied in you! My prayer is that through Jesus and Mary you may discover how to release more of your own amazing potential to be who you really are!

NOTES

1. There are many conflicting legends about the final days of Mary Magdalene; this chapter simply touches on the question.

2. "According to tradition, Mary Magdalene retired to Ephesus with the Virgin Mary and John." Marion J. Hatchett, *Commentary on the American Prayer Book*, Seabury Press, 1980, p. 68

3. Tom Kenyon and Judi Sion, *The Magdalen Manuscript*, p. 12, printed for the Magdalen Retreat in Sedona, Arizona, November 9-12, 2001

4. "In the Eastern Church she is treated as the equal of an apostles, since she was the first to see the risen Lord." Marion J. Hatchett, *Commentary on the American Prayer Book*, Seabury Press, 1980, p. 68

5. Susan Haskins, *Mary Magdalen, Myth and Metaphor*, Harcourt Brace & Company, 1993.

6. "The feast can be traced as far back as the Council of Oxford in 1222 which made it a day of obligation. It was retained with a prayer for the day in the 1549 Prayer Book, deleted in the revi-

sion of 1552, and restored as a black letter day in the revised cal-
endar of 1561. Some recent Prayer Book revisions have restored
it as a red letter day, but the Prayer Book of 1979 is the first
American edition which includes it." Marion J. Hatchett,
Commentary on the American Prayer Book, Seabury Press, 1980,
p. 68.

7. Note in particular the work of Betty Conrad Adam, *The
Magdalene Mystique*, Morehouse Publishing, 2006, and the annual observances by Brigid's Place and the Magdalene Community
of Houston, Texas. www.brigidsplace.org. You may also wish to
consider participating in the the Mary Magdalene Festivals in
Sedona, Arizona. For information, contact Barbara Litrell.
blitrell@aol.com

CHAPTER 73:
EXPERIENCING
THE MYSTERY NOW

DURING THEIR LIVES IN GALILEE, JESUS AND MARY Magdalene embark on spiritual journeys that lead them more and more deeply into the Amazing Pulsating Mystery of Life. With the assistance of John the Baptizer and so many others who serve as catalysts for them, they discover more and more of what Life is really all about, their essential identity, and creative ways to use their energies.

Countless other human beings are drawn to them, listen to their wisdom teachings, interact with them, and discover that they, too, can become chalices of Mystery.

The ability of Jesus and Mary to live freely and without fear empowers others, especially the powerless. Simultaneously the Powers that Be, that run on force and fear, feel threatened and react with violence.

When Jesus is arrested, tortured, and executed, the Roman authorities think they have solved this problem once and for all.

The amazing surprise is that the death of Jesus actually triggers an enormous release of spiritual Energy and power that continues to manifest ever since.

By gathering in his name, recalling his wisdom teachings, sharing stories of their experiences with him, praying, singing, breaking bread, and sharing the Cup, his friends and disciples continue to discover what it is to be really alive. Mary and others find themselves in positions of leadership, teaching others that the Seed of True Humanity is within them.

Jesus and Mary Magdalene have risen from the dead. Their archetypal energies are alive and well, readily available to manifest fully in you, me, and all who are open to becoming chalices of Mystery.

The process through which we can become aware that we are chalices of Mystery is clearly outlined in one succinct verse from the Gospel of Philip: "The Teacher did everything in a Mystery: a baptism, a chrism, a eucharist, a reconciliation, and a bridal chamber."[1] Here is revealed the sequence for entering into awareness of Mystery. The secret is hidden yet open to all who have eyes to see, ears to hear, minds and hearts ready for discovery. The simple challenge is to wake up to what already IS.

"Truth did not come into the world naked, but it came in types and images. The world will not receive truth in any other way. There is a rebirth and an image of rebirth. It is certainly necessary to be born again through the image. Which one? Resurrection. The image must arise again and again through the image. The bridal chamber and the image must enter through the image into the truth: this is the restoration."[2]

The Gospel of Philip provides us with the essence of what has come to be known as the incarnational and sacramental principle: outward and visible signs of inner and spiritual grace. In other words, Energy manifests in Matter. The theory of relativity and the sacramental principle are essentially the same, just a slightly different vocabulary.

More important than the theory, of course, is the experience, the actual awareness of coming to realize that we, like Jesus and Mary Magdalene are chalices, containers of Mystery. We deepen our experience by developing our own spiritual practice and by participating in Sacred Circles with others.

NOTES

1. Gospel of Philip 68
2. Gospel of Philip 67

CHAPTER 74:
CREATING YOUR OWN SPIRITUAL PRACTICE

JESUS AND MARY GO INTO THE HILLS TO PRAY ALONE OR together. Each day we find them praying with others, laying on hands, and anointing with oil. They have a rhythm of praying that is as natural to them as breathing.

"There is within each of us, I believe, a deep and holy hunger for sacred union. Our souls yearn to unite, to live in concert and connection with other souls. Collectively and individually we are crying for the solace of reconnection with Mystery."[1]

To keep one's awareness of Mystery heightened, it is helpful to create and maintain a daily spiritual practice. Core components include Silence, readings from sacred texts, prayer, and psalms or spiritual songs. Meditating when sitting, walking, swimming, or cycling often works well.

Other practices may include written dialogue prayer, journaling, and expression through the arts. Whatever one chooses, the practice needs to be simple and easily remembered. Participation in seminars and an annual retreat in a sacred place can also deepen and enhance one's awareness of living in Mystery.

When will you do your daily spiritual practice? Where? Will you have an altar and symbols? Light a chalice?

When designing or reevaluating your spiritual practice, simply follow the leading of the Spirit within you. Consulting with a reliable spiritual Guide may also be beneficial.

Your daily practice and intuition may reveal how to share your experience in your own natural circles of influence: family, friends, workplace, church, or other spiritual communities. Pay attention to synchronicities with individuals you meet.

By having specific times to pray we gradually discover that we are praying all the time.

NOTES

1. Sue Patton Thoele, *Heart Centered Marriage, Fulfilling Our Natural Desire for Sacred Partnership*, Conari Press, Berkeley, California, 1996, p. 1. Thoele's word is "God" for which I have substituted the word, "Mystery."

CHAPTER 75:
CREATING SACRED CIRCLES

MARY AND JESUS ARE LIVING CHALICES OF MYSTERY BOTH historically and archetypally. They share in a sacred partnership as teachers, catalysts for healing, and guides who initiate people into Mystery. They demonstrate how we, too, can be living Chalices embodying the same Mystery within, between, around, and beyond us.

The heart of their message is crystal clear: "The Seed of true Humanity is within you. Follow it."[1] They urge us to proclaim this central message, to become catalysts of healing, and "to do everything in Mystery: a baptism, a chrism, a eucharist, a reconciliation, and a bridal chamber."[2]

As with Jesus and Mary, so with us: it is through our own direct experience that we are able to know that the Seed of True Humanity does, indeed, live within us. Then we are ready to join them in proclaiming the same good news. So how will you respond to their invitation to experience more fully your own Immersion in Mystery? Perhaps you might consider asking for an Immersion in Mystery ritual? If so, you may choose to seek and find a guide who can facilitate your immersion.

Thich Nhat Hanh reminds us that "We are here to awaken from the illusion of our separateness." We human beings need to be intentional in the way we live in community as members of one living body of humanity.

We can think cosmically and act personally by reaching out to join others in awakening from the illusion. For most of us, a group of caring supportive "spiritual friends" can be crucial to our process. Awareness of our full humanity flourishes best in sacred circles.

Human beings have always come together in sacred circles around a camp fire, an altar, a sacred stone, or some other focal point. Circles may vary in size from just a few to many more, but the dynamics remain the same: there is no beginning and no end to a circle and everyone is equal. The Center is important; without a clear Center and commitment to that Center and one another, circles fall apart.

Sue Patton Thoele states it well when she says, "I have a pet theory about why circles are such nurturing symbols. First, with no beginning and no end, a circle is definitely feminine in character. A circle is whole and holy. But other reasons why it seems so sacred to me is that there is no hierarchy. When facing into the center of a circle, everyone can see everyone else. Eye contact, as well as body contact, is possible. Everyone around the circle is equally important, equally present, equally accessible. Similar to the adage that a chain is only as strong as its weakest link, each member of a circle is equally important in keeping the circle viable and intact.

"Sacred partnership creates circles that embrace a far wider spectrum than we can imagine. In times when we need to 'circle the wagons,' other people can watch out for our backs. If our circle faces outward, every direction is visible to at least one member of the group. Ideally, a circle of family, friends, community, and cosmos will support and protect us whether metaphorically facing in or out. Wrapped in the safety of both small and ever-enlarging circles, we are free to become the unique human beings that our souls long to be.

And as members of various valuable sacred circles, we have the opportunity to bring our unique sparks of divinity to the central fire that then warms us all.

"Balanced circles are composed of complementary opposites represented by dark, receptive feminine yin and light, dynamic masculine yang energies. The sacred circle within ourselves recognizes that yin and yang are not divided along gender lines, and both are essential for keeping the circle intact, and the fire, at its center, lighted.

"In gathering at the sacred circle... the queen, or Feminine/Yin Energy brings her gifts of vision, intuition, connectedness, wisdom, and the understanding of what is good, true, and beautiful within all members of the circle. Her consort, the Masculine/Yang Energy picks up the torch ignited within the sacred circle and takes the light out into the world, where he accomplishes what needs to be done...

"The fires of support and protection burn brightly within the sanctuary of the Sacred Circle. They stand as a lighthouse to guide us safely through the storms of life. It is our calling to complete the sacred circle of support not only by accepting blessings, but also by becoming a blessing. Each of us must feed both ourselves and our beloveds the feminine fruits of kindness, consideration, and reverence.

"When each person within our sacred circle is protected, nurtured, and has his or her emotional needs met, everyone's energy is freed up to care about others in a meaningful, unselfish way. Therefore, a circle of supportive, loving relationships is one of the best ways for gathering up the energy to move out into the world to right the wrongs and balance the imbalances. The energy from such sacred circles shines as a beacon of possibility for others, and spreads an aura of kindness and compassionate caring from which miracles can spawn."[3]

Sacred Circles have several essential components: study, sharing, silence, ritual, and, most importantly, the desire to live creatively in Mystery. Our pattern is manifestly clear in the life and teachings of Jesus and Mary. Their lives and sacred partnership can serve as a paradigm for our own. As a result, it will be natural for us to become intensely aware of injustice and suffering of other human beings and of our Mother the Earth. We will be moved to consider and then take focused, concerted action with others in confronting the powers that be, and working for creative change.

You may already belong to a church, spiritual community, or some other sacred circle. There are many helpful resources available. And you may decide to work with the material in this book and introduce some of the sacred rituals.

If you are a priest, pastor, or leader of a community, you have unique opportunities to use the stories and rituals of this book whenever you feel it is appropriate.

You can work within existing groups or you may feel moved by the Spirit to begin creating a new Sacred Circle by inviting a few people to join with you. In words ascribed to Jesus, we know that, "Wherever two or three are gathered together in my name, I will be there among them."[4]

Joan Norton in her book, *14 Steps to Awaken the Sacred Feminine*, describes how to form Magdalene Circles. She calls our attention to the importance of confidentiality. "It goes without saying that you should make a conscious and stated agreement with each other in the beginning not to tell each other's stories outside the group. It is destructive and will cause your group to dissolve."[5]

The challenge to us is put very succinctly in the title of a song, "What in the world will you do for heaven's sake?" We need to remember that heaven is not a place where we go to when we die, but a place within us that impels us to put our energy into social transformation and healing in this life. Like the early Quakers who sat in Silence and then worked for the abolition of slavery and then the emancipation of women, so we can keep the discipline of our own spiritual practice, participate in Sacred Circles, and work for the transformation of the world.

As one person said after her immersion in the gently flowing waters of Oak Creek, "I am energized, passionate, willing, ready and initiated into my role or roles that I will take on in this new world that is so rapidly unfolding. I feel officially a part of the 'transition team' now!"[6]

NOTES

1. Gospel of Mary 4:5

2. Gospel of Philip 68

3. Sue Patton Thoele, *Heart Centered Marriage, Fulfilling Our Natural Desire for Sacred Partnership*, Conari Press, Berkeley, California, 1996, p. 269-271.

4. Matthew 18:20

5. Joan Norton and Margaret Starbird, *14 Steps to Awaken the Sacred Feminine, Women in the Circle of Mary Magdalene*, Bear & Company, Rochester, Vermont, 2009.

6. Katherine DesJardins, Mary Magdalene Day, July 22, 2009.

CHAPTER 76:
CELEBRATING RITUALS

AUTHENTIC RITUAL IS DESIGNED TO ENHANCE YOUR awareness of Mystery by stimulating your imagination, arousing your senses, releasing your emotions, and awakening the Spirit.

A creative Convenor is needed as a guide and facilitator so that all who are ready and open will enter into Holy Union and become One Body.

Liturgical celebrations are empowered by chanting Odes, singing songs, praying spontaneously, and releasing other outpourings of the Spirit.

How long should a Celebration take? Good liturgy is like making love: allow yourselves to take whatever time you need. Let clock time fade into Eternal time. Let go of fear and release the Energy of the Spirit freely. Know and be known completely.

When we allow ritual to do its work, we are energized to practice mindfulness, live wisdom and compassion, relate freely and openly with all we meet, become catalysts for healing, work for justice and peace, and do our part in confronting the Powers that Be. Live creatively in the rhythm of movement and rest.

Our models are Jesus, Mary Magdalene, and their sacred Partnership.

As you gather others to join you in celebrating these rituals, may they serve as a doorway inviting you into deeper awareness of Amazing Mystery, Pulsating Energy of the Universe in whom we live and move and have our being who is our Mother, Father, Teacher, and Lover, the TAO of Ten Thousand Names.

CHAPTER 77:
CHALICES OF MYSTERY RITUAL

The people assemble at an agreed time in a quiet place in nature, a warm and friendly home, a church, or some other sacred space. A creative Convenor is responsible for guiding the people through the sacred ritual and enabling free, open, and natural participation by all who are present.

As the people gather, they will normally form a circle around a table, preferably one that is octagonal or round in shape. When there is a larger number of people, a series of concentric circles may form in a natural way around the table which serves as an altar.

On the altar is placed a chalice of water containing an oil lamp or floating candle in the center.

This ritual is a celebration of the Life and Wisdom Teachings of Jesus and Mary Magdalene. It reclaims the first century ritual of passing bread and three cups: first a cup of water, then a cup of milk and honey, and then a cup of wine.[1]

Smaller group of participants may use the same chalice for each of the elements. Larger groups may find it works best to have one chalice for water, a second for milk and honey, and a third for wine.

Participants in sacred rituals may experience greater empowerment by chanting Odes, singing songs, praying spontaneously, and releasing other outpourings of the Spirit.

A Convenor welcomes everyone to the celebration and states clearly the purpose of this ritual:

WELCOME

The Chalices of Mystery ritual is designed to enhance your awareness of Mystery by stimulating your imagination, arousing your senses, releasing your emotions, and awakening the Spirit. You are invited to celebrate this ritual with the intention of becoming One Body and experiencing Holy Union.

We begin by Lighting the Chalice, symbol of ourselves as open Chalices ready to be filled and ignited by the Fire of Mystery.

LIGHTING OF THE CHALICE

Jesus says, "When you are near me, you are near the fire."[2]

An opening tone is sounded on a Tibetan bowl, Japanese bowl, or similar instrument, creating a sound conducive to centering.

READINGS FROM SACRED SCRIPTURES

One or more passages from sacred writings and a selection from one of the Gospels are read. A chapter from this book might be appropriate to read and then invite reflections. Dialogue, song, dance, instrumental music, other art forms, and silence may be included.

VISUALIZING AND PRAYING

In silence and aloud, focused attention is given to Mother Earth, the people of the earth, contemporary events around the planet, personal concerns, and individual needs. When desired, there may be praying with laying on of hands. A vessel of oil may be available for anointing for healing and for releasing the Holy Spirit.

As the people remain seated, the Convenor or someone else may say the following with appropriate pauses for silence:

I invite you to close your eyes and join me in doing some visualizing and praying.

In your mind's eye, visualize Mother Earth:

What do you see?
What do you hear her saying?
In silence or aloud, what is your prayer for her?

In your mind's eye, visualize scenes of the people of the Earth:
Who do you see?
What do you hear them saying?
In silence or aloud, what is your prayer for them?

In your mind's eye, visualize people whom you know:
Who do you see?
What do you hear them saying?
In silence or aloud, what is your prayer for them?
In your mind's eye, look into yourself:
What do you see?
What do you hear yourself saying?
In silence or aloud,
what is your prayer for yourself?
The Convenor then asks
Would anyone like us to pray with you?
When someone responds, the Convenor may ask,
What do you want? How would you like us to pray for you?
Do you desire laying on of hands or anointing with oil?
People join in praying for one another.

PREPARING THE TABLE

Bread, a Chalice, and cruets of water, milk and honey, and wine are brought to the altar.

MAKING EUCHARIST

The Eucharistic Prayer may be offered by one person or by two people, preferably a man and a woman praying alternating paragraphs, or between men and women alternating:
Amazing Mystery, Pulsating Energy of the Universe!
You are Darkness and Light, You are Fullness and Emptiness,
You are Known and Unknown, You are Silence and Voice,
You are the Name of the Sound and the Sound of the Name.

You are the Mother and the Womb that gives shape to all.
You hide yourself in everyone and reveal yourself within them.
You move in every creature. You give life and take it away.
You shatter and You bring together.
You are union and dissolution.
You are the Holy Mystery, hidden and revealed,
And we praise you as long as we have breath.[3]
Jesus!
You are born of Mary and your Mother the Earth,
You are baptized by John and come out of the water laughing,
You are driven into the wilderness by the Spirit
and questioned by the Instructor
You return home to begin your Spirit filled ministry.
You invite us to join you by saying, "Come follow me."

Mary Magdalene!
You are baptized, Immersed in Mystery.
You know how to enter the very depths of your soul.
You know the healing power of inner transformation.
You are the woman who understands.

Jesus and Mary!
You are Companions on the *Way of Mystery*
You know each other completely and love each other devotedly
You kiss each other often, drink deeply from each other,
become each other, and hidden things are revealed to you!
You share in Sacred Partnership for Life and Work
You are Chalices on fire with Holy Mystery.

Jesus, you are true to the Spirit within you
You have the courage to engage and confront the Powers that Be
You are arrested, tried, tortured, and crucified,
You die and return to your Mother the Earth,
who lives in all who allow the same Spirit to breathe through
them.

Mary, you are with Jesus during his passion and death.
You are the first one to experience Jesus still living within you
and others who are becoming his Resurrected Body.

You are empowered by the Spirit to proclaim the Gospel
"The Seed of true humanity is within you, Follow it!"[4]
You encourage the other disciples when they are afraid.
You continue living in Sacred Partnerships.

The Convenor offers each line below as a call and the people repeat as
an echo:
Amazing Mystery!
Pulsating Energy of the Universe!
In You we live and move and have our being!
You are our Mother, Father, Teacher, and Lover!
You are the TAO of Ten Thousand Names!
We offer and present unto You, ourselves, our souls and bodies,
to be a reasonable, holy, and living sacrifice to You.
We offer as much as we know of ourselves
to as much as we know of You.
Break the bonds that constrain us and set us free!
Take our minds, passions, emotions, and wills!
Make us Your Living Chalices!
Empty us and rinse us out!
Fill us with all that You Are!
Energize and empower us!
Enlighten us and set us on fire!

One person takes bread in hand and gives voice to Mystery saying,
I AM the Bread of Life![5]
Take, eat, and become my Body.[6]
In Silence, Bread is passed around the circle
for each person to take and break off a piece.
One person gives voice to Mystery saying,
Drink from my Mouth and become like me;
I myself shall become you,
and the hidden things will be revealed to you."[7]

One person fills the Chalice with fresh water and gives voice to Mystery saying:
I AM the Living Water welling up from within you.[8]
Drink deeply and be refreshed.[9]

In Silence, the Chalice is passed around the Circle until it is empty.

One person fills the Chalice with milk and honey and gives voice to Mystery saying:
I AM Your True Mother.[10]
Drink from me Wisdom and Compassion.[11]

In Silence, the Chalice is passed around the circle until it is empty.

One person fills the Chalice with wine and gives voice to Mystery saying:
I AM The Vine and You are the Branches[12]
Drink and become the Fruit of the Vine.
In Silence, the Chalice is passed around the circle until it is empty.

The Convenor gives voice to Mystery and says:
Jesus looks at his friends and says, "This is my Body."[13]

THE PEACE
People in the Circle turn to each other, embrace, and share the Peace.

CLOSING MEDITATION
The Convenor leads a Call and Response:
We are Living Chalices of Holy Fire:
Live in Sacred Partnership with Jesus,
Mary Magdalene, and one another...
Practice Mindfulness...
Live Wisdom and Compassion...
Relate freely and openly with all you meet....
Become catalysts for healing...
Go in Peace and Justice...
Confront the Powers that be...

Know the *Way of the Mystery...*
Live In movement and rest...
AMEN!

EXTINGUISH THE CHALICE

NOTES

1. The practice of sharing bread and three cups was common in the first and second centuries as recorded in the Apostolic Tradition of Hippolytus, ca. 217 C.E.

2. Gospel of Thomas 82

3. The first two paragraphs of this Eucharistic Prayer are from Thunder, one of the energizing mystical documents found in the Nag Hammadi Scriptures. The rest of the Prayer is woven together from texts in the Gospels of Mark, Luke, Mary, and Philip.

4. Gospel of Mary 4:5

5. John 6:35

6. Matthew 26:26

7. Gospel of Thomas 108

8. John 4:10, 14

9. Odes of Solomon 30

10. Gospel of Thomas 101

11. Odes of Solomon 19

12. John 15:5

13. Luke 22:19

CHAPTER 78:
A FOOTWASHING RITUAL

FOOTWASHING RITUALS ORIGINATE IN THE STORY OF Jesus having an evening meal with his friends and after supper washing their feet and saying, "I have washed your feet. You ought to wash one another's feet." The story is in the Gospel of John chapter 13.

Following his example, we can gather in a warm and friendly home, a quiet place in nature, a church, or some other sacred space to share meals, and wash one another's feet.

The custom in the time of Jesus was for visitors to have their feet washed when they entered the home as a sign of welcome and hospitality. The meal would occur later.

But in John's account, Jesus washes the feet of his friends after the meal. So when doing the ritual, will you choose to do the washing before or after the meal?

In making the choice, you will be considering some practical considerations like keeping the food hot before it is served. Food may be provided by the host or participants can bring food to share. Serving buffet or family style allows free choices by everyone.

Leonardo da Vinci's painting of the Last Supper shows Jesus and his friends seated on one side of a table. But it is much more likely that they would have been seated on the floor with pillows or on couches arranged against the sides of the room as is often the custom in Middle East homes today.

Wherever people gather for sharing meals and footwashing, the seating should be as much as possible in the shape of a Sacred Circle. You will need a table that can serve as an altar. On the table rests a chalice filled with water and a floating oil lamp or candle symbolizing the union of opposites: fire and water, yin and yang, masculine and feminine living in harmony.

At a convenient place you will need one or more basins or foot tubs, pitchers for water, bars of soap or liquid soap, olive oil or massage oil, and a sufficient supply of towels.

Either before or after the meal, a creative Convenor is responsible for guiding the people through the ritual of Footwashing and enabling free, open, and natural participation by all who are present. The ritual begins with the Convenor welcoming everyone and giving thanks for the food and the evening. Someone is asked to light the chalice.

LIGHTING OF THE CHALICE AND MEDITATION

Jesus says, "Whoever is near me is near the fire."

An opening tone is sounded on a Tibetan bowl, Japanese bowl, or similar instrument, creating a sound conducive to centering. Then follows a period of meditation which concludes with a wakeup bell.

READING OF SACRED SCRIPTURE

After the meditation, the Convenor provides an introduction like this:

Mary Magdalene and Jesus are companions who are empowered to live a loving and compassionate life. They are in a Sacred Partnership for work and ministry of teaching, healing, baptizing, and forming sacred circles of disciples. They live freely, no matter what the cost, even when it brings them into conflict with the Powers that Be.

On more than one occasion, Mary Magdalene and other women take the initiative to anoint Jesus. Having first received loving atten-

326 | *John Beverley Butcher*

tion from them, Jesus becomes free to wash his disciples' feet. Listen now to the story as found in the Gospel of John.

The Convenor or someone appointed reads or tells the story:

Before the Passover celebration Jesus knew that the time had come for him to leave the world and return to the Father. He had loved his own in the world and would love them to the end. Now that the devil had planted it in the mind of Judas, Simon Iscariot's son, to turn him in, at supper Jesus could tell that the Father had left everything up to him and that he had come from God and was going back to God.

So he got up from the meal, took off his clothing, put it aside, and wrapped a towel around himself. Then he put water in a basin and began to wash the disciples' feet and to wipe them off with the towel around his waist.

He comes to Simon Peter. Peter says to him, "Master, you're going to wash my feet?" Jesus replied, "Right now you don't understand what I'm doing, but later you will."

"You'll never, ever wash my feet," Peter says. Jesus answered him, "Unless I wash you, you won't have anything in common with me." "In that case, Master, "wash not only my feet but my hands and my head too."

Jesus says, "People who have bathed need only to wash their feet; nevertheless, they're clean all over. And you are clean - but not quite all of you." (He knew, of course, who was going to turn him in; that's why he said, "You're not all clean.")

When he had washed their feet, he put his clothes back on and sat down at the table again, "Do you realize what I've done?" he asked. "You call me Teacher and Master, and you're right: that's who I am. So if I am your master and teacher and have washed your feet, you ought to wash each other's feet. In other words, I've set you an example: you're to do as I have done to you... I am giving you a new directive: Love each other. Just as I have loved you, you are to love each other." (John 13:1-15, 34, Scholars Version)

CONVERSATION ON THE MEANING OF THE STORIES

The Convenor or another member of the Circle leads a conversation on the meaning of the reading by asking open ended questions such as these:

Jesus removes his clothing and is wearing only his loin cloth, like a household slave.

+ How might Jesus be feeling as he assumes the role of a slave?

+ How might the disciples be feeling when Jesus assumes the role of a slave?

+ How might Peter be feeling when he says, "You'll never, ever wash my feet,"

+ What might Jesus want Peter to understand when he says, "Unless I wash you, you won't have anything in common with me" ?

+ What is needed for someone to be willing to wash another person's feet?

+ What does it take for someone to allow another to wash and anoint them?

INVITATION FOR THE RITUAL OF FOOTWASHING

The Convenor provides instructions like these for the footwashing and anointing:

Out of this experience, Jesus says to his disciples and to us, "Wash each other's feet... Love others as I have loved you."

Following their example, we are now invited to wash and anoint one another's feet. When you are ready, pick up a towel and place it around your neck or wrap it around your waist. Pick up a pitcher and fill it with warm water. Then return to pick up a basin, liquid soap, and massage oil.

Allow the Spirit within you to guide you to stand before someone in the Sacred Circle and ask, "May I wash your feet?"

When the person agrees, set the bowl and pitcher down. Then kneel and remove that person's shoes and socks. Wash the feet with care and compassion. After drying the feet with the towel, use the oil to massage the feet with care.

Meditate and pray in silence as you massage the feet. Allow your intuition to tell you which part of the foot needs special attention as it may correspond to other places in the body needing healing. Continue the anointing as long as you feel it is needed.

When the washing and anointings are completed, please take the basin to the sink to empty and rinse it out. Then return the basin to the place where you picked it up, along with the containers of liquid soap and oil. Return to your place in the Circle.

Please keep your own shoes and socks on until they are removed by someone else. This way we will know whose feet still need attention. The rule is simple: each one wash one. It works best if you wash the feet of someone other than the one who washed yours.

The ritual continues until all feet are clean and anointed with the oil of the Holy Spirit. As the Gospel of Philip says, "The fire is the chrism and the light is the fire. There is fire in chrism" (Gospel of Philip 66).

Are there any questions before we begin?

When all are ready, the Convenor says: "Let us now wash and anoint one another's feet with love and compassion. We will do this ritual in Silence." (*Or there may be singing of simple chants and songs.*)

REFLECTIONS AFTER THE FOOTWASHING

After the footwashing, the Convenor may invite people to share their feelings of this experience by asking questions like these:

+   What were your feelings as you washed another's person's feet?

+   What were your feelings as your feet were being washed?

+   How might this experience affect the way we live our lives?

After the sharing, the Convenor invites everyone to stand in a Circle, embrace one another, and say: "This is my Body."

The ritual either concludes with the extinguishing of the Chalice or continues with the Eucharistic Prayer and Communion in the Chalices of Mystery Ritual.

CHAPTER 79:
INTRODUCTION TO
IMMERSION IN MYSTERY RITUAL

IN THE STORY OF THE BAPTISM OF JESUS AND HIS VISION
Quest in the Wilderness we have the essence of his experience of
Enlightenment, his awareness of who he is in the whole scheme of
things. During his Baptism and Anointing in the Spirit, Jesus wakes
up to the Mystery of Life.

His Baptism and Anointing serve as the archetype for our own
journey into knowing who we really are and our own awareness of
the Mystery in whom we live and move and have our being.

How did Jesus and Mary Magdalene prepare people for their baptisms? The sequence of initiation into Holy Mystery that Jesus and
Mary use is quite clear: they "did everything in a Mystery: a baptism,
a chrism, a eucharist, a reconciliation, and a bridal chamber."[1]

However, we have no written record describing the process itself.
It is highly unlikely that such records ever existed in the first place.
Yet it is safe to assume that Jesus and Mary have a sensitivity to the
spiritual needs of each person. They would have known when specific teachings had been received and experienced by the Seeker.
Through the guidance of the Spirit, they would know intuitively
when to move with the Seeker into the next part of the initiation
process.

Our own enlightenment may begin occurring before, during, or after our baptism and anointing. Even though our baptism and our enlightenment may not occur simultaneously, yet the ritual of Immersion in Mystery has the potential for assisting us in deepening our awareness.

Careful preparation for Immersion with a reliable spiritual guide whom we trust is essential, focusing especially on the Eternal Questions. This may take a substantial period of time. The norm in the early church was three years of preparation. The Immersion in Mystery Ritual needs to occur when the Seeker and Guide together agree that the appropriate time has arrived.

The word "baptism" is from a Greek word meaning "to dip" or "to immerse." Being fully immersed in water allows the Seeker to experience more fully that he or she is, indeed, immersed in this Amazing Mystery we call Life. Immersions occur most naturally in an ocean, a creek, a river, a lake, hot springs, or a pool where a person can be completely immersed in water.

The Seeker and the Guide enter the water together, standing about waist high.

It will help if the Seeker will cross his or her arms over the chest. The Baptizer puts his or her left arm around the Seeker's back and places the right hand on the Seeker's crossed arms, thus holding the person securely front and back. During the immersion, the Seeker needs to bend the knees as the Baptizer dips the upper part of the body and head beneath the waters. In an ocean, the Seeker may face the shore while the Baptizer waits for the best wave for dipping the person. Thus the Ocean herself does the actual baptizing.

The Baptizer does not say, "I baptize you..." but rather, "You are immersed in Mystery: Mother, Father, Teacher, and Lover." The purpose is to wake up the person to awareness of already being immersed in Amazing Mystery, the pulsating Energy of the Universe who is within, between, around, and beyond us.

When they are ready, the Baptizer and the newly baptized emerge out of the water and walk ashore for anointing the body with Chrism. The anointing with oil serves as an outer sign of the anointing of the Spirit within. Its roots go back to the ceremonies of the anointing with oil of kings by the prophet or priest who invokes the release of the wisdom and power of the Spirit from within.

Anointing with oil is an essential part of Baptism used for empowering the person with the Holy Spirit and for activating the five senses and the seven energy centers known as chakras.

Anointing of the five senses includes eyes (closed), ears (lobes), nostrils, lips, hands, and feet.

Anointing of the chakras normally begins with the root chakra at the base of the spine, then moves to the second chakra at the pelvis, the third at the navel, and then the heart chakra. Next comes the throat chakra also known as the Third Ear at the base of the neck, the Third Eye in the center of the forehead, and then the crown chakra at the top of the head.

The purpose is to raise energy from the root chakra through the body and out the top of the head into space and the higher consciousness of the eighth chakra above the head and the ninth chakra which is in the farthest reaches of outer space.[2]

Being fully alive, one is empowered for living and loving freely and without fear especially in violent times when Empires reign and people are oppressed. Empowerment comes when the Truth sets you free.

After the anointing, the Baptizer places a towel around the neck of the newly baptized saying, "You are empowered for your ministries."

By being clothed in one's True Humanity and empowered by the Spirit, one is ready to serve others in energized work and ministries.

The incarnational and sacramental principle applies throughout the ritual, all in accordance with the central teaching of Jesus,

> "When you make the two into one,
> and when you make the inner like the outer,
> and the outer like the inner,
> and the upper like the lower,
> and when you make male and female into a single one,
> so that male will not be male nor female be female...
> then you will enter the Kindom of Father and Mother,
> the *Way of Mystery.*"[2]

The purpose is to actually put on your new Humanity: your entire body and total being need to be transformed so that, as Jesus says, you will

> "make eyes in place of an eye,
> a hand in place of a hand,
> a foot in place of a foot,
> an image in place of an image."[3]

For people who are more introverted, the transformation normally begins from within and radiates out. For people who are more extraverted, the transformation will often begin from outside and go inward to the core of one's being. When a person is living in the rhythm of Mystery, the process of transformational Energy will pulsate inwardly and outwardly, like breathing. Which is more important: inhaling or exhaling? Both are necessary.

Actually the process is so profoundly simple that when one enters into that place of truly Knowing, one might ask, "Why was it so hard to discover what is now so obvious?"

How do you know when you have touched that place of truly Knowing? Perhaps when you no longer have to ask the question.

Hear Jesus one more time, "When they ask you 'What is the evidence of the Father within you?' say to them, "It is movement and rest."[4]

The Gospel of Philip explains "Through the Holy Spirit we are indeed begotten again, but we are begotten through Christ in the two. We are anointed through the Spirit. None can see himself either in water or in a mirror without light. Nor again can you see in light without water or mirror. For this reason it is fitting to baptize in the two, in the light and the water. Now the light is the chrism."[5]

The Immersion in Mystery ritual serves as a mirror in which we can begin to see our true reflection. Or as one of the songs from the first century says,

Look, the Lord is our mirror,
Open your eyes and see your eyes in him.
Learn the way of your face,
and praise the Spirit of the Lord.
Wipe the make-up from your face

and love the Holiness of the Lord.

Dress yourself in the Lord,

Reveal your true humanity.[6]

The Immersion in Mystery ritual symbolizes our rebirth into Life. Like a mirror it reflects back to us who we really are. We are both dying and then rising to new Life. As the Gospel of Philip says so clearly, "Those who say they will die first and then rise are in error. If they do not first receive the resurrection while they live, when they die they will receive nothing."[7]

NOTES

1. Gospel of Philip 68

2. See the Discourse on the Eighth and Ninth in the Nag Hammadi Scriptures, Marvin Meyer, ed., HarperOne, 2007, p. 409

2. Gospel of Thomas 22:4-5, 7

3. Gospel of Thomas 22:6

4. Gospel of Thomas 50

5. Gospel of Philip 75

6. Odes 43 from the Odes of Solomon, the church's oldest song book, compiled by the end of the first century.

7. Gospel of Philip 90

CHAPTER 80:
IMMERSION IN MYSTERY RITUAL

THE PEOPLE GATHER ON AN OCEAN BEACH OR ON THE shores of a river, a creek, a lake, hot springs, or a pool where a person can be completely immersed in living water.

The celebration begins with everyone standing for a Call and Response:
Amazing Mystery!
Pulsating Energy of the Universe!
In You we live and move and have our being!
You are our Mother, Father, Teacher, and Lover!
You are the TAO of Ten Thousand Names!

The people are seated in a circle for the following readings or other selections from the Tao Te Ching and the Complete Gospels. After each reading, a meditation bowl may be invited to sound followed by a period of silent meditation and then a wake-up bell.
From the Tao Te Ching:

The Tao that can be spoken of is not the eternal TAO.
The name that can be named is not the eternal name.
The nameless is the beginning of heaven and earth.
The named is the Mother of the ten thousand things.

Send your desires away and you will see the Mystery.
Be filled with desire and you will see only the manifestation.
As these two come forth they differ in name.
Yet at their source they are the same.
This source is called Mystery.
Darkness within darkness,
the gateway to all Mystery.

From the Gospel of John:
In the beginning was the TAO...
Everything comes into being from TAO...
And the TAO becomes flesh within us...

Tone—Silence—Bell

Jesus Teaching about Seeking:
Jesus says, "Those who seek should not stop seeking until they find. When they find, they will be disturbed. When they are disturbed, they will marvel and will rule over all, and they will rest."

Jesus says, "If those who lead you say to you, 'See, the *Way of Mystery* is in the sky,' then the birds of the sky will precede you. If they say to you, 'It is in the sea', then the fish will precede you. Rather the *Way of Mystery* is inside of you, and it is outside of you. When you come to know yourselves, then you will become known and you will realize that it is you who are the offspring of the living Father. But if you will not know yourselves, you dwell in poverty and it is you who are that poverty."

Tone—Silence—Bell

Jesus' disciples said to him, "When will you appear to us, and when will we see you?"

Jesus said, "When you strip without being ashamed, and you take your clothes and put them under your feet like little children and trample them, then you will see the offspring of the living one and you will not be afraid."

336 | *John Beverley Butcher*

Tone—Silence—Bell

Jesus, the Teacher, did everything in a Mystery: a baptism, a chrism, a reconciliation, and a bridal chamber (Gospel of Philip 68).

ETERNAL QUESTIONS
The Seeker is asked each Question with enough time allowed for the depths of the soul to be revealed.

+ Where have you come from?Gospel of Thomas 50

+ Who are you?Gospel of Thomas 61

+ What do you want?Gospel of Matthew 20:21

+ What is the evidence of Mystery in you?Gospel of Thomas 50

+ Why do you want to be immersed in Mystery?

+ Who is Jesus for you?Gospel of Thomas 13, 61

IMMERSION IN MYSTERY
The Seeker enters the Water with a Baptizer. During the immersion the Baptizer says,

N., You are Immersed in Mystery: Mother, Father, Teacher, and Lover.

CHRISM: ANOINTING WITH THE HOLY SPIRIT
After emerging from the water, the newly immersed person is anointed with the oil of Chrism. Anointing may include the senses: eyes (closed), ears (lobes), nostrils, lips, hands, and feet. Anointing of the seven energy centers known as chakras may also be included, especially the Heart chakra, the throat chakra, known as the Third Ear, located at the base of the neck, the Third Eye in the center of the forehead, and the Crown chakra at the top of the head.

Salt may be placed on the tongue, with the words,
"You are the salt of the earth."

When the anointing is completed, the Baptizer says,
"Stand up on your feet in your True Humanity!"

The Baptizer places a towel around the neck of the newly immersed person and says,

"You are empowered for your work and ministries!"

THE PEACE

All share the Peace. Participants are invited to greet one another with a hug, handshake, or kiss, whatever is appropriate to the relationship.

Normally a Celebration of the Chalices of Mystery Ritual will follow.

CHAPTER 81:
TAKE INTO YOUR HANDS

IN YOUR HANDS YOU HAVE MY BEST EFFORT IN RESTORING
Mary Magdalene to her rightful place alongside Jesus in the Gospel
record by drawing on long hidden Sacred Scriptures now available
to us. I have invited you to focus on what we know of Jesus and
Mary's experience of Mystery individually and in their Sacred
Partnership. I have suggested that you participate in a Sacred Circle
and I have offered you several Sacred Rituals to help energize you for
creative living. Experiencing the mystical empowers the practical.

Now I hear Jesus and Mary giving Voice to Mystery who says to
us:

Take into your hands
this yeasty Bread I give to you.
Slip me now into your mouth:
Taste and savor without fear!
Take me down Into your Self
Let me find my home in you.
Come to Know that I am You
You are me and we are One.
Now take into your hands each cup

and drink the loving liquids they contain!
Let them flow into you fully,
fill your heart, your mind, your soul, and body.
Drink until you feel and know
that what I say to you is very Real:
I am the Living Water of your Life,
I am the sweetest milk you've ever tasted.
I am the Wine of Joy inside your Soul,
I am your vital Energy.

When you take into your Self
this sacred food and holy drink,
Allow my warm, exciting fire to flare
inside your tingling Body.
I am yours and You are mine.
Let nothing come between us now.
There is no separation, no division,
there is no conflict anymore.
Doubt and fear have flown away
anxious hesitation yields to freedom.
No need to clothe yourself
in those things anymore.
I am yours and you are mine.
I stand before you naked, unashamed.
Manifest our Oneness
Live Eternal Mystery!

ENERGIZING RESOURCES
WWW.SACREDPARTNERSHIP.NET

SACRED TEXTS

The Complete Gospels, Robert J. Miller, editor, Polebridge Press, Santa Rosa, CA 1994

The Nag Hammadi Scriptures, Marvin Meyer, editor, HarperOne, New York, 2007.

Tao Te Ching, Lao Tsu, a new translation by Gail-Fu Feng and Jane English, Vintage Books, 1972.

The Gnostic Bible, Willis Barnstone and Marvin Meyer, Shambala, 3003.

DAILY SPIRITUAL PRACTICE

The Tao of Jesus (New Revised Edition), John Beverley Butcher, Apocryphile Press, Berkeley, California, 2006.

Sounds of the Eternal, Morning and Night Prayer, J. Philip Newell, William B. Eerdmans, 2002.

Celtic Benediction, Morning and Night Prayer, J. Philip Newell, William B. Eerdmans, 2000.

An Uncommon Lectionary, John Beverley Butcher, Polebridge Press, Santa Rosa, California, 2002.

Anatomy of the Spirit, The Seven Stages of Power and Healing, Caroline Myss, Three Rivers Press, 1996.

Talking to God, Portrait of a World at Prayer, John Gattuso, editor, Stone Creek Publications, Milford, New Jersey, 2006.

ICONS

Reproductions of the icons of Jesus and Mary Magdalene by Lewis Williams are available in many formats from: www.trinity-stores.com

For giclee on stretched canvas: www.Sacredpartnership.net

CREATING SACRED CIRCLES

The Magdalene Mystique, Living the Spirituality of Mary Today, Betty Conrad Adam, Morehouse Publishing, Harrisburg, PA, 2006.

14 Steps to Awakening the Sacred Feminine, Women in the Circle of Mary Magdalene, Joan Norton and Margaret Starbird, Bear and Company, 2009.

www.MaryMagdaleneWithin.com

SONGS AND CHANTS

50 songs and Chants in the back of *The Tao of Jesus,* (New Revised Edition), John Beverley Butcher, Apocryphile Press, Berkeley, California, 2006.

Inclusive Hymns for Liberating Christians, Jann Aldredge-Clanton with Composer Larry E. Schultz, Eakin Press, Austin, TX. www.eakinpress.com

CD from Inclusive Hymns for Liberating Christians, CD: www.jannaldredgeclanton.com.

Thunder Perfect Mind, CD by Julia Haines. www.juliahaines .com

JESUS AND THE GOSPELS

The Five Gospels, Robert Funk, Roy W. Hoover, and the Jesus Seminar, A Polebridge Press Book, Macmillan Publishing, New York, 1993.

Jesus and Empire, Richard A. Horsley, Augsburg Fortress Press, 2003.

Son of Man, The Mystical Path to Christ, Andrew Harvey, Jeremy P. Tarcher/Putnam, New York, 1998.

Telling the Untold Stories, Encounters with the Resurrected Jesus, John Beverley Butcher, Trinity Press International, 2001.

The Tao Te Ching, a new translation with Commentary, Ellen M. Chen, Paragon House, 1989.

MARY MAGDALENE STUDIES

The Gospels of Mary, The Secret Tradition of Mary Magdalene the Companion of Jesus, Marvin Meyer, HarperSan Francisco, 2004. Note: here in one convenient volume are all the texts relating to Mary Magdalene.

The Gospel of Mary of Magdala, Karen L. King, Polebridge Press, 2003.

Woman With the Alabaster Jar, Margaret Starbird. Margaret Starbird website: www.MargaretStarbird.net

Mary Magdalene, Bride in Exile, Margaret Starbird, Bear & Company, Rochester, Vermont, 2005.

The Goddess in the Gospels, Reclaiming the Sacred Feminine, Margaret Starbird, Bear & Company, Rochester, Vermont, 2005.

Magdalene's Lost Legacy, Symbolic Numbers and the Sacred Union in Christianity, Margaret Starbird, Bear & Company, Rochester, Vermont, 2003.

Mary Magdalen, Myth and Metaphor, Susan Haskins, Harcourt Brace, San Diego,1993. Note: This book has many paintings of Mary Magdalene.

The Resurrection of Mary Magdalene, Legends, Apocrypha, and the Christian New Testament, Jane Schaberg, Continuum, New York, 2004.

Mary Magdalene, The First Apostle, The Struggle for Authority, Harvard University Press, Cambridge, MA, 2003.

Mary Magdalene, A Biography, Bruce Chilton, Random House, New York, 2005.

PARTNERSHIP STUDIES

The Center for Partnership Studies, www.partnershipway.org

The Chalice and the Blade, Our History, Our Future, Riane Eisler, Harper & Row, San Francisco, 1987.

The Power of Partnership, Seven Relationships that will Change Your Life, Riane Eisler, 2002

Sacred Pleasure, Sex, Myth, and the Politics of the Body, Riane Eisler, San Francisco: Harper, 1996.

The Real Wealth of Nations, Creating a Caring Economics, Riane Eisler, Berrett-Koehler Publishers, San Francisco, 2007

Tomorrow's Children, A Blueprint for Partnership Education in the 21st Century, Riane Eisler, 2000.

Life-Enriching Education, Nonviolent Communication Helps Schools Improve Performance, Reduce Conflict, and Enhance Relationships, Marshall B. Rosenberg, Puddle Dancer Press, Encinitas, CA, 2003.

Heart Centered Marriage, Fulfilling Our Natural desire For Sacred Partnership, Sue Patton Thoele, Conari Press, Berkeley, California, 1996.

DATABASE FOR JESUS AND MARY MAGDALENE

Until recently, most people have been under the impression that the basic information on the life and teachings of Jesus and Mary Magdalene would be found in the Gospels of the conventional New Testament.

With the discovery of the Nag Hammadi Library and other early documents our data base is expanded:

Gospels in Chronological Order
Gospel of Thomas, first edition, ca. 50
Q Gospel, ca. 50
Gospel of Peter, ca. 50-100
Dialogue of the Savior, ca. 50-100
Gospel of Philip, ca. 70
Gospel of Mark, first edition, ca. 70
Gospel of Matthew, ca. 80
Gospel of Luke, ca. 90
Gospel of John, ca. 90
Gospel of Mary, ca. 90

Other Writings in *The Nag Hammadi Scriptures* where Mary Magdalene is named:
Sophia of Jesus Christ, ca. 90
First Apocalypse of James, second century

Translation of texts woven into Sacred Partnership are normally drawn from *The Complete Gospels*, Annotated Scholars Version, Robert J. Miller, editor, Polebridge Press, Santa Rosa, CA 1992 and 1994.

Acknowledgments

AS A BOY, I WAS FASCINATED BY PLAYING WITH A magnifying glass that allowed me to focus the rays of the sun and set fire to paper or burn my name into a piece of wood. Ever since then I have been filled with an intense desire to unscrew the Inscrutable and experience the Mystery who drives me in the research that results in this book.

During my undergraduate days at Harvard I majored in philosophy beginning with the Greeks on through history into the existentialists who thrust me into a study of psychology, especially the work of Carl Gustav Jung, Emma Jung, and Toni Wolf.

Berkeley Divinity School at Yale gave me a grounding in Sacred Scripture, theology, liturgy, and pastoral care. Edward Rochie Hardy taught me to go to original sources. Elmer Cook laid out a variety of interpretations from competent New Testament scholars and concluded with, "You pays your money and you takes your choice." Lansing Hicks conveyed to me his deep reverence for the Holy Name and a love of the Sacred Scriptures informed by responsible critical scholarship. He challenged me to "Read, read, read," and I have been reading ever since.

Since 1989 I have been engaged with the scholars of the Jesus Seminar and Westar Institute especially Elaine Pagels, Karen King, James M. Robinson, Marvin Meyer, Robert J. Miller, Marcus Borg, John Dominic Crossan, Barbara Thiering, Stephen Patterson, and John Shelby Spong. I identify with Jesus Seminar founder Robert Funk when he says, "I write to find out what I think."

Additional scholars and writers whose work has had a profound affect on my own include Willis Barnstone, Richard A.Horsley, Robert Eisenman, Riane Eisler, Andrew Harvey, Susan Haskins, Margaret Starbird, Jane Schaberg, liturgical scholars Thomas Cranmer, Dom Gregory Dix, and Starhawk.

My continuing philosophical work is grounded in Lao Tsu, Alan Watts, Barry Wood, Wee Chong Tan, and Matthew Fox.

My psychological work is deepened by the Guild for Psychological Studies and seminars led by Elizabeth Boyden Howes, Sadie Gregory, Luella Sibbald, Joan Gibbons, John Petroni, and Manuel Costa along with the writings of Thomas William Doane, John Sanford, Edward Edinger, Joseph Campbell, Charles Webster Leadbeater, and Caroline Myss.

My research associates engage with me in intense study, retreat work, and experiential rituals: Joanna Percival, Nancy Gwin Walker, John R. Mabry, Kimberly Elliot, Victoria MacDonald, Philip Russell West, Irene Laudeman, Judy Ford Massey, the people of Pescadero Community Church and St. Peter's Episcopal Church in San Francisco. Springing from this collaborative work are the rituals and liturgies published in this book: Chalices of Mystery, A Footwashing Ritual, and Immersion in Mystery,

Journeys into the depths of my soul have been facilitated by my spiritual Companions who have taken the risk of igniting within ourselves the Holy Fire of the Burning Bush. Most important of all are Jesus of Nazareth and Mary Magdalene who embody vibrant Holy Mystery and show us the Way to be energized by the gentle fiery Spirit.

Special thanksgiving to the Amazing Mystery for my family especially Alfred James Butcher and Clara Alice Buckingham, Edwin Pierson Ford and Louise Chapin Shepard, Harold Butcher and Elizabeth Van Dyck Ford, Geoffrey Ford Butcher, Elizabeth Tertia

West, Connie Jones Butcher, Grace Elise Vilez, Marie Butcher, Maher Essi, and Suraya Noor Elizabeth Essi.

Great appreciation to my Readers and their constructive criticism in preparing this manuscript: Grace Vilez, Patrick Andersen, Antonnette Vaglia Graham, Bruce Huston, Sandy Havens, Victoria MacDonald, Mark Tyx, Detlef Matthies, Rosamonde Miller, Norman McMullen, Ruth McMullen, Philip West, Judy Ford Massey, Margaret Starbird, Eric Brandt, Larry Alexander, Jon Graham, and Steve Scholl.

I stand with deep appreciation for Chauncie Kilmer Myers, William Edwin Swing, and Marc Handley Andrus, my bishops, who have enthusiastically encouraged my explorations into the depths of the Amazing Mystery in whom we live and move and have our being.

And I feel enormous gratitude to my publisher John R. Mabry and the staff of Apocryphile Press who have done the work to put this book into your hands.

I have discovered that, if the truth be known, I am the composite of my ancestors, family, friends, teachers, lovers, opponents, people in my congregations, and countless others who ride around inside me influencing my life and work. To all of them, named and unnamed members of the Web of Life, I say a heart felt THANK YOU!

ABOUT THE AUTHOR

JOHN BEVERLEY BUTCHER IS A STUDENT OF JESUS, MARY Magdalene, and Lao Tzu of China. His research is centered in reclaiming their Wisdom Teachings and spiritual practice through study of *The Complete Gospels*, the Tao Te Ching, and other sacred texts.

He is seeking to integrate Holy Scripture, archetypal psychology, Taoist philosophy, and personal experience with the arts and lively Spirit filled liturgy. His primary purpose in life is to discover how to become more fully human.

Out of his research, he offers seminars, lectures, and retreats. In addition to editing *The Tao of Jesus*, Harper San Francisco 1994 and Apocryphile Press 2006, he is author of *Telling the Untold Stories, Encounters with the Resurrected Jesus*, Trinity Press International, 2001, and *An Uncommon Lectionary, A Companion to the Common Lectionary*, Polebridge Press, 2002.

John Beverley is a son of Harold Butcher, an English freelance journalist and lecturer, and Elizabeth Ford, an American musician and teacher. He was born in New York City and raised in Prescott, Arizona. He received his Bachelor of Arts in philosophy and psychology from Harvard College and a Master of Divinity from Berkeley Divinity School at Yale.

He was ordained priest in the Missionary District of Arizona in 1960 and served as pastor of Episcopal congregations in Sedona, Clarkdale, and Winslow, Arizona, and chaplain of the Arizona State Prison at Florence. Moving to California in 1969, he became pastor of Holy Trinity Church, Menlo Park, and then rector of St. Peter's, San Francisco.

His continuing education includes seminars with the Guild for Psychological Studies in San Francisco and Four Springs, a retreat center near Middletown, California. He is an Associate Fellow of the Jesus Seminar and a Fellow of the Canadian College for Chinese Studies in Victoria, British Columbia.

He is a priest of the Episcopal Diocese of California, rector emeritus of St. Peter's, San Francisco, and a minister of Pescadero Community Church which is in the town of Pescadero on the Pacific coast just south of San Francisco. He serves on the steering committee of MultiFaith Voices for Peace and Justice in Palo Alto.

John and his beloved wife, Grace, live on the San Francisco Peninsula.

Contact: www.sacredpartnership.net

CPSIA information can be obtained at www.ICGtesting.com
Printed in the USA
267703BV00001B/4/P

9 781937 002046